.NET Windows Forms Custom Controls

Controls

Richard Weeks

201 West 103rd St., Indianapolis, Indiana, 46290 USA

.NET Windows Forms Custom Controls

Copyright © 2002 by Sams Publishing

International Standard Book Number: 0-672-32333-8

Library of Congress Catalog Card Number: 2001118745

Printed in the United States of America

First Printing: February 2002

05   04   03   02   4   3   2   1

Trademarks

Warning and Disclaimer

ASSOCIATE PUBLISHER
Linda Engelman

ACQUISITIONS EDITOR
Neil Rowe

DEVELOPMENT EDITOR
Ginny Bess

MANAGING EDITOR
Charlotte Clapp

PROJECT EDITOR
Carol Bowers

COPY EDITOR
Cheri Clark

INDEXER
Sandy Henselmeier

PROOFREADER
Andrea Dugan

TECHNICAL EDITOR
Chris Crane

TEAM COORDINATOR
Lynne Williams

MEDIA DEVELOPER
Dan Scherf

INTERIOR DESIGNER
Anne Jones

COVER DESIGNER
Aren Howell

PAGE LAYOUT
Mark Walchle

Contents at a Glance

Contents

About the Author

Richard Weeks has been writing software for the better part of 10 years, specializing in C++, MFC, COM, ATL, and now C#. His major areas of interest include custom control development, compiler theory, distributed applications development, and design patterns. During the past 10 years, he managed to make time to earn his B.S. degree in Computer Science from Western Carolina University; it proudly hangs next to his G.E.D. When not working, he enjoys video games, go-cart racing, and good beer. Richard Weeks can be reached at rweeks@nc.rr.com.

Dedication

This book is dedicated to my grandfather, Howard R. Henry, a two-time survivor of cancer now in his third battle. His positive can-do attitude has been an inspiration to everyone in my family and especially to me. I love you, Granddad.

Acknowledgments

Writing a book is not a one-person task, and without the guidance from the editors and technical reviewers at Sams, there is no way I could have written this book. I would like to thank Neil Rowe, my acquisitions editor for the second time and survivor of driving with me through the Georgia Dome in a utility cart.

I would also like to thank my friends and family who have supported my efforts and have been most understanding of the countless hours required to write such a book. And last but not least is my friend Bob Powell, who asked me to co-author with him in my first writing venture. Oh, be sure to buy his books too.

Tell Us What You Think!

As the reader of this book, *you* are our most important critic and commentator. We value your opinion and want to know what we're doing right, what we could do better, what areas you'd like to see us publish in, and any other words of wisdom you're willing to pass our way.

As an Associate Publisher for Sams Publishing, I welcome your comments. You can fax, email, or write me directly to let me know what you did or didn't like about this book—as well as what we can do to make our books stronger.

Please note that I cannot help you with technical problems related to the topic of this book, and that due to the high volume of mail I receive, I might not be able to reply to every message.

When you write, please be sure to include this book's title and author, as well as your name and phone or fax number. I will carefully review your comments and share them with the author and editors who worked on the book.

Fax: 317-581-4770

Email: feedback@samspublishing.com

Mail: Linda Engelman
          Associate Publisher
          Sams Publishing
          201 West 103rd Street
          Indianapolis, IN 46290 USA

Introduction

Why write a book on custom controls? Well, there's an adage that says "sex sells." The premise of that adage is the same for developing custom controls and application development. Consumers tend to buy the pretty box, or the application with the slickest, most modern user interface. Prettiness also sells. Often, consumers make purchase decisions regardless of functionality. Custom control development serves two purposes: The first is to mimic user interface elements found in leading commercial products, and the second is to provide controls not found in the standard set of Windows common controls.

Examples of useful custom controls include spreadsheet-style controls, such as Spread from FarPoint Technologies, and the Outlook-style shortcut bar provided by various Toolkit vendors. These custom controls provide elements not found in the standard set of common controls and allow for application developers to concentrate on building the core logic of their application without having to spend time developing UI components. Custom controls often fill a specific need, as in the case of Spread, and other times merely enhance common UI elements such as customizable toolbars and menus.

In general, Microsoft has set the standard for application user interfaces. In fact, an entire industry has been created whose sole purpose is providing developers with UI Toolkits that emulate the same UI elements found in most Microsoft applications. Consider MS Office and VS .NET (Visual Studio .NET). Both of these applications have defined the expected UI elements in other commercial Windows applications such as Act, Work Force Vision by Peopleclick, and Visio. Companies that make their living selling custom controls are already releasing updated Toolkits to provide the UI elements found in VS .NET.

Developing custom controls has often been considered a poorly documented, Windows guru-only task. This doesn't have to be the case. Although poor documentation does exist, anyone with the proper documentation can create stunning, modern UI custom controls like those found in MS Office and VS .NET. Such a journey begins with this book.

Before you start this journey, it might be helpful to know how custom controls are defined. A custom control is just a common control that has been altered in either appearance or functionality to produce a desired effect. A custom control can also be a new control that doesn't have a counterpart within the Windows common controls. There's no hard-and-fast definition for what constitutes a custom control. Basically, just keep in mind that a custom control is not part of the Windows common controls.

The process of developing controls is not a single-sided effort. In fact, the .NET base class library provides an overwhelming set of base classes and interfaces targeted at control development and support. The base class library provides not only several control base classes, but also several designer base classes that can be extended to provide the design-time behavior for the control.

For those of you who've had the pleasure (read "torment") of developing ActiveX controls with Microsoft Foundation Class (MFC) or even ActiveX Template Library (ATL), you'll appreciate the amount of reusable code provided by the base class libraries. In fact, for simple controls it's possible to merely use one of the existing designers to support your new control.

The .NET Windows Forms framework has the capability to host both classic ActiveX controls and .NET controls, thus extending the life of existing ActiveX controls. I would expect that third-party UI control vendors will eventually port all of their existing ActiveX controls over to native .NET controls to benefit from the added support afforded by the base class libraries.

Who Should Read This Book

To create custom controls it is assumed that you, the reader, have some knowledge of C# and .NET. In addition, you should be familiar with Windows Forms development. No prior knowledge of control development is required. The goal of this book is to teach control development.

It is also helpful if you have some knowledge of advanced C# topics such as attributes, custom events, and reflection. However, I have provided the needed information about these topics during the course of each control's development and as necessary. If you are new to programming, I suggest that you choose another avenue for learning, because this book is not geared toward teaching C# or .NET; rather, it shows you how to use C# and .NET to create your own controls.

This Book's Approach

To gain an understanding of what it takes to build controls for Windows Forms, this book takes a sample-based approach. The first control presented is a simple IconButton control. The IconButton control acts as a standard Windows Forms button, and in addition it allows for an icon image to be displayed on the control (see Figure 1).

FIGURE 1

The IconButton control developed in Chapters 2 and 3.

The `IconButton` serves as our first foray into custom control development. Although not very complicated, it shows how to get started with building controls and using the various services offered by VS .NET for control development.

With the basics of control development covered, we'll move on to advanced control development topics, including designer services, design-time verses runtime behavior, serialization, and licensing. To explore these topics, we'll develop an `OutlookBar` control, which is similar to the custom control found in MS Outlook. Figure 2 shows the `OutlookBar` control we will develop as the advanced sample for this book.

FIGURE 2
An advanced control, the `OutlookBar`.

After you understand the concepts and tasks related to developing the `IconButton` control and the `OutlookBar` control, you will be well equipped to create other custom controls. You'll learn that the necessary requirements for creating custom controls are the development of a sense of flair and style, and, of course, knowledge of the requirements for building controls. This book arms you with that knowledge, and hopefully you will confidently develop your own sense of style with the knowledge and experience you gain from the samples in this book.

Again, the main goal of this book is to teach by example. I've packed as much code as possible into each section, including the appendix, which deals with Extender Providers. The code provided serves as a stepping-stone from which to extend the provided controls or to use as the building blocks for new controls.

Each chapter builds on the concepts and code examples of the preceding chapter. The controls built over the course of this book represent a starting point on which you should expand by adding your own features and support. The goal is to cover key concepts rather than extraneous features that don't contribute to understanding the process of custom control development.

Windows Controls

IN THIS CHAPTER

One of the early premises of the Windows operating system was to define a common set of user interface elements to be shared by all applications. The idea was that a user could learn one application and apply that knowledge to other applications. Each application shared common user interface elements such as menus, toolbars, and dialog boxes, thereby creating a sense of unity between all Windows-based applications.

Over the years, the Windows common controls set has been expanded to include more and more user interface elements that have become commonplace in applications. Of course, these common controls stem from the Windows operating system itself and the advances of its own user interface.

The development of the Windows UI (User Interface) controls has not been limited to just advances in the Microsoft Windows environment; rather, many third-party companies have built their entire livelihood off of creating custom controls for Windows developers. Often, these custom controls mimic the various UI elements found within the latest Microsoft products, such as Visual Studio and the popular Microsoft Office line of products.

The reason for the thriving market is customer driven. Customers expect that applications have the latest UI elements found in typical Microsoft products. Somehow a slick up-to-date UI translates to a more powerful application. This assumption is not always accurate, but a modern UI goes a long way in selling software—just ask any commercial software developer.

I have often been asked, "Why doesn't Microsoft release its UI components for use by other developers?" Well, the answer is not very straightforward. Each development team at Microsoft typically creates its own UI controls, and devoting a single group to creating UI components is not cost-efficient or profitable for a company the size of Microsoft. A top Toolkit company, as custom control development companies are called, can expect to see revenues of $5 to $7 million annually. For Microsoft, this would probably cover the landscaping for the main campus.

Developing custom controls is a rewarding experience that allows for a deeper understanding of Windows development and the development environment, such as Visual Studio. Gaining a solid understanding of the Windows subsystem, GDI+ (Graphics Device Interface+), and user interaction, such as a mouse and keyboard, tends to push custom control developers to create more powerful and feature-packed controls and applications.

The remainder of this chapter discusses basic control concepts such as runtime verses design-time support. In addition, the basic anatomy of controls is covered.

Control Concepts

Regardless of the type of control being developed, its use should be immediately obvious to the user of the control. After all, if the user doesn't know what the control does, then the control serves no valid use. In addition, users expect some basic concepts to be universal among all controls. For example, users expect a left mouse click to result in an action.

Consider a menu, a toolbar, and a command button. Although each control looks different, users expect that when they left-click the control, some action will take place within the application. The action is, of course, application specific; however, the control's behavior is common among all applications. This common functionality is the cornerstone of Windows development because it allows users to learn one application and apply that knowledge to other Windows-based applications.

All Windows-based controls, both common and custom, share several common traits. These traits include the various properties and events used to define the control's appearance and behavior. Common properties include `Text`, `ForeColor`, `BackColor`, `Size`, and `Location`, to name a few. Standard events include `Click`, `Focused`, `MouseEnter`, `MouseLeave`, and basic keyboard events. These events allow for an application to respond to a user's current action. Properties and events are discussed later in this chapter.

NOTE

The subject of properties and events as defined within .NET development should be already familiar to you; therefore, only a brief discussion of their use is covered here.

Control Anatomy 101

Controls all have the same basic anatomy. Just as human anatomy is mostly the same and differs only slightly based on function and form, so is a control's anatomy. Humans share basic properties, such as eye color, hair color, height, and weight. These properties can be used to describe an individual and help form a visual image of the individual. In the same way, various properties of a control define its outward appearance.

A control has one physical part and two logical parts. The physical part is the control window. The control window is the physical space the control occupies on the screen. Within the physical boundary of the control are two logical regions: client and non-client areas. Figure 1.1 shows a basic form showing these areas.

The form itself represents the control window. The title bar containing the control box represents the non-client area of the control. The control box contains the `minimize`, `maximize`, and `close` buttons in the upper-right corner of the window. The remaining area of the control window is considered the client area. The client area is where child controls would be located and all painting logic, such as drawing a pie chart, is clipped to the client area. The control window, the client area, and the non-client area are discussed in more detail in the following sections.

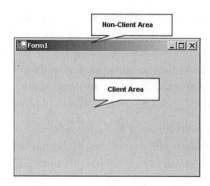

FIGURE 1.1
Basic Windows Forms control anatomy.

Control Window

The main window of a control defines the physical boundary of the control. All messages, such as mouse and keyboard, are sent to the main control window for dispatching. These messages are generated based on user interaction with the current window in focus. The main control window may or may not contain a non-client, or NC, area. Normally, only top-level windows and dialogs contain NC areas. The NC area is generally reserved for the window's main caption and the control box. The remainder of the control area is known as the client area. This is where all other child controls and custom painting logic typically take place.

NC (Non-Client) Area

Often it is not necessary to manage the NC area of a control because the framework handles the painting and management of this area. The underlying windowing framework takes care of providing the system menu, painting the title bar, and placing the control box. In addition, the windowing framework handles the dispatching of commands for the various items, such as system menu items and the minimize/maximize controls.

In recent years, applications have begun to take over the painting and logic of the NC area by providing for gradient-filled title bars or bitmap images within the title-bar area. Such custom painting of the NC area is in the realm of skinning or applying a theme to an application's appearance. Examples of this custom painting logic include WinAmp and Microsoft Media Player. Custom painting makes the application look more individual rather than appearing as part of the collective.

Client Area

As stated previously, the client area of a control is where most of the work, such as child controls and painting, takes place. The client area represents a logic boundary within the main control. This logic boundary can be the same size as the control itself. In the case of a common button, the control consists entirely of a client area. The logical boundary for the client area is not restricted to the size of the control container, but rather the logical client area can be any size. Only the client area visible within the boundaries of the parent control will be rendered on the screen, but the logical size of the client area could be 100 square miles. Of course, I don't suggest a client area that large.

Control Appearance and Behavior

During development of a custom control, the main goal is to produce a control that is concise in its intended use. After all, if the control's use eludes the end user, the control's development is really pointless. The user might as well have chosen a better-known control or one of the common controls. Make sure that your users understand the intended use of your control.

When you are developing a control that is useful, it is also important to know your targeted audience. When you are developing custom controls, there are two target audiences. The first is the developer who will use your control when building an application, and the second is the end user of the application. Although the developer may understand the use of the control, you must ensure that the end user of the application will also understand how to use the control. Custom control developers sometimes forget about end users and focus solely on the developers who will be purchasing the controls and using them to build applications. However, when end users complain that the application is difficult to use, don't expect the developers to come back and purchase any more custom controls from you.

Custom control development consists of four major areas: properties, events, runtime, and design-time. Each of these is discussed in the following sections and throughout this book.

Properties

Properties are the main mechanism for controlling the appearance of a control. Aspects from color and size to text and images are defined using properties.

Using properties to define characteristics of a control is part of the Rapid Application Development, or RAD, style of application development. Coupled with RAD is the capability to create small reusable modules of code such as custom controls. This capability spawned a huge success for Microsoft Visual Basic.

The basic premise of properties was to replace the method call style invocation with a dot style notation. Under the covers, the dot style notation is actually a method call, but to the developer the dot style notation provides a layer of abstraction. Listing 1.1 shows a method call and a property reference or dot notation that sets a person's name.

LISTING 1.1   Method Call Versus Dot Notation Properties

```
1: //Method Calls to set person's name
2: Person me;
3: me.SetFirstName( "Richard" );
4: me.SetLastName( "Weeks" );
5:
6: //Property or Dot Notation
7: Person grandfather;
8: grandfather.FirstName = "Howard";
9: grandfather.LastName = "Henry";
```

The code snippet in Listing 1.1 shows the stylistic difference between using method calls, lines 3 and 4, and using the dot notation of properties, lines 8 and 9. The result is the same in both cases. The first and last name of the Person object is set. The debate over which is better or preferred is often discussed; however, know that properties and the dot notation are a requirement for developing well-behaved and well-received custom controls.

Events

Events provide a basic mechanism for notification between various components. When the left mouse button is clicked on a control, the control in turn fires off a click event to be handled by the application. These events allow for an application to respond to user- or system-generated actions. Controls fire events to notify the application that some action has taken place and the application should in turn do something. That "something" is, of course, application specific.

Runtime

The runtime appearance and behavior of a control are what the end user of an application experiences. Thus, when an application is being used, the controls within the application have a defined appearance and a set of behaviors that are controlled by the application itself. Certain aspects of a control can be modified during runtime, such as the color and font used. The properties of a control can be modified in the application code, and may even be exposed to the user of the application. End users of the application do not typically modify the appearance of a control; rather, modifications to the control are performed by application code.

For the most part, however, when an application is running, the control cannot be altered in terms of its behavior. The behavior of the control—that is, the logic handling the control's events—is defined during the design and development of the application.

Design-Time

With the RAD style of development, application developers work with a design-time tool such as Visual Studio to create applications. During the design of an application, the developer will assign values to various properties of a control and write custom code to handle any events fired by the control. The design-time cycle of a project is interactive between the developer and the controls being used within the application. To a custom control developer, it is of paramount importance to create a control with solid design-time support. Figure 1.2 shows the Outlook-style control. You are shown an Outlook-style control as it is developed at design-time in Chapters 7, 8, and 9.

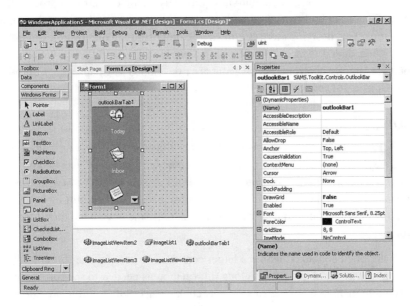

FIGURE 1.2
Design-time development using the Outlook-style control.

It is during the design-time development of an application that the developers (one of your target audiences) are addressed. If the custom control is hard for the developer to use to build applications, chances are the developer will give up and purchase a different custom control to get the job done.

Pleasing developers is a difficult task. It is important to get feedback from the developers using your custom control and to incorporate their comments into the control's design and usability. It is also helpful to look at the current set of controls and their design-time support. Perfecting the design-time support of a control takes time and several iterations of the controls designer. Designers are covered in Chapter 3, "Designer Basics."

Composite Controls

The discussion of custom controls to this point has assumed a single control or single component. As with most development projects, the end result is a composition of smaller components that in turn create the final product. The same case holds for custom control development. Rather than create a single monolithic control, custom controls are often created by using one or more smaller controls.

Simple controls, such as a command button, require only a single control to provide the necessary functionality. A combo box is a composite control that uses smaller controls to implement the larger control. This design pattern is known as Composition. Composition is a useful design pattern you should explore when creating any custom control that contains several aspects found in simpler controls. The `UserControl` developed in Chapter 2, "Control Basics," is based on the idea of Composition.

Soft Controls

In the days before 128MB of RAM was standard, developers had to save as many system resources as they could. This is when soft controls came into play. The idea behind soft controls is that the control is not a real control. The control does not have an HWND, or handle to a physical window, but rather is a logical area on the screen. A soft control looks and acts just like a standard control as far as the user is concerned. Only the developer knows that it's not a real control.

Soft controls are often contained within a larger control. The host for the soft control handles the processing of user input and passes along information as needed to the soft control. Such information might include mouse events such as click events. Soft controls provide a lightweight alternative to full-blown controls and are rather easy to implement. Soft controls generally provide painting logic and hit-testing. Hit-testing is used to determine whether a point is located within the boundaries of the soft control. In Chapter 9, "`ImageListView` Control," a small soft-control scroll button, similar to those found on scrollbars, is developed to demonstrate this useful technique.

VS .NET Integrated Development Environment (IDE)

Before we dive into control development in the next chapter, a tour of the VS .NET IDE is in order. Understanding the development environment is essential when developing custom controls. After all, custom controls must interact with the environment during design-time to support code-serialization and design-time feedback for the developer using the control. Figure 1.3 shows the IDE during the design of a Windows application.

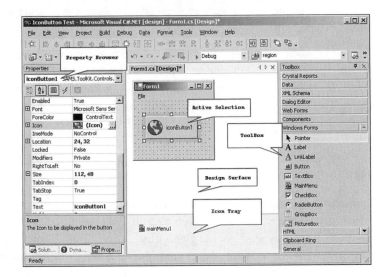

FIGURE 1.3
The parts of the VS .NET IDE.

The VS .NET IDE is geared toward RAD-style development and makes heavy use of the Toolbox and Property Browser for quickly creating Windows-based applications. During the development of custom controls, it is important to understand how to properly coexist and make use of the services exposed via the IDE. These interactions and services are discussed in later chapters as they become important.

When it comes to custom control development, understanding how the Toolbox, Icon Tray, and Property Browser work is very important. Each of these items reacts to controls and offers different services to be used by a custom control developer.

The Toolbox, for instance, displays the control name and associated bitmap for the control. In addition, the Toolbox exposes a service for querying the actively selected control within the Toolbox. This service is needed for providing drag-and-drop support during design-time.

In addition, it is possible to exclude controls from the Toolbox by specifying that a control should not be visible in the Toolbox. This is accomplished through the use of a custom attribute. These topics are discussed in later chapters.

The Property Browser is the most widely used of the IDE components. The Property Browser offers several areas of extensibility, such as custom editors for property values, and the capability to hide and dynamically add properties. Each of these topics is covered in later chapters. In addition, the Property Browser, known as the PropertyGrid control, can be used in your own applications. By default, the PropertyGrid control does not appear within the Toolbox. Adding the PropertyGrid is just a simple matter of customizing the Toolbox and adding the control. This too is covered in later chapters.

The Icon Tray is used to hold components that require design-time support but are not necessary controls. For instance, the Menu component is not a control; however, it requires extensive design-time support. In addition to the Menu, a Tooltip is also a component that requires design-time support. The Tooltip, like the Menu, is not a control but rather a component. The Icon Tray serves as a bucket to hold these components and allow for a user to select the component and access its properties via the Property Browser.

Summary

Developing custom controls is not a difficult task, and by the end of this book you will have all the knowledge necessary to create advanced custom controls. The intent of this chapter was to familiarize you with the necessary terms and to give a general overview of control development. The key requirement for developing custom controls is a desire to create cool components for other developers to drool over.

Control Basics

IN THIS CHAPTER

Controls provide a means for user interaction with an application. Every control defines a set of properties, events, and a user interface that represents the control and the intended use the control has. Control development consists of two parts: runtime and design-time. Runtime has to do with how the control looks and acts during the execution of the application, whereas design-time refers to the WYSIWYG editor used by VS .NET to create an application. In this chapter the runtime aspect of control development is the focus; Chapter 3, "Designer Basics," covers the design-time aspects of control development.

This chapter covers the basics for creating a simple button control—the `IconButton` control. The `IconButton` control allows an `Icon` image to be displayed along with the standard text found on the Windows Forms button control (see Figure 2.1).

FIGURE 2.1
The `IconButton` *control.*

The `IconButton` control is a custom control. To build it, you need to understand the following topics:

- Control base classes
- Properties
- Events

The process of developing custom controls is the same as that of developing a set of classes. The process begins by determining the required functionality and the necessary classes that will be responsible for implementing the functionality. In addition, it is necessary to determine the proper base class for the custom control. Each class can inherit from a base class and implements zero or more interfaces. Classes also provide properties and even events. As you'll see in the following sections, custom controls behave much like classes do.

Control Base Classes

The .NET base Class Library provides base classes that provide various levels of support for building controls. The .NET base Class Library is at the heart of the .NET platform. You can think of the .NET base Class Library as similar to the C runtime or VB runtime on steroids. In addition to providing common types such as `Int32` and `string`, the base Class Library provides for database access, collections, windows forms, and Web forms development, to name a few.

Each derived control base class extends the functionality provided by the base class from which it inherits. Figure 2.2 shows the control classes provided by the base Class Library.

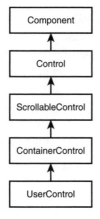

FIGURE 2.2
Control base classes.

The control hierarchy shown in Figure 2.2 should be used to determine where to begin when a new custom Windows Forms control is being built. Each derived class extends and in some cases modifies the behavior of its parent class. Every common control available with VS .NET derives from one of the classes in the control hierarchy.

Component

At the very root of all control base classes is the Component class or the fully qualified name System.ComponentModel.Component. The Component base class serves as the base class for all classes within the System.Windows.Forms namespace. Any class that inherits from the Component base class basically states that the class will free up any resources it uses through the invocation of its Dispose method. In essence, any class that inherits from the Component base class can be told when to clean up without waiting for the object instance to be collected by the .NET Garbage Collector.

Control

The Control class represents the single most significant base class in that it provides all the necessary plumbing for control development. The Control base class provides for message routing, both keyboard and mouse, security, size and position, and the creation of the underlying window handle or hWnd, for instance. Although the Control base class does not provide any default painting, it does provide for all the basic services of a .NET control, including the implementation of ActiveX control interfaces. By providing all the ActiveX control interfaces, custom controls developed in .NET can be hosted within Internet Explorer and other ActiveX control hosts.

According to the documentation, classes do not typically inherit from the `Control` base class directly, but rather from the `UserControl` class. The developers for the Windows Forms controls apparently didn't read that documentation, because the controls found in the Windows Forms namespace typically inherit directly from the `Control` base class. The `System.Windows.Forms.Control` class serves as the base class for the `DataGrid`, `DateTimePicker`, `Label`, `GroupBox`, `ListControl`, and so on. Actually, the intention is that most developers will be developing simple `UserControl` derived controls and do not require the low-level control afforded by twiddling with the underpinnings of the control framework.

ScrollableControl

As the name suggests, the `ScrollableControl` base class provides the capability for a control to scroll its contents. Setting the `AutoScroll` property to `true` provides the scrolling. The `Panel` control inherits from this control base class.

ContainerControl

The `ContainerControl` base class provides the necessary wiring for hosting other controls such as buttons, labels, and the like, and it serves as the base class for the `UserControl`, the `PropertyGrid`, and the `Form` class. The main benefit derived from using the `ContainerControl` is focus management and mnemonic handling for child controls contained within the `ContainerControl`. Focus management deals with handling the Tab key and setting focus to the next control based on the tab order of the child controls. Mnemonic handling is the processing of shortcut or accelerator keys to set focus to the corresponding control.

Using the `ContainerControl` object provides processing of events such as the Tab key and focus information about child controls. It is important to note that a `ContainerControl` will not receive focus but rather focus will be set to the first child control of the container.

UserControl

The .NET `UserControl` is very much the same as the `User` control concept found in earlier versions of Visual Basic. Essentially, a `UserControl` is a simple method for creating a composite control consisting of one or more controls. Because the `UserControl` class derives from the `ContainerControl` base class, it inherits all the focus management and control management implemented by the `ContainerControl`. Control management entails hosting child controls and managing the events of the child controls. In essence, a `UserControl` is a fully self-contained control that also generally includes some amount of business logic such as data entry validation and even database access if necessary.

The `UserControl` base class provides a solid foundation for creating reusable controls consisting of presentation and data validation to be reused in an application. Consider building an application in which it is necessary to obtain a customer's address, suppliers' addresses, and other various addresses. Each of these addresses will be subject to similar data validation, such as verifying the zip code for a city and the city within a state.

When a `UserControl` is created to handle this common task, the `UserControl` can then be used anywhere within the application that requires validating the user-entered address.

Address `UserControl`

To gain an understanding of basic control development, designing and creating a simple `UserControl` provides an easy starting point. Taking the address validation scenario presented previously, designing and implementing a basic `UserControl` to fulfill this purpose requires only the following few simple steps:

1. Create a new C# Windows application.
2. Add a new `UserControl` to the project.
3. Design the `UserControl` user interface (see Figure 2.3).
4. Compile the project.
5. Select the new `UserControl` from the Toolbox and drag it onto the main form (see Figure 2.4).

Beginning with step 1, create a new Windows application project with the name "Address `UserControl`." This project will serve to contain both the custom `UserControl` and the Windows Form that will be used to host the `AddressControl`. After the project is created, it's time to add a new `UserControl` to the project. You can do this by selecting Add New Item from the File menu or by right-clicking on the project in the Solution explorer and selecting New UserControl from the Add menu item. Name the new `UserControl` `AddressControl`.

If the `AddressControl` is not currently in design mode, double-click the `AddressControl.cs` file in the Solution explorer to bring up the `UserControl` in design mode. Next, construct the `AddressControl` UI so that it matches the control shown in Figure 2.3.

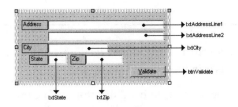

FIGURE 2.3

The user interface for the `AddressControl` `UserControl`.

2

CONTROL BASICS

After the UI for the control has been constructed, double-click the Validate button to bring up the code window for the control. Listing 2.1 provides the implementation for the click event handler and a small helper method for the control.

LISTING 2.1   Logic for the AddressControl Validate Button

```
 1: private void btnValidate_Click(object sender, System.EventArgs e) {
 2:     //Ensure there are no empty text boxes
 3:     if( !ValidateTextBox( txtAddressLine1 ) ) {
 4:         txtAddressLine1.Focus( );
 5:         return;
 6:     }
 7:     if( !ValidateTextBox( txtAddressLine2 ) ) {
 8:         txtAddressLine2.Focus( );
 9:         return;
10:     }
11:     if( !ValidateTextBox( txtCity ) ) {
12:         txtCity.Focus( );
13:         return;
14:     }
15:     if( !ValidateTextBox( txtState ) ) {
16:         txtState.Focus( );
17:         return;
18:     }
19:     if( !ValidateTextBox( txtZip ) ) {
20:         txtZip.Focus( );
21:         return;
22:     }
23: }
24:
25: private bool ValidateTextBox( TextBox textBox ) {
26:     if( textBox.Text.Length == 0 ) {
27:         MessageBox.Show( this, string.Format( "{0} is empty",
➥textBox.Name ) );
28:         return false;
29:     }
30:     return true;
31: }
```

The code for the AddressControl is fairly simple in all respects. Each TextBox on the control is tested to ensure that the user in fact entered something.

With the code in place, the next step is to build the project. The project must be compiled before the new AddressControl can be used and placed on the main form. Attempting to use the AddressControl without building the project results in a rather cryptic message from the IDE about not being able to create the control.

After the project has been compiled, switch back to the main form, which should be `Form1.cs`. Now available on the bottom of the Toolbox in the Windows Forms tab is the newly created `AddressControl`. As with any other control within the Toolbox, this new control can be dragged onto the form and sized appropriately (see Figure 2.4).

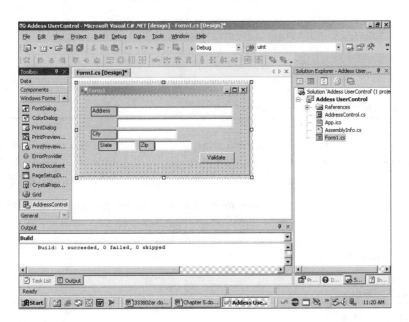

FIGURE 2.4
The AddressControl *placed on* Form1.

Custom `UserControl` style controls are handy when building applications in which the UI and business logic are seemingly tied together, such as in the case of data validation. Also, because `UserControls` are by far the simplest style of control to construct, they allow for implementing quick and simple solutions rather than constructing complex controls from scratch.

Properties

Properties are syntactic shorthand for accessor and mutator methods. In place of coding methods that retrieve or modify a particular member variable, properties provide both a get and a set submethod. Support for property style methods can be found in Visual Basic, C#, C++ (using `__declspec()`) and COM, to name a few. Consider the code snippet in Listing 2.2.

LISTING 2.2 Get/Set Methods

```
1: class Person {
2:
3:     private string name;
4:
5:     public void SetName( string Name ) { name = Name; }
6:     public string GetName( ) { return name; }
7: }
8:
9: Person me = new Person( );
10: me.SetName( "Richard" );
11:  Console.WriteLine( me.GetName( ) );
```

The code in Listing 2.2 shows two methods whose sole purpose is to expose the underlying private data member: name. Before the notion of properties, this style of set/get methods for allowing access to data members was common practice among Object-Oriented developers.

Without support for properties, accessing member fields requires the explicit invocation of a method. The property syntax merely shortens the code; however, the syntax offers a more natural expression. Listing 2.3 shows the same Person class using a property instead of methods to access the name member field.

LISTING 2.3 Properties

```
1: class Person {
2:
3:     private string name;
4:
5:     public string Name {
6:         get { return name; }
7:         set { name = value; }
8:     }
9: }
10:
11: Person me = new Person( );
12: me.Name = "Richard";
13:  Console.WriteLine( me.Name );
```

The property syntax is shorthand notation for calling the accessor/mutator method. In fact, line 12 of Listing 2.3 is represented as me.set_Name("Richard") in Intermediate Language and is the actual call made to the Person object.

Controls have several properties already defined by the Control base class. These properties include Text, Size, ForeColor, BackColor, and a host of others. Table 2.1 shows some of the common properties of the Control base class.

TABLE 2.1   Control Properties

Property	Description
Text	Text to be displayed in the control.
ForeColor	Foreground color of text and graphics in the control.
BackColor	Background color of the control.
Dock	Get/set edge of parent to dock the control to.
Font	Font to use for text within the control.
Size	Size of the control.
Visible	Determines whether the control is visible at runtime.
Enabled	Determines whether the control is enabled.
Width	Get/set width of the control.
Height	Get/set height of the control.

2

CONTROL BASICS

NOTE

At last count, the Control base class provides 59 properties of its own; for a complete listing of Control properties, see the MSDN help topic for Control Members.

When creating new controls, you will also be defining additional properties that relate to the expected functionality of the control. The IconButton control developed in this chapter adds a property for the icon to be drawn on the button. Properties are in many respects the attributes of a control. As such, when deciding what properties a control should have, try to think in terms of "What are the attributes of this control?" With respect to the IconButton control to be developed, the Icon property defines the associated icon image of the control.

Events

Events are one of the more interesting additions to VB .NET and are an integral part of the C# language and the .NET platform. The event mechanism provides a method of communication or notification between objects. Consider the Windows Forms Button control. When a mouse-click event occurs, the button notifies any subscriber that a Click event has occurred. The subscriber can then perform processing based on the event received from the publisher of the event.

Subject-Observer

The event paradigm is an implementation of the Subject-Observer pattern. In the Subject-Observer model, also known as Publish-Subscribe, the Subject notifies registered Observers when the state of the Subject has changed. Figure 2.5 shows a UML, or Unified Modeling Language, diagram of the Subject-Observer pattern classes.

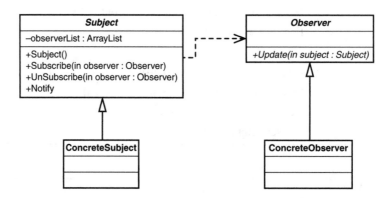

FIGURE 2.5

The Subject-Observer pattern.

The Subject-Observer is a very useful design pattern and can be easily implemented in both C# and VB .NET. In addition, it is often helpful to understand the fundamental concepts when dealing with a high-level abstraction such as events. The event model used in .NET reduces the dependency on having known methods for a subject and observer as in the Subject-Observer pattern. Rather than requiring an Observer to provide a known method such as Update, the .NET event model allows for loosely coupled events and event handlers.

Delegates

To provide a loosely coupled event system, .NET introduces the concept of delegates. For C/C++ programmers, delegates are like function pointers on steroids. In VB parlance, delegates are similar to passing the address of a function to another function using the AddressOf opera-tor. For an object to subscribe to an event, it need only implement a member method with the required delegate signature, the signature being the return type and parameters for the method.

As an example, consider the Click method on a Button control. To handle the event, a method must exist that accepts two parameters: object sender and EventArgs e. As long as the member method conforms to this method signature, that method can be used to attach to the published event. Events and delegates go hand in hand as delegates are used by events to invoke the specified method.

Defining Events

To expose an `event`, a class needs to define the event within the class declaration. Listing 2.4 shows an example of defining an event.

LISTING 2.4   Declaring a Public Event

```
1: public class MyControl {
2:
3:     public event System.EventHandler        MyEvent;
4:
5:
6:     protected virtual void OnMyEvent( EventArgs e ) {
7:         if( MyEvent != null )
8:             MyEvent( this, e );
9:     }
10: }
```

The `MyEvent` member of the `MyControl` class defines an event with a delegate type of `System.EventHandler` and, as recommended by the coding standards, implements a `protected virtual` method `OnMyEvent` to handle dispatching the event. The reason for the `protected virtual` method is so that derived classes can have a first crack at the event and can decide whether the event should be propagated to all registered listeners.

The `MyControl` class uses the method `OnMyEvent` internally to raise the event. Anytime it is necessary to invoke the event, code within the `MyControl` class would merely make a call to the protected `OnMyEvent` method, passing it a new instance of the `EventArgs` type. In turn, the `MyEvent` member is tested to determine whether it is null, and if not, all observers of this event are notified.

In addition to using predefined `delegate` types, you can create your own delegate signatures. Listing 2.5 provides for a custom `delegate` signature and `EventArgs` derived class.

LISTING 2.5   Custom Delegate/Event

```
1: public class MyEventArgs : EventArgs {
2:     //MyEventArgs implementation
3: }
4:
5: public delegate void MyEventHandler( object sender, MyEventArgs e );
6:
7:
8: public class MyControl {
9:
10:     public event MyEventHandler     MyEvent;
```

LISTING 2.5   Continued

```
11:
12:      protected virtual void OnMyEvent( MyEventArgs e ) {
13:           if( MyEvent != null )
14:                MyEvent( this, e );
15:      }
16: }
17:
18:
19:
20:
21: public class MyForm {
22:
23:      private MyControl myControl;
24:
25:
26:      public void InitializeComponent( ) {
27:
28:           myControl = new MyControl( );
29:           myControl.MyEvent += new MyEventHandler( this.OnMyEvent );
30:      }
31:
32:
33:      public void OnMyEvent( object sender, MyEventArgs e ) {
34:           //TODO: Handle the event
35:      }
36: }
```

Listing 2.5 creates a custom `EventArgs` derived class used by the custom `MyEventHandler` delegate that is then consumed by a client declaring a method whose signature matches that of the `MyEventHandler` delegate.

The `IconButton` Control

Okay, time for something interesting. With the basics covered, it's time to dive in and create a simple control based on the information provided so far. The example we'll use creates a custom pushbutton that displays an icon to the left of the text. In addition to providing the C# implementation, the `IconButton` has also been implemented in VB .NET to show that it is possible to create the same types of controls regardless of language choice.

Choosing the base class for a custom control requires evaluating the functionality needed by the control. Because the `IconButton` control doesn't scroll and is not going to host other controls, the `System.Windows.Forms.Control` base class provides all the required functionality needed to serve as a starting point from which to build. Figure 2.6 shows the IconButton being used in an application.

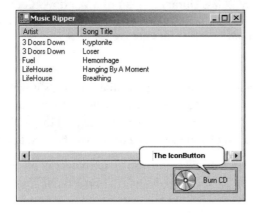

FIGURE 2.6
The IconButton.

To create the IconButton control the following three steps are required:

1. Create a new Class Library project.
2. Add references to System.Drawing.dll and System.Windows.Forms.dll.
3. Create the IconButton.cs source.

To create the IconButton, start by creating a new Class Library project in VS .NET, as shown in Figure 2.7, with the name IconButton.

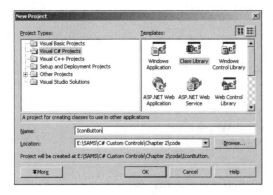

FIGURE 2.7
The IconButton *project.*

> **NOTE**
>
> The reason for creating a Class Library instead of a Windows Control Library is that a Windows Control Library assumes you are going to build a UserControl. As such, unnecessary references and project files are created.

As always, VS .NET provides a default class1.cs file and opens it within the editor. You can delete this file, or rename it to IconButton.cs as you chose. Next, add references to System.Drawing.dll and System.Windows.Forms.dll to the project. Right-clicking the project name and choosing the Add Reference menu option can be used to add the references.

With the project workspace set up and the necessary references in place, all that remains is to copy the source from Listing 2.6 for C# or Listing 2.7 for VB .NET, depending on the project language type you chose.

LISTING 2.6   IconButton.cs C# Source

```
 1: /////////////////////////////////////////////////////////////////////////
 2: ///File        :IconButton.cs
 3: ///Author      :Richard L. Weeks
 4: ///
 5: /// Copyright (c) 2001 by Richard L. Weeks
 6: /// This file is provided for instructional purposes only.
 7: /// No warranties.
 8: /////////////////////////////////////////////////////////////////////////
 9:
10: using System;
11: using System.Windows.Forms;
12: using System.Drawing;
13:
14:
15: namespace SAMS.ToolKit.Controls {
16:     /// <summary>
17:     /// IconButton Class
18:     /// </summary>
19:     [System.ComponentModel.Description( "SAMS IconButton Control" )]
20:     public class IconButton : System.Windows.Forms.Control {
21:
22:
23:         #region STATIC MEMBER FIELDS
24:
25:         protected static int       EDGE_PADDING = 4;
26:
```

LISTING 2.6   Continued

```
27:          #endregion
28:
29:          #region Implementation Member Fields
30:
31:          protected ButtonState         buttonState;
32:          protected Icon                buttonIcon;
33:          protected int                 iconDrawWidth;
34:          protected bool                mousePressed;
35:
36:          #endregion
37:
38:   #region IconButton Properties
39:
40:          [
41:          System.ComponentModel.Description(
➡"The Icon to be displayed in the button" ),
42:          System.ComponentModel.Category( "Appearance" ),
43:          System.ComponentModel.DefaultValue( null )
44:          ]
45:          public Icon Icon {
46:              get { return buttonIcon; }
47:              set {
48:                  buttonIcon = value;
49:                  Invalidate( );
50:                  Update( );
51:              }
52:          }
53:
54:          #endregion
55:
56:
57:          #region Construction / Initialization
58:          /// <summary>
59:          /// Simple Constructor
60:          /// </summary>
61:          public IconButton( ) {
62:              InitializeComponent(  );
63:          }
64:
65:          /// <summary>
66:          /// Initialize the default values for the IconButton
67:          /// </summary>
68:          private void InitializeComponent( ) {
69:              buttonIcon        = null;
70:              buttonState        = ButtonState.Normal;
```

LISTING 2.6   Continued

```
 71:              mousePressed     = false;
 72:          }
 73:          #endregion
 74:
 75:          #region Control Method Overrides
 76:
 77:          /// <summary>
 78:          ///
 79:          /// </summary>
 80:          /// <param name="e"></param>
 81:          protected override void OnGotFocus( EventArgs e ) {
 82:              Invalidate( );
 83:      base.OnGotFocus( e );
 84:          }
 85:
 86:          protected override void OnLostFocus( EventArgs e ) {
 87:              Invalidate( );
 88:              base.OnLostFocus( e );
 89:          }
 90:
 91:          protected override void OnTextChanged( EventArgs e ) {
 92:              Invalidate( );
 93:              Update( );
 94:              base.OnTextChanged( e );
 95:          }
 96:
 97:          /// <summary>
 98:          ///
 99:          /// </summary>
100:          /// <param name="e"></param>
101:          protected override void OnSizeChanged( EventArgs e ) {
102:              base.OnSizeChanged( e );
103:              this.Invalidate( );
104:              this.Update( );
105:          }
106:
107:          /// <summary>
108:          /// Render the IconButton
109:          /// </summary>
110:          /// <param name="e"><see cref="PaintEventArgs"/></param>
111:          protected override void OnPaint( PaintEventArgs e ) {
112:              base.OnPaint( e );
113:              Draw( e.Graphics );
114:          }
115:
```

LISTING 2.6   Continued

```
116:          /// <summary>
117:          ///
118:          /// </summary>
119:          /// <param name="e"></param>
120:          protected override void OnMouseDown( MouseEventArgs e ) {
121:              if( e.Button == MouseButtons.Left ) {
122:      Focus( );
123:                  Capture           = true;
124:                  buttonState       = ButtonState.Pushed;
125:                  mousePressed     = true;
126:                  Invalidate( );
127:                  Update( );
128:              } else
129:                  base.OnMouseDown( e );
130:          }
131:
132:          /// <summary>
133:          ///
134:          /// </summary>
135:          /// <param name="e"></param>
136:          protected override void OnMouseUp( MouseEventArgs e ) {
137:
138:              if( mousePressed && e.Button == MouseButtons.Left ) {
139:                  Capture           = false;
140:                  buttonState       = ButtonState.Normal;
141:                  Invalidate( );
142:                  Update( );
143:              } else
144:                  base.OnMouseUp( e );
145:
146:              mousePressed     = false;
147:          }
148:
149:
150:
151:      #endregion
152:
153:      #region Implementation
154:
155:          /// <summary>
156:          /// Render the IconButton
157:          /// </summary>
158:          /// <param name="g"></param>
159:          protected virtual void Draw( Graphics g ) {
160:
```

LISTING 2.6   Continued

```
161:            DrawButton( g );
162:
163:            if( buttonIcon != null )
164:                DrawIcon( g );
165:
166:            DrawText( g );
167:
168:            if( base.Focused )
169:                DrawFocusClues( g );
170:        }
171:
172:        /// <summary>
173:        ///
174:        /// </summary>
175:        /// <param name="g"></param>
176:    protected virtual void DrawButton( Graphics g ) {
177:            Rectangle rcButton = new Rectangle( 0, 0,
➥this.Width, this.Height );
178:            if( Focused )
179:                rcButton.Inflate(-1,-1);
180:
181:            ControlPaint.DrawButton( g, rcButton, buttonState );
182:        }
183:
184:        /// <summary>
185:        ///
186:        /// </summary>
187:        /// <param name="g"></param>
188:        protected virtual void DrawText( Graphics g ) {
189:            int left    = (buttonIcon == null ?
190:                IconButton.EDGE_PADDING :
191:                iconDrawWidth + IconButton.EDGE_PADDING);
192:            int width   = Width - left;
193:            int top     = IconButton.EDGE_PADDING;
194:            int height  = Height - (2*IconButton.EDGE_PADDING);
195:
196:            RectangleF layoutRect = new RectangleF( left, top,
➥ width, height );
197:            if( ButtonState.Pushed == buttonState )
198:                layoutRect.Offset( 1f, 1f );
199:
200:            StringFormat fmt    = new StringFormat( );
201:            fmt.Alignment       = StringAlignment.Center;
202:            fmt.LineAlignment   = StringAlignment.Center;
203:
```

LISTING 2.6   Continued

```
204:            SolidBrush textBrush    = new SolidBrush( this.ForeColor );
205:            g.DrawString( Text, Font, textBrush, layoutRect, fmt );
206:
207:            textBrush.Dispose( );
208:        }
209:
210:        /// <summary>
211:        ///
212:        /// </summary>
213:        /// <param name="g"></param>
214:        protected virtual void DrawIcon( Graphics g ) {
215:            System.Diagnostics.Debug.Assert( buttonIcon != null,
➥ "IconButton Icon is null" );
216:
217:            int top      = ((Height/2) - (buttonIcon.Height/2));
218:            int height   = buttonIcon.Height;
219:            int width    = buttonIcon.Width;
220:
221:            if( (top + height) >= Height ) {
222:        //Scale the image to fit in (w,h) of button
223:            top = IconButton.EDGE_PADDING;
224:            int drawHeight = Height - (2*IconButton.EDGE_PADDING);
225:            float scale = ((float)drawHeight / (float)height);
226:            width = (int)((float)width*scale);
227:            height = drawHeight;
228:        }
229:            Rectangle iconRect = new Rectangle( IconButton.EDGE_PADDING,
➥ top, width, height);
230:
231:            if( buttonState == ButtonState.Pushed )
232:                iconRect.Offset(1,1);
233:
234:            g.DrawIcon( buttonIcon, iconRect );
235:
236:            this.iconDrawWidth = iconRect.Width;
237:        }
238:
239:        /// <summary>
240:        ///
241:        /// </summary>
242:        /// <param name="g"></param>
243:        protected virtual void DrawFocusClues( Graphics g ) {
244:            System.Drawing.Pen p =
➥new Pen( System.Drawing.Color.Black, 1f );
```

LISTING 2.6   Continued

```
245:             Rectangle frameRect =
➡new Rectangle( 0, 0, this.Width, this.Height );
246:             g.DrawRectangle( p, frameRect );
247:
248:             p.DashStyle = System.Drawing.Drawing2D.DashStyle.Dot;
249:             frameRect = new Rectangle( 2, 2, this.Width - 6,
➡ this.Height - 6);
250:             if( buttonState == ButtonState.Pushed )
251:                 frameRect.Offset( 1, 1 );
252:             g.DrawRectangle( p, frameRect );
253:
254:             p.Dispose( );
255:         }
256:     #endregion
257:
258:     }
259: }
```

Even a small control can quickly reach a couple hundred lines of code. The C# version of the IconButton control, from Listing 2.6, is designed to mimic the standard Windows button in terms of look and feel while also providing the capability to associate an icon to be drawn on the button.

The drawing code for the button is broken down into three tasks. The first task is to draw the button itself. The method DrawButton on line 176 handles drawing the basic button control. After the button has been rendered, the next step is to draw the associated icon if there is one. The DrawIcon method on line 214 handles this task.

Rather than simply drawing the icon image as is, the DrawIcon method scales the icon as necessary to fit within the button. The final width of the renderend icon must also be tracked because the text for the button will need this information to align itself properly. The final basic drawing step is to render the button text using the DrawText method on line 188.

The DrawText method determines the alignment for the text depending on factors such as the icon draw width and the current state of the button. If the button is in a pushed state, the text is offset by one pixel. This offsetting makes it appear as if the button is being pushed down and gives a sense of movement to the user.

The next major area of the IconButton is dealing with events. The most common events deal with the mouse. The IconButton overrides both the OnMouseDown and the OnMouseUp events of the control base class. The mouse events are used to change the state of the button from normal to pushed and back to normal, depending on the actions of the mouse. Other events include the paint and size events, along with responding to the TextChanged event.

Listing 2.7 is the VB .NET equivalent of the C# source found in Listing 2.6. In every way, these two code listings provide for the same functionality.

LISTING 2.7 IconButton VB .NET Source

```
 1: Imports System.Windows.Forms
 2: Imports System.Drawing
 3:
 4: Namespace SAMS.ToolKit.VB.Controls
 5:
 6:     <System.ComponentModel.Description("SAMS IconButton Control (VB)")> _
 7:     Public Class IconButton
 8:         Inherits System.Windows.Forms.Control
 9:
10: #Region "Const Member Fields"
11:         Protected Const EDGE_PADDING As Integer = 4
12: #End Region
13:
14: #Region "Implementation Member Fields"
15:         Protected buttonState As System.Windows.Forms.buttonState
16:         Protected buttonIcon As System.Drawing.Icon
17:         Protected mousePressed As Boolean
18:         Protected iconDrawWidth As Integer
19: #End Region
20:
21: #Region "Properties"
22:
23:         <System.ComponentModel.Description(
➥"The Icon to be displayed in the button"), _
24:         System.ComponentModel.Category("Appearance")> _
25:         Public Property Icon() As Icon
26:             Get
27:                 Icon = buttonIcon
28:             End Get
29:             Set(ByVal value As Icon)
30:                 buttonIcon = value
31:                 Invalidate()
32:                 Update()
33:             End Set
34:         End Property
35: #End Region
36:
37:
38: #Region "Construction"
39:
40:         Public Sub IconButton()
```

LISTING 2.7   Continued

```
41:                buttonState = buttonState.Normal
42:                buttonIcon = Nothing
43:                iconDrawWidth = 0
44:            End Sub
45:
46: #End Region
47:
48: #Region "Control Overrides"
49:
50:        Protected Overrides Sub OnMouseDown(ByVal e As
➥System.Windows.Forms.MouseEventArgs)
51:            If (e.Button = MouseButtons.Left) Then
52:                Focus()
53:                Capture = True
54:                buttonState = buttonState.Pushed
55:                mousePressed = True
56:                Invalidate()
57:                Update()
58:            Else
59:        MyBase.OnMouseDown(e)
60:            End If
61:        End Sub
62:
63:
64:        Protected Overrides Sub OnMouseUp(ByVal e As
➥System.Windows.Forms.MouseEventArgs)
65:            If (mousePressed And (e.Button = MouseButtons.Left)) Then
66:                Capture = False
67:                mousePressed = False
68:                buttonState = buttonState.Normal
69:                Invalidate()
70:                Update()
71:            Else
72:                MyBase.OnMouseUp(e)
73:            End If
74:        End Sub
75:
76:        Protected Overrides Sub OnPaint(ByVal e As
➥ System.Windows.Forms.PaintEventArgs)
77:            Draw(e.Graphics)
78:            MyBase.OnPaint(e)
79:        End Sub
80:
81:        Protected Overrides Sub OnSizeChanged(ByVal e As System.EventArgs)
82:            Invalidate()
```

LISTING 2.7   Continued

```
83:                 MyBase.OnSizeChanged(e)
84:         End Sub
85:
86:         Protected Overrides Sub OnTextChanged(ByVal e As System.EventArgs)
87:             Invalidate()
88:         End Sub
89:
90:         Protected Overrides Sub OnLostFocus(ByVal e As System.EventArgs)
91:             Invalidate()
92:         End Sub
93:
94:         Protected Overrides Sub OnGotFocus(ByVal e As System.EventArgs)
95:             Invalidate()
96:         End Sub
97:
98: #End Region
99:
100: #Region "Implementation"
101:        Protected Overridable Sub Draw(ByRef g As System.Drawing.Graphics)
102:            DrawButton(g)
103:            If (Not buttonIcon Is Nothing) Then
104:                DrawIcon(g)
105:            End If
106:            DrawText(g)
107:
108:   If (MyBase.Focused) Then
109:                DrawFocusClues(g)
110:            End If
111:        End Sub
112:
113:         Protected Overridable Sub DrawButton(ByRef g As
➥System.Drawing.Graphics)
114:            Dim rcButton As New Rectangle(0, 0, Width, Height)
115:            If (Focused) Then
116:                rcButton.Inflate(-1, -1)
117:            End If
118:            ControlPaint.DrawButton(g, rcButton, buttonState)
119:        End Sub
120:
121:         Protected Overridable Sub DrawIcon(ByRef g As
➥System.Drawing.Graphics)
122:            System.Diagnostics.Debug.Assert(Not buttonIcon Is Nothing,
➥"IconButton is null")
123:
124:            Dim top, height, width As Integer
```

LISTING 2.7 Continued

```
125:
126:                top = (Me.Height / 2) - (buttonIcon.Height / 2)
127:                height = buttonIcon.Height
128:                width = buttonIcon.Width
129:
130:                If ((top + height) >= Me.Height) Then
131:                    'Scale the image to fit in (w,h) of button
132:                    top = EDGE_PADDING
133:                    Dim drawHeight As Integer = Me.Height - (2 * EDGE_PADDING)
134:                    Dim scale As Single = drawHeight / height
135:                    width = width * scale
136:                    height = drawHeight
137:                End If
138:
139:                Dim iconRect As New Rectangle(EDGE_PADDING, top,
➥width, height)
140:                If (buttonState.Pushed = buttonState) Then
141:                    iconRect.Offset(1F, 1F)
142:                End If
143:
144:                g.DrawIcon(buttonIcon, iconRect)
145:                iconDrawWidth = iconRect.Width
146:            End Sub
147:
148:            Protected Overridable Sub DrawText(ByRef g As
➥System.Drawing.Graphics)
149:                Dim top, left, width, height As Integer
150:
151:   top = EDGE_PADDING
152:                left = IIf(buttonIcon Is Nothing, EDGE_PADDING,
➥ iconDrawWidth + EDGE_PADDING)
153:                width = Me.Width - left
154:                height = Me.Height - (2 * EDGE_PADDING)
155:
156:                Dim layoutRect As New RectangleF(left, top, width, height)
157:                If (buttonState.Pushed = buttonState) Then
158:                    layoutRect.Offset(1F, 1F)
159:                End If
160:
161:                Dim fmt As New StringFormat()
162:                fmt.Alignment = StringAlignment.Center
163:                fmt.LineAlignment = StringAlignment.Center
164:
165:                Dim textBrush As New SolidBrush(Me.ForeColor)
166:
```

2

LISTING 2.7 Continued

```
167:                 g.DrawString(Text, Font, textBrush, layoutRect, fmt)
168:
169:                 textBrush.Dispose()
170:
171:             End Sub
172:
173:             Protected Overridable Sub DrawFocusClues(
➥ByRef g As System.Drawing.Graphics)
174:                 Dim p As New System.Drawing.Pen(System.Drawing.Color.Black,
1F)
175:                 Dim frameRect = New Rectangle(0, 0, Me.Width, Me.Height)
176:                 g.DrawRectangle(p, frameRect)
177:
178:                 p.DashStyle = Drawing.Drawing2D.DashStyle.Dot
179:                 frameRect = New Rectangle(2, 2, Me.Width - 6, Me.Height - 6)
180:                 If (buttonState.Pushed = buttonState) Then
181:                     frameRect.offset(1, 1)
182:                 End If
183:                 g.DrawRectangle(p, frameRect)
184:
185:                 p.Dispose()
186:             End Sub
187: #End Region
188:
189:     End Class
190:
191: End Namespace
```

The code for both C# and VB .NET is remarkably similar in structure and syntax. In fact, all the topics covered in this book can be implemented in C# or VB .NET with ease. The .NET base class libraries have finally leveled the playing field such that you may use the language of your choice to accomplish the task at hand.

Most of the code for the IconButton is fairly simple in nature and makes use of GDI+, Graphics Device Interface, to draw the associated icon for the button. The topic of GDI+ is covered in Chapter 4, "GDI+." In addition, the IconButton uses the ControlPaint class to draw the button itself. Controls have two basic parts: presentation and logic.

The logic of a control depends on the purpose it's supposed to serve, and as such, developing two complete controls, both presented in this book, will help give you an understanding on that front. The presentation of a control consists of runtime and design-time behavior and the control's look and feel. Chapter 4, "GDI+," covers the use of GDI+ for dealing with the drawing aspects of a control, and the remaining chapters cover VS .NET support for control development.

Testing the `IconButton` Control

Testing the `IconButton` is as simple as creating a new Windows Forms project and customizing the Toolbox to display the `IconButton`. Create a new Windows Forms project and then right-click on the Toolbox to bring up the context menu shown in Figure 2.8, and select Customize Toolbox. This brings up the Customize Toolbox dialog, which you can use to browse for the compiled DLL created for the `IconButton` (see Figure 2.9).

FIGURE 2.8

The Toolbox context menu.

Click OK and a Toolbox item for the `IconButton` appears at the bottom of the Windows Forms tab. As with any other controls, select the `IconButton` and drag it onto the form. With the `IconButton` selected, use the property browser to assign an icon to the button. Notice that a dialog appears and that when an icon file is selected, the property browser is updated and the control renders the icon. How does this happen? Well, this is the subject of the next chapter.

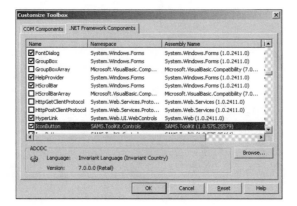

FIGURE 2.9
The Customize Toolbox dialog.

Summary

By now you should realize that there is nothing difficult about developing custom controls. All that is really necessary is to be armed with the information about control base classes and a desire to create your own custom control. This chapter covered the basics of control classes and what it takes to get up and running with building controls. The next chapter deals with the design-time of custom controls, whereas this chapter focused on the runtime behavior. To build professional-quality controls, equal effort must be spent on runtime and design-time. And now, on to the design-time experience.

Designer Basics

IN THIS CHAPTER

A control designer defines the behavior and UI presentation of a control during design-time. In VS .NET, forms can be created using the Forms Designer. This Forms Designer allows controls, such as buttons, menus, and toolbars, to be drawn on the form rather than being created pragmatically. Each control has an associated designer that defines the behavior of the control during the visual design-time process of building a Windows Forms application.

During design-time, a control's properties can be manipulated using the Property Grid. The control should appear very similar to the runtime look while being designed, with a few exceptions. These exceptions include the handling of a control's `Visible` property and any designer clues such as the placement grid. The placement grid is the series of dots used for aligning controls during design-time that are not shown at runtime. In general, however, a control's appearance during design-time should give an accurate representation of the control's appearance during runtime.

> **NOTE**
>
> Certainly, setting the control's `Visible` property to `false` during design-time should not make the control invisible. If this were the case, there would be no way to select the control and continue to visually design it.

Designers are an important part of the equation in developing custom controls. By providing a rich design-time experience, application developers can visually build applications using the custom control you've created. The UI presentation is not a designer's sole responsibility; designers must also provide for proper serialization of the code generated for the control, in order for the control to work properly at runtime. The code for the construction of the control, along with the necessary property settings, is serialized within the `InitializeComponent` method of the form hosting the control. This is the reason for the all-too-familiar comment on the method stating, "This code should not be modified as the designer will OVER WRITE this method when serializing the form's design state."

The `ControlDesigner` Base Class

Just as .NET provides base classes for developing controls, there also exists a set of base classes for implementing designers. In Chapter 5, "Advanced Control Development," the designer base classes are covered in more detail; for now, the `ControlDesigner` base class is the focus.

The `ControlDesigner` base class provides the bare-bones functionality for designing a control. Figure 3.1 shows a UML diagram of the `ControlDesigner` inheritance chain and supported interfaces. UML, or Unified Modeling Language, diagrams are helpful tools for visualizing the various components and classes of any software project.

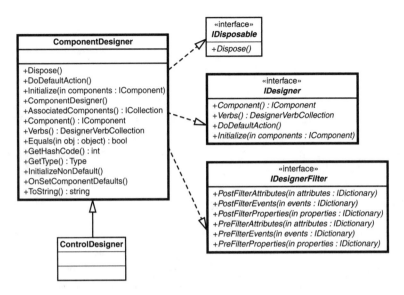

FIGURE 3.1
The ControlDesigner *hierarchy.*

The base class for ControlDesigner is ComponentDesigner. The ComponentDesigner base class provides support for general component design and is not intended to be used directly for providing design-time support for controls. Its purpose is to provide common functionality for component design-time support.

The ControlDesigner base class serves as a starting point for creating control designers and implements the necessary interfaces for VS .NET. The ControlDesigner base class will serve as the base class for the IconButtonDesigner developed in this chapter. Remember that each control has an associated designer class. This association between the control and its designer class is created by specifying the designer class of a control through the use of an attribute. The DesignerAttribute is used for this purpose.

DesignerAttribute

To specify the designer for a control, the System.ComponentMode.Design.DesignerAttribute is used to decorate the control class. The word *decorate* is used to denote the fact that the DesignerAttribute provides extra information about the control class. The control class itself does not use the specified designer class; however, VS .NET uses this information to locate and create the specified designer. In the case of the IconButton, the DesignerAttribute would be declared as shown here:

```
1: [
2: System.ComponentModel.Design.Designer (
3:                 typeof( SAMS.ToolKit.Design.IconButtonDesigner )
4:                                        )
5: ]
6: public class IconButton : ... { //rest of class }
```

The declaration for the designer assumes that the `IconButtonDesigner` resides in the name-space `SAMS.ToolKit.Design` and uses the fully qualified name as the argument for the `DesignerAttribute`. In C# it's not necessary to include the `Attribute` part when declaring and using an attribute; the class `DesignerAttribute` can be referenced as `Designer`.

The IconButton Designer

It's time to create a simple designer for the `IconButton` control. The designer will be built in two stages. The first stage of the designer will filter properties of the control to remove the `BackColor` and `BackgroundImage` properties. The next stage of development will introduce the concept of *verbs*; verbs are actions that can be associated with a control.

As with any project, the first step involves setting up the development environment. After the VS .NET Solution is created, the process of creating and testing the `IconButtonDesigner` can begin.

Setting Up the SAMS.ToolKit Solution

Before we venture into designer development, now would be a good time to set up a VS .NET Solution that will be used throughout the remainder of the book. In VS .NET a Solution is used to contain one or more related projects. For those of you familiar with Visual Studio 6, a Solution is orthogonal to a workspace.

Start by creating a new C# class library with the name `SAMS.ToolKit`. This will create a new VS .NET Solution, and the output when compiling the Solution will be `SAMS.ToolKit.dll`. In addition, the default namespace will also be `SAMS.ToolKit`.

With the Solution in place, create two folders:

- Controls
- Design

The new Solution should look similar to what's shown in Figure 3.2.

FIGURE 3.2

The SAMS.ToolKit *Solution.*

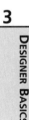

As with any .NET project, the familiar References folder and the AssemblyInfo.cs source file are automatically created. The folders within the Solution allow for a convenient way to organize code within the project. In addition, any new classes that are created within the folders will have the folder name added to the default namespace.

The Controls folder will need to contain the IconButton.cs file that was created in the preceding chapter. Right-click the Controls folder, select Add Existing Item from the Add menu, and locate the IconButton.cs source file. It is important to note that this operation will *copy* the source file to the new destination *rather than referencing* it. This means that there will be two copies of the source and changes to the new source will not be reflected in the original source. Open the IconButton.cs source file and change the namespace to SAMS.ToolKit.Controls.

Filtering Properties

During development of a new custom control, it is sometimes necessary to remove any unwanted or unneeded properties inherited from the base class from which the new custom control derives. The process of adding or removing properties and events is known as filtering. The reason behind filtering, in this case filtering properties, is to alter the available options during the design of the control rather than to provide unnecessary or unused properties/events.

The first designer will be used to remove or filter out two properties from the IconButton: BackColor and BackgroundImage. These properties are inherited from the Control base class and serve no purpose for the IconButton control because neither of these properties has any effect on the control.

The capability to filter properties, events, and attributes comes from implementing the IDesignerFilter interface. Table 3.1 lists the IDesignerFilter interface methods.

TABLE 3.1   The IDesignerFilter Interface Methods

Method	Description
PostFilterAttributes	Allows a designer to change or remove attributes.
PostFilterEvents	Allows a designer to change or remove events.
PostFilterProperties	Allows a designer to change or remove properties.
PreFilterAttributes	Allows a designer to add attributes.
PreFilterEvents	Allows a designer to add events.
PreFilterProperties	Allows a designer to add properties.

Advanced uses of the IDesignerFilter interface are covered in Chapter 5, "Advanced Control Development."

As the first venture into developing a designer, the first pass of the IconButton designer will remove the unused properties BackColor and BackgroundImage. Currently, the IconButton provides both of these properties as they are implemented by the Control base class. The default properties are supplied when the control is created and can be seen in the property grid when the control is selected on the form (see Figure 3.3).

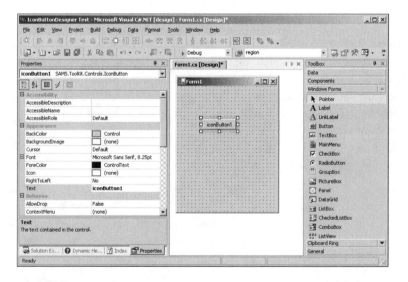

FIGURE 3.3

The IconButton default properties.

> **NOTE**
>
> The `BackgroundImage` property has the value of `(none)`. This means that currently there is no image associated with this property. One of the responsibilities of a `Designer` class is to provide such feedback to the developer and to the property grid.

Notice the `BackColor` and `BackgroundImage` properties displayed in Figure 3.3. To remove these properties, the `IconButtonDesigner` class will implement the method `PostFilterProperties` and remove the unwanted properties from the properties collection. Because the `ControlDesigner` base class implements the `IDesignerFilter` interface, the `IconButtonDesigner` class needs to override the implementation of the `PostFilterProperties` method. Listing 3.1 contains the C# source for the `IconButtonDesigner`.

LISTING 3.1   Designer Stage One

```
 1: //////////////////////////////////////////////////////////////////////
 2: ///File        :IconButton.cs
 3: ///Author      :Richard L. Weeks
 4: ///
 5: /// Copyright (c) 2001 by Richard L. Weeks
 6: /// This file is provided for instructional purposes only.
 7: /// No warranties.
 8: //////////////////////////////////////////////////////////////////////
 9:
10: using System;
11: using System.ComponentModel;
12: using System.ComponentModel.Design;
13: using System.Collections;
14: using System.Drawing;
15:
16:
17: namespace SAMS.ToolKit.Design
18: {
19:     /// <summary>
20:     /// Simple Designer for IconButton
21:     /// </summary>
22:     public class IconButtonDesigner :
➥System.Windows.Forms.Design.ControlDesigner {
23:
24:
25:
```

LISTING 3.1   Continued

```
26:        public IconButtonDesigner()    {
27:        }
28:
29:
30:        //Overrides
31:
32:        /// <summary>
33:        /// Remove some basic properties that are not supported by the
➥IconButton
34:        /// </summary>
35:        /// <param name="Properties"></param>
36:        protected override void PostFilterProperties(
➥IDictionary Properties ) {
37:            Properties.Remove( "BackgroundImage" );
38:            Properties.Remove( "BackColor" );
39:        }
40:
41:
42:
43: }
44: }
```

The `PostFilterProperties` method receives an `IDictionary` interface to a collection of properties associated with the control being designed. As with any collection, the `Remove` method is
used to remove the specified item from the collection. In the case of the `IconButtonDesigner`,
the code on lines 37 and 38 of Listing 3.1 remove or filter out the unwated properties:
`BackgroundImage` and `BackColor`.

With the unwanted properties filtered out, they will no longer be displayed within the property
grid during the design-time of the `IconButton` control. However, pragmatic access to the properties is still available to the developer.

To enable the designer for the `IconButton` control, add the following attribute to the
`IconButton` class:

`System.ComponentModel.Designer(typeof(SAMS.ToolKit.Design.IconButtonDesigner))`

The `IconButton` class should now look similar to what's shown in Listing 3.2.

LISTING 3.2   Updated Attributes for the IconButton

```
1:[
2:System.ComponentModel.Description( "SAMS IconButton Control" ),
3:System.ComponentModel.Designer(
➥ typeof( SAMS.ToolKit.Design.IconButtonDesigner ) )
```

LISTING 3.2   Continued

```
4:]
5:public class IconButton : System.Windows.Forms.Control {
6: //IconButton implementation
7: }
```

Rebuild the SAMS.ToolKit Solution to produce the new control library. To test the results of the designer, start a new Windows Forms Solution and add the IconButton to the form. Notice that the BackColor and BackgroundImage properties are no longer displayed in the property grid, as shown in Figure 3.4.

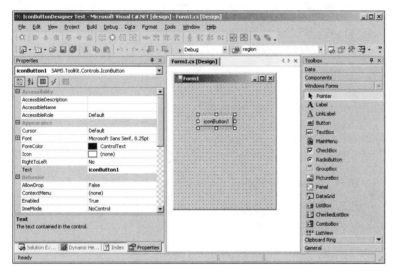

FIGURE 3.4
The first phase of the IconButtonDesigner.

Designer Verbs

Verbs are best described as actions that can be applied to the control being designed. Verbs for a control are linked to an event handler and are added to the context menu for the control, as well as the property window. The best way to understand the role of verbs is to implement them, and that's exactly what the second phase of the IconButtonDesigner is about.

To support adding verbs for a control, the designer needs to implement the Verbs property. The Verbs property returns a DesignerVerbsCollection of DesignerVerbs that the control designer supports. The IconButtonDesigner will be extended to provide verbs for changing the `ForeColor` property of the control to Red, Green, or Blue. The event handler for custom verbs uses the following `EventHandler` signature:

```
void EventHandler( object sender, EventArgs e )
```

Listing 3.3 shows the updated `IconButtonDesigner` with the `Verbs` property implemented.

LISTING 3.3   Designer Stage Two

```
 1: //////////////////////////////////////////////////////////////////////
 2: ///File      :IconButton.cs
 3: ///Author    :Richard L. Weeks
 4: ///
 5: /// Copyright (c) 2001 by Richard L. Weeks
 6: /// This file is provided for instructional purposes only.
 7: /// No warranties.
 8: //////////////////////////////////////////////////////////////////////
 9:
10: using System;
11: using System.ComponentModel;
12: using System.ComponentModel.Design;
13: using System.Collections;
14: using System.Drawing;
15:
16:
17: namespace SAMS.ToolKit.Design
18: {
19:     /// <summary>
20:     /// Simple Designer for IconButton
21:     /// </summary>
22:     public class IconButtonDesigner :
➥System.Windows.Forms.Design.ControlDesigner {
23:
24:
25:
26:         public IconButtonDesigner()    {
27:         }
28:
29:         public override DesignerVerbCollection Verbs {
30:             get {
31:   DesignerVerb[] verbs = new DesignerVerb[3];
32:                 verbs[0] = new DesignerVerb( "Red",
➥new EventHandler( this.OnRedVerb ) );
33:                 verbs[1] = new DesignerVerb( "Green",
➥new EventHandler( this.OnGreenVerb ) );
34:                 verbs[2] = new DesignerVerb( "Blue",
➥new EventHandler( this.OnBlueVerb ) );
```

LISTING 3.3   Continued

```
35:                    return new DesignerVerbCollection( verbs );
36:             }
37:         }
38:
39:
40:        //Overrides
41:
42:        /// <summary>
43:        /// Remove some basic properties that are not supported by the
➡IconButton
44:        /// </summary>
45:        /// <param name="Properties"></param>
46:        protected override void PostFilterProperties(
➡IDictionary Properties ) {
47:            Properties.Remove( "BackgroundImage" );
48:            Properties.Remove( "BackColor" );
49:        }
50:
51:
52:        //Verb Handlers
53:        protected void OnRedVerb( object sender, EventArgs e ) {
54:            this.Control.ForeColor = System.Drawing.Color.Red;
55:        }
56:        protected void OnGreenVerb( object sender, EventArgs e ) {
57:            this.Control.ForeColor =  System.Drawing.Color.Green;
58:        }
59:        protected void OnBlueVerb( object sender, EventArgs e ) {
60:            this.Control.ForeColor =  System.Drawing.Color.Blue;
61:        }
62:
63:
64:  }
65: }
```

Line 29 of Listing 3.3 implements the Verbs property. Each verb defines a text string for the menu and an EventHandler to be invoked when the menu handler is selected. Figure 3.5 shows the context menu and property grid of the IconButton using the revised IconButtonDesigner class.

3

DESIGNER BASICS

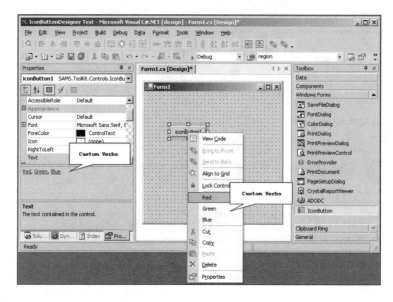

FIGURE 3.5

Verbs support.

VS .NET handles the context menu and property grid support for displaying the supported verbs or commands that the current control designer supports. When one of the supported verbs is selected, the designated EventHandler is invoked so that the verb can be executed. In the case of the IconButtonDesigner, the ForeColor property of the IconButton being designed is updated accordingly.

Designer verbs also allow for user feedback such as providing a check mark for the current ForeColor selected. To provide this feedback, the Checked property of the DesignerVerb item needs to be set. The current implementation of the IconButtonDesigner merely creates the supported designer verbs within the context of the Verbs property rather than as an implementation member. Listing 3.4 updates the IconButtonDesigner to support providing the DesignerVerbs as members and makes use of the Checked property.

LISTING 3.4   The Updated IconButtonDesigner Class

```
1: /////////////////////////////////////////////////////////////////////////
2: ///File        :IconButton.cs
3: ///Author      :Richard L. Weeks
4: ///
5: /// Copyright (c) 2001 by Richard L. Weeks
6: /// This file is provided for instructional purposes only.
7: /// No warranties.
8: /////////////////////////////////////////////////////////////////////////
```

LISTING 3.4 Continued

```
 9:
10: using System;
11: using System.ComponentModel;
12: using System.ComponentModel.Design;
13: using System.Collections;
14: using System.Drawing;
15:
16:
17: namespace SAMS.ToolKit.Design
18: {
19:     /// <summary>
20:     /// Simple Designer for IconButton
21:     /// </summary>
22:   public class IconButtonDesigner :
➥System.Windows.Forms.Design.ControlDesigner {
23:
24:         private enum VERBS {
25:             Red,
26:             Green,
27:             Blue
28:         }
29:
30:         private DesignerVerb[]          designerVerbs;
31:
32:         public IconButtonDesigner()    {
33:             designerVerbs = new DesignerVerb[3];
34:             DesignerVerb[] verbs = new DesignerVerb[3];
35:             designerVerbs[(int)VERBS.Red] =
➥new DesignerVerb( "Red", new EventHandler( this.OnRedVerb ) );
36:             designerVerbs[(int)VERBS.Green] =
➥new DesignerVerb( "Green",  new EventHandler( this.OnGreenVerb ) );
37:             designerVerbs[(int)VERBS.Blue] =
➥new DesignerVerb( "Blue",  new EventHandler( this.OnBlueVerb ) );
38:         }
39:
40:   public override DesignerVerbCollection Verbs {
41:         get {
42:             return new DesignerVerbCollection( designerVerbs );
43:         }
44:     }
45:
46:
47:     //Overrides
48:
49:     /// <summary>
```

LISTING 3.4 Continued

```
50:        /// Remove some basic properties that are not supported by the
➥IconButton
51:        /// </summary>
52:        /// <param name="Properties"></param>
53:        protected override void PostFilterProperties(
➥ IDictionary Properties ) {
54:            Properties.Remove( "BackgroundImage" );
55:            Properties.Remove( "BackColor" );
56:        }
57:
58:
59:        //Verb Handlers
60:    protected void OnRedVerb( object sender, EventArgs e ) {
61:            this.Control.ForeColor = System.Drawing.Color.Red;
62:            UpdateCheckMarks( VERBS.Red );
63:        }
64:        protected void OnGreenVerb( object sender, EventArgs e ) {
65:            this.Control.ForeColor =  System.Drawing.Color.Green;
66:            UpdateCheckMarks( VERBS.Green );
67:        }
68:        protected void OnBlueVerb( object sender, EventArgs e ) {
69:            this.Control.ForeColor =  System.Drawing.Color.Blue;
70:            UpdateCheckMarks( VERBS.Blue );
71:        }
72:
73:
74:        private void UpdateCheckMarks( VERBS ActiveVerb ) {
75:            foreach( DesignerVerb dv in designerVerbs )
76:                dv.Checked = false;
77:            designerVerbs[ (int)ActiveVerb ].Checked = true;
78:        }
79:    }
80: }
```

As a result of the updated IconButtonDesigner, the custom verbs on the context menu will show a check mark next to the currently selected foreground color corresponding to the selected verb (see Figure 3.6).

With the addition of verbs, the IconButtonDesigner class is beginning to take shape. In Chapter 5, "Advanced Control Development," the designer will be extended to provide even more features. By now you should have the basic idea of what is involved in developing a designer.

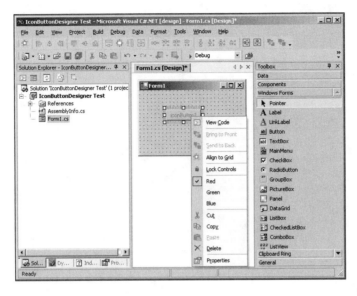

FIGURE 3.6
Using the designer verb Checked *property.*

Adding a Toolbox Bitmap

Before this chapter ends, I'd like to add a Toolbox bitmap for the IconButton. A Toolbox bitmap is the 16×16 image that appears in the Toolbox tab for the IconButton. Adding a bitmap for a control is a simple task, to say the least. All that needs to be done is to add a bitmap with the same name as the control to the project. Figure 3.7 shows the Solution with the IconButton.bmp file added in the Controls folder of the Solution.

The bitmap must reside in the same namespace as the control and be compiled as an embedded resource. The Toolbox uses this as the default search for locating the associated Toolbox image to associate with the control. In the case of the IconButton, this means adding the bitmap to the Controls folder of the Solution. To enable the bitmap as an embedded resource, right-click the bitmap file and select the Properties menu item. From the Properties page, set the Build Action to Embedded Resource, as shown in Figure 3.8.

FIGURE 3.7

The IconButton.bmp *file.*

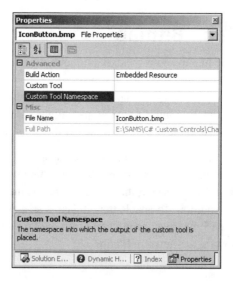

FIGURE 3.8

IconButton.bmp *properties.*

The bitmap that will act as the Toolbox bitmap for the control must also have the following properties:

- Height of 16
- Width of 16
- 16 colors

With these conditions satisfied, the new bitmap image will appear next to the name of the IconButton control when loaded in the Toolbox. Figure 3.9 shows the Toolbox with the IconButton bitmap enabled.

FIGURE 3.9
The IconButton *Toolbox bitmap.*

Again, the Toolbox will search the assembly manifest for an embedded bitmap with the same qualified name as the control. If found, the bitmap will be used as a visual representation of the control within the Toolbox.

Summary

The intent of this chapter was to produce a simple designer for the IconButton that was developed in the preceding chapter. In addition, I wanted to point out that there is no voodoo or black art to developing custom controls and the designers for those controls. All that is needed is an understanding of what is expected of a designer and the support provided by VS .NET. In addition, all the C# code presented in this chapter can easily be directly ported to VB .NET or any other .NET language. By now you should have a sense of the basic requirements for developing controls and their designers.

3

DESIGNER BASICS

GDI+

IN THIS CHAPTER

Before this chapter dives into the details of control development, a brief tour of GDI+ is in order. GDI stands for Graphics Device Interface, an abstraction for drawing to a graphics-capable device such as the screen or printer. GDI+ is the next stage of evolution in the development of the Win32 GDI API.

One of the major tasks associated with Windows development is the task of rendering or painting on the screen or printer. Humans are visual creatures, and as such the capability to provide information and feedback through visual means is important. Consider data within a spreadsheet. Although the actual figures and formulas detail the exact data and necessary information, providing different styles of graphs of the data often helps us visualize the information. This presentation of data is just as important when developing various user interface elements such as custom buttons, menus, and toolbars.

GDI+ represents the latest Graphics Device Interface API provided by the .NET framework. GDI+ is a major improvement over the somewhat archaic Win32 GDI calls of yesteryear, and it provides a simple object model for a graphics interface.

One of the major portions of control development is the user interface it presents to the user. In fact, a lot of time and effort will be spent on the painting code necessary to create just the right look and feel you're after for the control. The goal of this chapter is to explore some of the objects associated with GDI programming. Issues such as different styles of brushes, pens, fonts, and image formats are covered because they are likely to be a common theme when developing custom controls and Windows applications in general.

The Graphics Class

At the root of GDI+ is the `System.Drawing.Graphics` class. This class encompasses methods for drawing text, icons, images, rectangles, ellipses, curves, and everything in between. The `Graphics` class is the heart and sole of GDI+, and you'd do well to familiarize yourself with the services it offers, as well as its limitations.

Although the `Graphics` class provides the means to render basic shapes and images to a window, it requires a supporting cast. This supporting cast comprises brushes, pens, fonts, and even images. All of these objects work together to produce the final result displayed on the screen or printer.

An important note about GDI+ is that the programming model is a static model, whereas previous versions of GDI were stateful models. This means that for GDI+ to work, it requires resources such as brushes and pens to be managed by the developer rather than the GDI API. For seasoned Win32 GDI developers, this new model requires some getting used to; however, the new GDI+ offers increased performance and ease of use.

Brushes

Brushes are used to fill basic geometric shapes such as rectangles, ellipses, and polygons. The System.Drawing.Brush class is an abstract base class and cannot be instantiated directly. The Brush class serves as a base class for various brush styles. Figure 4.1 shows four of the common brush styles in action.

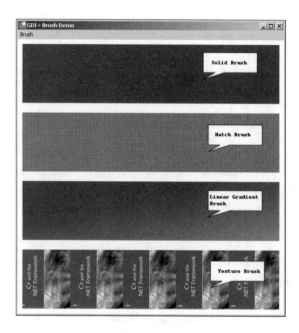

FIGURE 4.1
Basic brushes.

The following sections describe the Brush class styles.

SolidBrush

A SolidBrush is just as its name implies: it creates a solid color that fills a graphics primitive such as a triangle, circle, or rectangle. All graphics primitives are constructed from the most basic primitive, the point. Points can be used to construct lines, circles, and polygons. From these basic shapes, more complex shapes can be constructed. Creating a SolidBrush is a simple matter of knowing the color of the brush to create and passing the color to the constructor of the SolidBrush class. In the case of Figure 4.1, the SolidBrush was created with the following code:

```
SolidBrush solidBrush = new SolidBrush( System.Drawing.Color.Blue );
```

The `SolidBrush` object is created by specifying the color of the brush. The color can be specified either by using a predefined color found in the `Color` class or by using the `FromArgb` method of the `Color` class.

With the brush created, a call to the `FillRectangle` method of the graphics object creates a solid blue rectangle. Listing 4.1 shows the code snippet from the Brush Demo used to create and render the `SolidBrush`.

LISTING 4.1   Creating a `SolidBrush`

```
1: protected override void OnPaint( PaintEventArgs e ) {
2:  SolidBrush solidBrush = new SolidBrush( System.Drawing.Color.Blue );
3:  e.Graphics.FillRectangle( solidBrush, rcDisplayRect );
4:  solidBrush.Dispose( );
5: }
```

Notice the call to the `Dispose` method of the `solidBrush` object. GDI+ objects tend to be resource intensive, and it's recommended that the `Dispose` method should be invoked to free the associated resources when the GDI+ object is no longer needed.

HatchBrush

A `HatchBrush` defines a brush with a foreground and background color, along with a `HatchSytle` enum or pattern for the brush. The `HatchBrush` displayed in Figure 4.2 uses a foreground color of `white`, a background color of `black`, and the `Cross` hatch style. At last count 56 hatch styles were defined within the `HatchSytle` enum. If you're interested in seeing all of them, use the code snippet in Listing 4.2 and change the `HatchStyle` accordingly. A complete listing of the various hatch styles can be found by searching the online help for `System.Drawing.Drawing2D.HatchStyle` enum value.

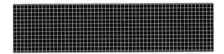

FIGURE 4.2
The `HatchBrush`.

LISTING 4.2   Creating a `HatchBrush`

```
1: protected override void OnPaint( PaintEventArgs e ) {
2: HatchBrush hatchBrush = new HatchBrush( HatchStyle.Cross,
➥System.Drawing.Color.White, System.Drawing.Color.Black );
```

LISTING 4.2   Continued

```
3: e.Graphics.FillRectangle( hatchBrush, rcDisplayRect );
4:   hatchBrush.Dispose( );
5:}
```

Providing a sample of every style of HatchStyle available would consume far too much space, but you should experiment with different HatchSytles to see the result. The following code snippet shows how to create a Weave hatch style with a blue foreground color and a gray background:

```
HatchBrush hatchBrush = new HatchBrush( HatchStyle.Weave, Color.Blue,
Color.Grey );
```

LinearGradientBrush

A linear gradient is a transition from one color to another. The LinearGradientBrush class defines a starting and ending color and creates a smooth transition from one color to another. In addition, it is also possible to define an angle for the transition. Figure 4.3 shows a gradient from Black to White with a 45-degree slope for the transition.

FIGURE 4.3
The LinearGradientBrush.

As with the other brushes, creating a gradient style brush is a simple matter of providing the desired parameters during construction. Listing 4.3 shows the code used to create the image shown in Figure 4.3.

LISTING 4.3   The LinearGradientBrush

```
1: protected virtual void OnPaint( PaintEventArgs e ) {
2: Rectangle rcDisplayRect = new Rectangle( 0, 0, 100, 100 );
3: LinearGradientBrush lgb = new LinearGradientBrush( rcDisplayRect,
4:                                                    Color.Black,
5:                                                    Color.White,
6:                                                    45f );
7:   e.Graphics.FillRectangle( lgb, rcDisplayRect );
8:   lgb.Dispose( );
9: }
```

The last parameter for the LinearGradientBrush constructor is the angle or rotation for the transition. In C# it is necessary to post-fix a float constant with the lowercase letter *f* in order for proper type safety. Such post-fixing of constants is found in languages such as C, C++, and even Visual Basic.

Also, the angle parameter is based on a left-handed coordinate system, meaning that the rotation is counterclockwise. To produce a downward slope, you can use a negative value or provide angle values greater than 90 degrees. Only extermination will help to make this clear.

GDI+ uses both 2D and 3D graphics concepts to accomplish rotation, scaling, and translation. Before panic sets in, be aware that the most 2D or 3D graphics fundamentals require nothing more than basic geometry, trigonometry, and matrix manipulation. Books solely devoted to 2D and 3D graphics are widely available in just about every bookstore.

TexturedBrush

The last brush covered is the TexturedBrush. The TexturedBrush allows for an image to be used as a repeating pattern for the brush. The image can be any image format such as a bitmap, jpeg, or gif, to name a few. Figure 4.4 shows the TexturedBrush using a jpeg as the repeating image.

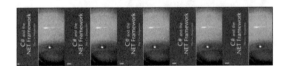

FIGURE 4.4
The TexturedBrush.

As with all the brushes presented so far, no real skill is needed to create the TexturedBrush. Listing 4.4 shows the code to create the TexturedBrush shown in Figure 4.4.

LISTING 4.4   Creating a TexturedBrush

```
1: protected override void OnPaint( PaintEventArgs e ) {
2:   System.Drawing.Image samsImage = Image.FromFile( "sams.jpg" );
3:   TextureBrush tb = new TextureBrush( samsImage );
4:   e.Graphics.FillRectangle( tb, new Rectangle( 0, 0, 500, 100 ) );
5:   samsImage.Dispose( );
6:   tb.Dispose( );
7: }
```

Listing 4.4 starts by loading a jpg image from a disk and then uses the newly created image to create a `TextureBrush`. This `TextureBrush` is then used to fill a rectangle much in the same manner as a solid brush or any other GDI+ brush.

This covers the basics of brushes. Listing 4.5 shows the complete source for the Brush Demo from Figure 4.1.

LISTING 4.5   Brush Demo Source

```
 1: using System;
 2: using System.Drawing;
 3: using System.Drawing.Drawing2D; //TexturedBrush, HatchBrush,
➥LinearGradientBrush
 4: using System.Collections;
 5: using System.ComponentModel;
 6: using System.Windows.Forms;
 7: using System.Data;
 8:
 9: namespace BrushDemo
10: {
11:     /// <summary>
12:     /// Summary description for Form1.
13:     /// </summary>
14:     public class Form1 : System.Windows.Forms.Form
15:     {
16:         /// <summary>
17:         /// Required designer variable.
18:         /// </summary>
19:         private System.ComponentModel.Container components = null;
20:
21:         public Form1()
22:         {
23:             //
24:             // Required for Windows Form Designer support
25:             //
26:             InitializeComponent();
27:             this.Paint += new PaintEventHandler(
➥this.OnPaintEventHandler );
28:             this.SizeChanged += new EventHandler(
➥this.OnSizeChangedEventHandler );
29:
30:             //Default the brushes
31:
32:         }
33:
34:         protected void OnSizeChangedEventHandler( object sender,
```

LISTING 4.5   Continued

```
➥EventArgs e ) {
35:             this.Invalidate( );
36:         }
37:
38:         protected void OnPaintEventHandler( object sender,
➥ System.Windows.Forms.PaintEventArgs e ) {
39:             int width = this.ClientRectangle.Width - 20;
40:             int height = this.ClientRectangle.Height / 4;
41:             int top = 0;
42:             int left = 10;
43:             int step = height;
44:             Rectangle rcDisplayRect = new Rectangle( left, top, width,
height );
45:             rcDisplayRect.Inflate(0,-10);
46:
47:             SolidBrush solidBrush = new SolidBrush(
➥System.Drawing.Color.Blue );
48:             e.Graphics.FillRectangle( solidBrush, rcDisplayRect );
49:             solidBrush.Dispose( );
50:
51:     rcDisplayRect.Offset( 0, step );
52:             HatchBrush hatchBrush = new HatchBrush( HatchStyle.Weave,
➥System.Drawing.Color.Blue, System.Drawing.Color.Gray );
53:             e.Graphics.FillRectangle( hatchBrush, rcDisplayRect );
54:             hatchBrush.Dispose( );
55:
56:             rcDisplayRect.Offset( 0, step );
57:             LinearGradientBrush lgb = new
➥LinearGradientBrush( rcDisplayRect,
58:                         System.Drawing.Color.Blue,
59:                         System.Drawing.Color.Red,
60:                         45f );
61:             e.Graphics.FillRectangle( lgb, rcDisplayRect );
62:             lgb.Dispose( );
63:
64:
65:             rcDisplayRect.Offset( 0, step );
66:             System.Drawing.Image samsImage = Image.FromFile("sams.jpg");
67:             TextureBrush tb = new TextureBrush( samsImage );
68:             e.Graphics.FillRectangle( tb, rcDisplayRect );
69:             samsImage.Dispose( );
70:             tb.Dispose( );
71:
72:         }
73:
```

LISTING 4.5   Continued

```
 74:         /// <summary>
 75:         /// Clean up any resources being used.
 76:         /// </summary>
 77:         protected override void Dispose( bool disposing )
 78:         {
 79:             if( disposing )
 80:             {
 81:                 if (components != null)
 82:                 {
 83:                     components.Dispose();
 84:                 }
 85:             }
 86:             base.Dispose( disposing );
 87:         }
 88:
 89:     #region Windows Form Designer generated code
 90:         /// <summary>
 91:         /// Required method for Designer support - do not modify
 92:         /// the contents of this method with the code editor.
 93:         /// </summary>
 94:         private void InitializeComponent()
 95:         {
 96:             //
 97:             // Form1
 98:             //
 99:             this.AutoScaleBaseSize = new System.Drawing.Size(5, 13);
100:             this.BackColor = System.Drawing.SystemColors.Window;
101:             this.ClientSize = new System.Drawing.Size(528, 517);
102:             this.Name = "Form1";
103:             this.Text = "GDI+ Brush Demo";
104:
105:         }
106:         #endregion
107:
108:         /// <summary>
109:         /// The main entry point for the application.
110:         /// </summary>
111:         [STAThread]
112:         static void Main()
113:         {
114:             Application.Run(new Form1());
115:         }
116:  }
117: }
```

Listing 4.5 reprents a fairly typical Windows Forms application as developed using the IDE. Note the comments on lines 91 and 92 which specifiy that the code within the `InitializeComponent` method should not be modified. This is due to the fact that the IDE and the Forms Designer use this method to persist code for creating controls placed on the form during design-time. This interaction between the designer and generated code is covered in Chapter 3, "Designer Basics."

All the painting code takes place within the `OnPaintEventHandler` method. Most of the code is derived from the previous code listings for creating and using GDI+ brushes. As with any new programming endeavor, you should modify the sample and experiment with the various brush properties and styles.

Pens

Pens are used for all drawing methods of the `Graphics` object with the exception of the `DrawString` method. A pen can be used to draw solid lines, dash patterns, and even brush-style lines such as gradient or hatch. To create brush-style pens, use the property `Pen` constructor for a new pen, or assign the existing brush to the pen's `Brush` property.

Figure 4.5 shows the interface for the Pen Demo. The property grid allows for changing the properties of the current pen to see the result.

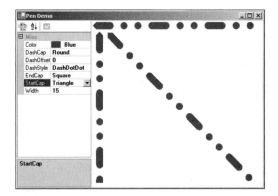

FIGURE 4.5
The Pen Demo.

Unfortunately, pens are not very exciting and a lengthy explanation of their use is not necessary. However, the Pen Demo is interesting with regard to the use of the property grid. To attach the property grid to the current pen, the Pen Demo application creates a small class named `PenProperties`. The `PenProperties` class provides some of the properties of a pen and is used to hook up the property grid to the underlying pen. The best part of this is the minimal amount of effort needed to use the property grid. Listing 4.6 shows the source for the Pen Demo application.

LISTING 4.6 Pen Demo Source

```
 1: using System;
 2: using System.Drawing;
 3: using System.Collections;
 4: using System.ComponentModel;
 5: using System.Windows.Forms;
 6: using System.Data;
 7:
 8: namespace Pen_Demo
 9: {
10:
11:     //Used by the property grid
12:     public class PenProperties {
13:
14:         //Implementation members
15:         private System.Drawing.Pen      thePen;
16:
17:         //Events
18:         public event EventHandler PropertyChanged;
19:
20:         //Properties
21:         public System.Drawing.Color Color {
22:             get { return thePen.Color; }
23:             set {
24:                 thePen.Color = value;
25:                 OnPropertyChanged( new EventArgs( ) );
26:             }
27:         }
28:
29:         public System.Drawing.Drawing2D.DashCap DashCap {
30:             get { return thePen.DashCap; }
31:             set {
32:                 thePen.DashCap = value;
33:                 OnPropertyChanged( new EventArgs( ) );
34:             }
35:         }
36:
37:         public System.Drawing.Drawing2D.DashStyle DashStyle {
38:             get { return thePen.DashStyle; }
39:             set {
40:             thePen.DashStyle = value;
41:                 OnPropertyChanged( new EventArgs( ) );
```

LISTING 4.6   Continued

```
42:                }
43:            }
44:
45:        public float Width {
46:            get { return thePen.Width; }
47:            set {
48:                thePen.Width = value;
49:                OnPropertyChanged( new EventArgs( ) );
50:            }
51:        }
52:
53:        public float DashOffset {
54:            get { return thePen.DashOffset; }
55:            set {
56:                thePen.DashOffset = value;
57:                OnPropertyChanged( new EventArgs( ) );
58:            }
59:        }
60:
61:        public System.Drawing.Drawing2D.LineCap StartCap {
62:            get { return thePen.StartCap; }
63:            set {
64:                thePen.StartCap = value;
65:                OnPropertyChanged( new EventArgs( ) );
66:            }
67:        }
68:
69:        public System.Drawing.Drawing2D.LineCap EndCap {
70:            get { return thePen.EndCap; }
71:            set {
72:                thePen.EndCap = value;
73:                OnPropertyChanged( new EventArgs( ) );
74:            }
75:        }
76:
77:        public PenProperties( Pen p ) {
78:            thePen = p;
79:        }
80:
81:        protected void OnPropertyChanged( EventArgs e ) {
82:            if( PropertyChanged != null )
83:                PropertyChanged( this, e );
84:        }
85:    }
86:
```

LISTING 4.6   Continued

```
 87:        /// <summary>
 88:        /// Summary description for Form1.
 89:        /// </summary>
 90:        public class Form1 : System.Windows.Forms.Form
 91:        {
 92:            /// <summary>
 93:            /// Required designer variable.
 94:            /// </summary>
 95:            private System.ComponentModel.Container        components = null;
 96:            private System.Windows.Forms.PropertyGrid      propertyGrid1;
 97:            private System.Drawing.Pen                     thePen = null;
 98:            private PenProperties                          penProps = null;
 99:
100:            public Form1()
101:            {
102:                //
103:                // Required for Windows Form Designer support
104:                //
105:                InitializeComponent();
106:
107:                thePen = new Pen( System.Drawing.Color.Black );
108:                penProps = new PenProperties( thePen );
109:                penProps.PropertyChanged +=
➥new EventHandler( this.OnPenPropertyChangedEventHandler );
110:                propertyGrid1.SelectedObject = penProps;
111:                propertyGrid1.Refresh( );
112:
113:
114:
115:            }
116:
117:            protected  override void OnSizeChanged( EventArgs e ) {
118:                base.OnSizeChanged( e );
119:                this.Invalidate( );
120:            }
121:
122:
123:            protected override void OnPaint( PaintEventArgs e ) {
124:                base.OnPaint( e );
125:                Rectangle drawZone = new Rectangle( ClientRectangle.Left,
126:                                                    ClientRectangle.Top,
127:                                                    ClientRectangle.Width,
128:                                                    ClientRectangle.Height );
129:
130:                //Offset for Property Grid
```

LISTING 4.6   Continued

```
131:            drawZone.X += this.propertyGrid1.Width;
132:
133:
134:        drawZone.Inflate(-10,-10);
135:
136:            //Draw horizontal line
137:            e.Graphics.DrawLine( thePen, drawZone.Left, drawZone.Top,
➥drawZone.Width, drawZone.Top );
138:
139:            //Draw vertical line
140:            e.Graphics.DrawLine( thePen, drawZone.Left + (thePen.Width/2),
➥ drawZone.Top + thePen.Width + 5, drawZone.Left + (thePen.Width/2),
➥drawZone.Bottom  );
141:
142:            //Draw diag line
143:            e.Graphics.DrawLine( thePen, drawZone.Left + (2*thePen.Width)
➥,drawZone.Top + thePen.Width + 5, drawZone.Width , drawZone.Bottom  );
144:        }
145:
146:        protected void OnPenPropertyChangedEventHandler( object sender,
➥EventArgs e ) {
147:            this.Invalidate( );
148:        }
149:
150:
151:
152:        /// <summary>
153:        /// Clean up any resources being used.
154:        /// </summary>
155:        protected override void Dispose( bool disposing )
156:        {
157:            if( disposing )
158:            {
159:                if (components != null)
160:                {
161:                    components.Dispose();
162:                }
163:            }
164:            base.Dispose( disposing );
165:        }
166:
167:        #region Windows Form Designer generated code
168:        /// <summary>
169:        /// Required method for Designer support - do not modify
170:        /// the contents of this method with the code editor.
```

LISTING 4.6 Continued

```
171:        /// </summary>
172:        private void InitializeComponent()
173:        {
174:            this.propertyGrid1 = new System.Windows.Forms.PropertyGrid();
175:        this.SuspendLayout();
176:            //
177:            // propertyGrid1
178:            //
179:            this.propertyGrid1.CommandsBackColor =
➥System.Drawing.SystemColors.Window;
180:            this.propertyGrid1.CommandsVisibleIfAvailable = true;
181:            this.propertyGrid1.Dock = System.Windows.Forms.DockStyle.Left;
182:            this.propertyGrid1.LargeButtons = false;
183:            this.propertyGrid1.LineColor =
➥System.Drawing.SystemColors.ScrollBar;
184:            this.propertyGrid1.Name = "propertyGrid1";
185:            this.propertyGrid1.Size = new System.Drawing.Size(160, 357);
186:            this.propertyGrid1.TabIndex = 0;
187:            this.propertyGrid1.Text = "propertyGrid1";
188:            this.propertyGrid1.ViewBackColor =
➥System.Drawing.SystemColors.Window;
189:            this.propertyGrid1.ViewForeColor =
➥System.Drawing.SystemColors.WindowText;
190:            //
191:            // Form1
192:            //
193:            this.AutoScaleBaseSize = new System.Drawing.Size(5, 13);
194:            this.BackColor = System.Drawing.SystemColors.Window;
195:            this.ClientSize = new System.Drawing.Size(520, 357);
196:            this.Controls.AddRange(new System.Windows.Forms.Control[] {
197:                                        this.propertyGrid1 } );
198:            this.Name = "Form1";
199:            this.Text = "Pen Demo";
200:            this.ResumeLayout(false);
201:
202:        }
203:        #endregion
204:
205:        /// <summary>
206:        /// The main entry point for the application.
207:        /// </summary>
208:        [STAThread]
209:        static void Main()
210:        {
211:            Application.Run(new Form1());
```

4

GDI+

LISTING 4.6   Continued

```
212:            }
213:    }
214: }
```

As stated earlier, no work is necessary to make use of the property grid; just assign the
SelectedObject property to the object you want the property grid to work with. The demo
allows you to see the result of changing the properties of the underlying Pen object and how
those changes affect the output generated by using the pen.

One item that requires explanation is the PropertyChanged event provided by the
PenProperties class. This event is used to notify the parent form that the properties of the pen
have been changed and the screen needs to be updated to reflect these changes. Events are an
intrinsic part of .NET, C#, and Windows/Web Forms development. When a property of the
PenProperties class has been modified, the protected method OnPropertyChanged is invoked.
Having a protected virtual method for events is recommended by the current .NET coding
standards available on the MSDN Web site. This allows for derived classes to have the first
crack at the event and determine whether the event needs to be propagated to all event
listeners.

The overall intent of the demo is to allow for a visual reference of the various effects the pen
properties have when the pen is used to draw to the screen or printer. In addition, the
PropertyGrid is a nice addition to the standard set of controls provided with Visual Studio;
understanding how it works will soon become necessary as you begin developing custom controls. This is the same PropertyGrid used by the IDE during design-time, and custom controls
are expected to work properly with the grid to provide manipulation of various design-time
properties. Interaction with the property grid is covered from time to time as it relates to the
current project.

Fonts

Working with various fonts has never been a trivial task. Each font has specific characteristics
such as its height, width, ascent, and decent. Fortunately, working with the Font class provided
by the base class libraries makes working with fonts a painless task.

Fonts, like brushes and pens, can be solid or textured and can be any size or color. Included
with the .NET Framework SDK is a wonderful font example that includes textured fonts, drop
shadows, internalization, and font rotation. For the sake of completeness, the Font Demo
application will be shown to illustrate the following topics:

- Drop shadows
- Textured fonts
- Background images
- Graphics transformations

The Font Demo will be in the style of the Pen Demo presented earlier in this chapter, enabling the property grid to be used to manipulate the various properties and options. Figure 4.6 shows the Font Demo application with the source given in Listing 4.7.

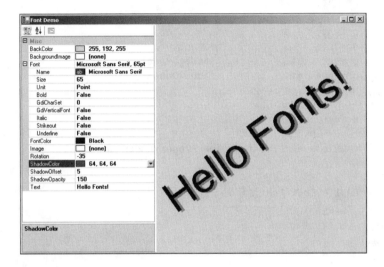

FIGURE 4.6

The Font Demo.

4

LISTING 4.7   Font Demo Source

```
 1: using System;
 2: using System.Drawing;
 3: using System.Drawing.Drawing2D;
 4: using System.Collections;
 5: using System.ComponentModel;
 6: using System.Windows.Forms;
 7: using System.Data;
 8:
 9: namespace FontDemo
10: {
11:
```

LISTING 4.7   Continued

```
12:      public class FontProperties {
13:          private Font        theFont;
14:          private Color       fontColor;
15:          private Brush       theFontBrush;
16:          private Image       theImage;
17:
18:          private Color       backgroundColor;
19:          private Image       backgroundImage;
20:          private Brush       backgroundBrush;
21:
22:          private Color       shadowColor;
23:          private Brush       theShadowBrush;
24:          private int         shadowOffset;
25:          private int         shadowOpacity;
26:          private float       rotation;
27:
28:          private string      text;
29:
30:          public event EventHandler PropertyChanged;
31:
32:
33:          public Font Font {
34:              get { return theFont; }
35:              set {
36:                  theFont = value;
37:                  OnPropertyChanged( new EventArgs( ) );
38:              }
39:      }
40:
41:          public Color FontColor {
42:              get { return fontColor; }
43:              set {
44:                  fontColor = value;
45:                  theFontBrush = new SolidBrush( fontColor );
46:                  OnPropertyChanged( new EventArgs( ) );
47:              }
48:          }
49:
50:          public Color ShadowColor {
51:              get { return shadowColor; }
52:              set {
53:                  shadowColor = value;
54:                  theShadowBrush =
➥new SolidBrush( Color.FromArgb( shadowOpacity, shadowColor ) );
```

LISTING 4.7 Continued

```
55:                     OnPropertyChanged( new EventArgs( ) );
56:                 }
57:             }
58:
59:         public int ShadowOpacity {
60:             get { return shadowOpacity; }
61:             set {
62:                 shadowOpacity = value;
63:                 theShadowBrush =
➥new SolidBrush( Color.FromArgb( shadowOpacity, shadowColor ) );
64:                 OnPropertyChanged( new EventArgs( ) );
65:             }
66:         }
67:
68:         public int ShadowOffset {
69:             get { return shadowOffset; }
70:             set {
71:                 shadowOffset = value;
72:                 OnPropertyChanged( new EventArgs( ) );
73:             }
74:         }
75:         public Image Image {
76:             get { return theImage; }
77:             set {
78:                 theImage = value;
79:                 theFontBrush = new TextureBrush( theImage );
80:                 OnPropertyChanged( new EventArgs( ) );
81:             }
82:         }
83:
84:         public Color BackColor {
85:             get { return backgroundColor; }
86:             set {
87:                 backgroundColor = value;
88:                 backgroundBrush = new SolidBrush( backgroundColor );
89:                 OnPropertyChanged( new EventArgs( ) );
90:             }
91:         }
92:
93:         public Image BackgroundImage {
94:             get { return backgroundImage; }
95:             set {
96:                 backgroundImage = value;
97:                 if( backgroundImage != null )
98:                     backgroundBrush = new TextureBrush(backgroundImage);
```

4

GDI+

LISTING 4.7   Continued

```
 99:                    else
100:                        backgroundBrush = new SolidBrush( backgroundColor );
101:                    OnPropertyChanged( new EventArgs( ) );
102:            }
103:        }
104:
105:        public string Text {
106:            get { return text; }
107:            set {
108:                text = value;
109:                OnPropertyChanged( new EventArgs( ) );
110:            }
111:        }
112:
113:        public float Rotation {
114:            get { return rotation; }
115:            set {
116:                rotation = value;
117:                OnPropertyChanged( new EventArgs( ) );
118:            }
119:        }
120:
121:
122:            //Properties to be used by Font Demo
123:            //The BrowsableAttribute is used by the Property
124:            //Grid to determine if the property should be
125:            //accessable or not.
126:
127:            [System.ComponentModel.Browsable( false )]
128:            public Brush FontBrush {
129:            get { return theFontBrush; }
130:            set { theFontBrush = value; }
131:        }
132:
133:        [System.ComponentModel.Browsable( false )]
134:        public Brush ShadowBrush {
135:            get { return theShadowBrush; }
136:            set { theShadowBrush = value; }
137:        }
138:
139:        [System.ComponentModel.Browsable( false )]
140:        public Brush BackgroundBrush {
141:            get { return backgroundBrush; }
142:            set { backgroundBrush = value; }
143:        }
```

LISTING 4.7   Continued

```
144:
145:          protected void OnPropertyChanged( EventArgs e ) {
146:              if( PropertyChanged != null )
147:                  PropertyChanged( this, e );
148:          }
149:      }
150:
151:
152:
153:
154:
155:      public class Form1 : System.Windows.Forms.Form
156:      {
157:          private FontProperties                       fontProperties;
158:          private System.Windows.Forms.PropertyGrid    propertyGrid1;
159:          private System.Windows.Forms.Splitter        splitter1;
160:          /// <summary>
161:          /// Required designer variable.
162:          /// </summary>
163:          private System.ComponentModel.Container components = null;
164:
165:
166:          public Form1()
167:          {
168:              //
169:              // Required for Windows Form Designer support
170:              //
171:              InitializeComponent();
172:
173:              this.SetStyle( ControlStyles.ResizeRedraw, true );
174:
175:              fontProperties = new FontProperties( );
176:
177:              //set default values
178:              fontProperties.Font = (Font)this.Font.Clone( );
179:              fontProperties.FontColor = Color.Black;
180:              fontProperties.ShadowColor = Color.LightGray;
181:              fontProperties.ShadowOpacity = 100; //range 0 to 255
182:              fontProperties.BackgroundBrush = new SolidBrush(Color.White);
183:              fontProperties.Text = "Hello Fonts!";
184:              fontProperties.PropertyChanged +=
➥new EventHandler( this.OnFPPropertyChangedEventHandler );
185:              propertyGrid1.SelectedObject = fontProperties;
186:              propertyGrid1.Refresh( );
187:
```

LISTING 4.7   Continued

```
188:
189:            this.Invalidate( );
190:
191:        }
192:
193:
194:
195:        protected void OnFPPropertyChangedEventHandler( object sender,
➥ EventArgs e ) {
196:            this.Invalidate( );
197:        }
198:
199:        protected override void OnPaint( PaintEventArgs e ) {
200:            Rectangle drawZone = new Rectangle( DisplayRectangle.Left +
➥propertyGrid1.Width,
201:                                        DisplayRectangle.Top,
202:                                        DisplayRectangle.Width -
➥propertyGrid1.Width,
203:                                DisplayRectangle.Height );
204:
205:            //Fill the background image
206:            e.Graphics.FillRectangle( fontProperties.BackgroundBrush,
➥ drawZone );
207:
208:
209:
210:            SizeF stringSize = e.Graphics.MeasureString(
➥fontProperties.Text, fontProperties.Font );
211:
212:
213:            System.Drawing.Drawing2D.GraphicsState gs =
➥e.Graphics.Save( );
214:
215:            //Center the Text
216:            Point ptCenter   = new Point(drawZone.X + (drawZone.Width/2),
➥ drawZone.Height / 2 );
217:
218:            //Set the Transform to the center of the drawZone
219:            e.Graphics.TranslateTransform(ptCenter.X, ptCenter.Y );
220:
221:            e.Graphics.RotateTransform( fontProperties.Rotation );
222:
223:        //The Coordinate system now stems from the center of the DrawZone
224:
225:            Point ptText = new Point( );
```

LISTING 4.7   Continued

```
226:                    ptText.X = -(int)(stringSize.Width / 2);
227:                    ptText.Y = -(int)(stringSize.Height / 2);
228:
229:
230:                    //Draw the Shadowed Text
231:                    int offset = fontProperties.ShadowOffset;
232:                    e.Graphics.DrawString( fontProperties.Text,
233:                                           fontProperties.Font,
234:                                           fontProperties.ShadowBrush,
➥new Point(ptText.X + offset,ptText.Y + offset) );
235:
236:                    e.Graphics.DrawString( fontProperties.Text,
237:                                           fontProperties.Font,
238:                                           fontProperties.FontBrush, ptText);
239:
240:
241:    e.Graphics.Restore( gs );
242:
243:        }
244:        /// <summary>
245:        /// Clean up any resources being used.
246:        /// </summary>
247:        protected override void Dispose( bool disposing )
248:        {
249:            if( disposing )
250:            {
251:                if (components != null)
252:                {
253:                    components.Dispose();
254:                }
255:            }
256:            base.Dispose( disposing );
257:        }
258:
259:        #region Windows Form Designer generated code
260:        /// <summary>
261:        /// Required method for Designer support - do not modify
262:        /// the contents of this method with the code editor.
263:        /// </summary>
264:        private void InitializeComponent()
265:        {
266:            this.splitter1 = new System.Windows.Forms.Splitter();
267:            this.propertyGrid1 = new System.Windows.Forms.PropertyGrid();
268:            this.SuspendLayout();
```

4

LISTING 4.7   Continued

```
269:              //
270:              // splitter1
271:              //
272:              this.splitter1.Location = new System.Drawing.Point(160, 0);
273:              this.splitter1.Name = "splitter1";
274:              this.splitter1.Size = new System.Drawing.Size(3, 341);
275:              this.splitter1.TabIndex = 1;
276:              this.splitter1.TabStop = false;
277:              this.splitter1.SplitterMoved +=
➥new System.Windows.Forms.SplitterEventHandler(
➥this.splitter1_SplitterMoved);
278:              //
279:              // propertyGrid1
280:              //
281:              this.propertyGrid1.CommandsBackColor =
➥System.Drawing.SystemColors.Window;
282:              this.propertyGrid1.CommandsVisibleIfAvailable = true;
283:            this.propertyGrid1.Dock = System.Windows.Forms.DockStyle.Left;
284:              this.propertyGrid1.LargeButtons = false;
285:              this.propertyGrid1.LineColor =
➥System.Drawing.SystemColors.ScrollBar;
286:              this.propertyGrid1.Name = "propertyGrid1";
287:              this.propertyGrid1.Size = new System.Drawing.Size(160, 341);
288:              this.propertyGrid1.TabIndex = 0;
289:              this.propertyGrid1.Text = "propertyGrid1";
290:              this.propertyGrid1.ViewBackColor =
➥System.Drawing.SystemColors.Window;
291:              this.propertyGrid1.ViewForeColor =
➥System.Drawing.SystemColors.WindowText;
292:              //
293:    // Form1
294:              //
295:              this.AutoScaleBaseSize = new System.Drawing.Size(5, 13);
296:              this.BackColor = System.Drawing.SystemColors.Window;
297:              this.ClientSize = new System.Drawing.Size(528, 341);
298:              this.Controls.AddRange(new System.Windows.Forms.Control[] {
299:                                                    this.splitter1,
300:                                                  this.propertyGrid1});
301:              this.Name = "Form1";
302:              this.Text = "Font Demo";
303:              this.ResumeLayout(false);
304:
305:          }
306:        #endregion
307:
```

LISTING 4.7   Continued

```
308:        /// <summary>
309:        /// The main entry point for the application.
310:        /// </summary>
311:        [STAThread]
312:        static void Main()
313:        {
314:            Application.Run(new Form1());
315:        }
316:
317:        private void splitter1_SplitterMoved(object sender,
➥System.Windows.Forms.SplitterEventArgs e) {
318:            this.Invalidate( );
319:        }
320:    }
321: }
```

The Font Demo application makes use of the `System.ComponentModel.Browsable` attribute. This attribute is used by the property grid; it determines whether the property will be available with the property grid. Expect to make use of this attribute to specify properties that are not appropriate for design-time editing.

The Font Demo uses the same basic application shell as the Pen Demo. The property grid is used to manipulate the various properties of the current font object, and those properties determine how the font will appear when rendered.

Working with Images

Working with image files has never been one of the easiest tasks to undertake. Acquiring proficiency with image formats such as bitmap, jpeg, gif, tiff, and countless others requires a significant investment of time and effort. Fortunately, the base class libraries provide support for the common image formats and allow for simple loading, displaying, and conversion of various image formats. Table 4.1 lists the currently supported image formats.

4

GDI+

TABLE 4.1   Supported Image Formats

Image Format	Description
Bmp	Bitmap image format
Emf	EnhancedWindows metafile image format
Exif	Exchangeable image format
Gif	Graphics interchange format

TABLE 4.1   Continued

Image Format	Description
Icon	Windows icon file format
Jpeg	Joint Photographic Experts Group (Jpeg) image format
MemoryBmp	Memory bitmap image format
Png	WC3 Portable Network Graphics image format
Tiff	Tag image file format
Wmf	Windows metafile image format

Unless you have plans to create a custom imaging application such as PaintShop Pro or Adobe PhotoShop, the Image class should serve the basic needs of loading and displaying images. Figure 4.7 shows the UI for the ImageStudio Demo application.

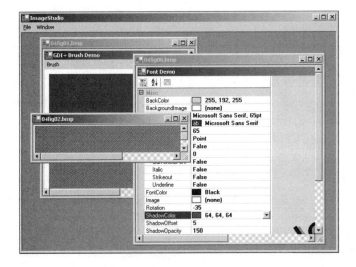

FIGURE 4.7
ImageStudio.

The ImageStudio Demo allows for viewing various image formats and for saving loaded images into other supported formats. The following listings describe the ImageStudio Demo source files.

ImageStudio will be developed in a pseudo-MVC-style framework. MVC refers to Model-View-Control and is a popular framework for developing large applications. Visual C++ developers will see this as similar to the Doc/View architecture employed by MFC. The basic premise of these two framework styles, MVC and MFC, is to separate the data, in this case the image, from the onscreen representation and the parent form or controller that handles user input. In addition, ImageStudio is an MDI application allowing for multiple images to be loaded and viewed at the same time. Listing 4.8 presents the Model or Document class used by ImageStudio.

LISTING 4.8   ImageDocument Class

```
 1: using System;
 2: using System.Drawing;
 3: using System.Drawing.Imaging;
 4:
 5: namespace ImageStudio
 6: {
 7:     public class ImageDocument
 8:     {
 9:
10:         private Image    image;
11:
12:         public event EventHandler DocumentChanged;
13:
14:         public Image Image {
15:             get { return image; }
16:         }
17:
18:         public ImageDocument()    {        }
19:
20:         public bool Open( string FileName ) {
21:             try {
22:                 image = Image.FromFile( FileName );
23:                 OnDocumentChanged( new EventArgs( ) );
24:                 return true;
25:             } catch( Exception e ) {
26:                 System.Diagnostics.Debug.WriteLine( e.Message );
27:                 return false;
28:             }
29:         }
30:
31:         public bool Save( string Filename, ImageFormat Format ) {
32:             try {
33:                 image.Save( Filename, Format );
34:                 return true;
35:             } catch( Exception e ) {
36:                 System.Diagnostics.Debug.WriteLine( e.Message );
37:                 return false;
```

LISTING 4.8 Continued

```
38:                 }
39:             }
40:
41:         protected virtual void OnDocumentChanged( EventArgs e ) {
42:             if( DocumentChanged != null )
43:                 DocumentChanged( this, e );
44:         }
45:     }
46: }
```

The ImageDocument class handles the loading and saving of images. Notice on line 22 of
Listing 4.8 that the Image.FromFile static method requires only the filename of the image to
load. The method uses the extension of the file to determine the format of the file and as such
does not require that the format be specified. The Image.Save method can also use the file
extension to determine the format, or override to save to a new format based on the
ImageFormat argument.

Listing 4.9 is the ImageView class, which is derived from Panel and supports scrolling of the
image. As its name suggests, the ImageView class represents the View component of MVC or
Doc/View MFC framework-style development.

LISTING 4.9 ImageView Class

```
 1: using System;
 2: using System.Windows.Forms;
 3: using System.Drawing;
 4: using System.Drawing.Imaging;
 5:
 6:
 7: namespace ImageStudio
 8: {
 9:
10:     public class ImageView : System.Windows.Forms.Panel
11:     {
12:         private ImageDocument    imageDocument;
13:
14:         public ImageView( ImageDocument Document )
15:         {
16:             this.BorderStyle = BorderStyle.Fixed3D;
17:             imageDocument = Document;
18:             if( imageDocument.Image != null )
19:                 AutoScrollMinSize = imageDocument.Image.Size;
20:
21:         }
```

LISTING 4.9   Continued

```
22:
23:         protected override void OnSizeChanged( EventArgs e ) {
24:             base.OnSizeChanged( e );
25:             this.Invalidate( );
26:         }
27:
28:         protected override void OnPaint( PaintEventArgs e ) {
29:             base.OnPaint( e );
30:             if( imageDocument.Image != null )
31:                 e.Graphics.DrawImage( imageDocument.Image,
32:                                       AutoScrollPosition.X,
33:                                       AutoScrollPosition.Y,
34:                                       imageDocument.Image.Width,
35:                                       imageDocument.Image.Height );
36:         }
37:     }
38: }
```

The sole purpose of the ImageView class is to render the loaded image and support scrolling when the window is smaller than the image size.

The ImageStudio Demo is an MDI application. Listing 4.10 contains the source for the ImageFrameChild class. The ImageFrameChild ties together a single instance of an ImageDocument and one or more ImageView classes. In the ImageStudio Demo application, only a single ImageView class is hosted within the ImageFrameChild.

LISTING 4.10   ImageFrameChild MDI Child Form

```
 1: using System;
 2: using System.Drawing;
 3: using System.Collections;
 4: using System.ComponentModel;
 5: using System.Windows.Forms;
 6:
 7: namespace ImageStudio
 8: {
 9:     /// <summary>
10:     /// Summary description for ImageFrameChild.
11:     /// </summary>
12:     public class ImageFrameChild : System.Windows.Forms.Form
13:     {
14:         private ImageDocument     imageDocument;
15:         private ImageView         imageView;
```

LISTING 4.10   Continued

```
16:
17:
18:         /// <summary>
19:         /// Required designer variable.
20:         /// </summary>
21:         private System.ComponentModel.Container components = null;
22:
23:
24:         public ImageDocument Document {
25:             get { return imageDocument; }
26:         }
27:
28:         public ImageFrameChild( ImageStudio.ImageDocument Document )
29:         {
30:             InitializeComponent();
31:
32:             imageDocument = Document;
33:             imageView = new ImageView( Document );
34:             imageView.Dock = DockStyle.Fill;
35:             this.Controls.Add( imageView );
36:         }
37:
38:         /// <summary>
39:         /// Clean up any resources being used.
40:         /// </summary>
41:         protected override void Dispose( bool disposing )
42:         {
43:             if( disposing )
44:             {
45:                 if(components != null)
46:                 {
47:                     components.Dispose();
48:                 }
49:             }
50:             base.Dispose( disposing );
51:         }
52:
53:         #region Windows Form Designer generated code
54:         /// <summary>
55:         /// Required method for Designer support - do not modify
56:         /// the contents of this method with the code editor.
57:         /// </summary>
58:         private void InitializeComponent()
59:         {
```

LISTING 4.10 Continued

```
60:               //
61:               // ImageFrameChild
62:               //
63:               this.AutoScaleBaseSize = new System.Drawing.Size(5, 13);
64:               this.ClientSize = new System.Drawing.Size(600, 373);
65:               this.Name = "ImageFrameChild";
66:               this.Text = "ImageFrameChild";
67:
68:           }
69:    #endregion
70:       }
71: }
```

The `ImageFrameChild` ties a specific instance of an `ImageDocument` class to the `ImageView` class that is responsible for displaying the loaded image. The goal of implementing all these classes, `ImageFrameChild`, `ImageDocument`, and `ImageView`, is to focus the responsibilities of the application where they make sense. Such a design might be somewhat overkill for this demo; however, understanding such design patterns and their usage is important when creating large-scale applications and even complex custom controls. The final component of the application is the `MainFrame` window or the Controller from the MVC architecture. The supporting cast is in place and all that remains is a host to oversee the user interaction and to dispatch responsibilities to the various components of the application.

Listing 4.11, the final listing for the ImageStudio Demo, is the `MainFrame` MDI parent window. The `MainFrame` provides handling of menu items and manages the MDI children, `ImageFrameChild` class, for the demo application.

LISTING 4.11 MainFrame MDI Parent Form

```
 1: using System;
 2: using System.Drawing;
 3: using System.Collections;
 4: using System.ComponentModel;
 5: using System.Windows.Forms;
 6: using System.Data;
 7: using System.Drawing.Imaging;
 8:
 9: namespace ImageStudio
10: {
11:     public class MainFrame : System.Windows.Forms.Form
12:     {
13:         private System.Windows.Forms.MainMenu mainFrameMenu;
14:         private System.Windows.Forms.MenuItem fileOpenMenuItem;
```

LISTING 4.11   Continued

```
15:        private System.Windows.Forms.MenuItem fileCloseMenuItem;
16:        private System.Windows.Forms.MenuItem fileSaveAsMenuItem;
17:        private System.Windows.Forms.MenuItem fileExitMenuItem;
18:        private System.Windows.Forms.MdiClient mdiClient1;
19:        private System.Windows.Forms.MenuItem fileSep2MenuItem;
20:        private System.Windows.Forms.MenuItem fileSep1MenuItem;
21:        private System.Windows.Forms.MenuItem fileMenuItem;
22:        private System.Windows.Forms.OpenFileDialog openFileDialog;
23:        private System.Windows.Forms.SaveFileDialog saveFileDialog;
24:        /// <summary>
25:        /// Required designer variable.
26:        /// </summary>
27:        private System.ComponentModel.Container components = null;
28:        private System.Windows.Forms.MainMenu mainMenu1;
29:        private System.Windows.Forms.MenuItem windowMenuItem;
30:
31:
32:        private ArrayList                          fileFormats;
33:
34:        public MainFrame()
35:        {
36:            //
37:            // Required for Windows Form Designer support
38:            //
39:            InitializeComponent();
40:
41:            fileFormats = new ArrayList( );
42:            fileFormats.Add( ImageFormat.Bmp );
43:            fileFormats.Add( ImageFormat.Gif );
44:            fileFormats.Add( ImageFormat.Jpeg );
45:            fileFormats.Add( ImageFormat.Png );
46:            fileFormats.Add( ImageFormat.Tiff );
47:        }
48:
49:    protected override void Dispose( bool disposing )
50:        {
51:            if( disposing )
52:            {
53:                if (components != null)
54:                {
55:                    components.Dispose();
56:                }
57:            }
58:            base.Dispose( disposing );
59:        }
```

LISTING 4.11   Continued

```
60:
61:          #region Windows Form Designer generated code
62:          /// <summary>
63:          /// Required method for Designer support - do not modify
64:          /// the contents of this method with the code editor.
65:          /// </summary>
66:          private void InitializeComponent()
67:          {
68:            this.openFileDialog = new System.Windows.Forms.OpenFileDialog();
69:            this.fileExitMenuItem = new System.Windows.Forms.MenuItem();
70:            this.mdiClient1 = new System.Windows.Forms.MdiClient();
71:            this.saveFileDialog = new System.Windows.Forms.SaveFileDialog();
72:            this.fileSep1MenuItem = new System.Windows.Forms.MenuItem();
73:            this.fileSep2MenuItem = new System.Windows.Forms.MenuItem();
74:            this.fileOpenMenuItem = new System.Windows.Forms.MenuItem();
75:            this.fileCloseMenuItem = new System.Windows.Forms.MenuItem();
76:            this.mainFrameMenu = new System.Windows.Forms.MainMenu();
77:            this.fileMenuItem = new System.Windows.Forms.MenuItem();
78:            this.fileSaveAsMenuItem = new System.Windows.Forms.MenuItem();
79:            this.mainMenu1 = new System.Windows.Forms.MainMenu();
80:            this.windowMenuItem = new System.Windows.Forms.MenuItem();
81:            this.SuspendLayout();
82:                //
83:        // openFileDialog
84:                //
85:            this.openFileDialog.DefaultExt = "bmp";
86:            this.openFileDialog.Filter =
➥"Bitmaps|*.bmp|Gif|*.gif|Jpeg|*.jpg|Tiff|*.tiff|Png|*.png";
87:            this.openFileDialog.Title = "Open Image File";
88:                //
89:            // fileExitMenuItem
90:                //
91:            this.fileExitMenuItem.Index = 5;
92:            this.fileExitMenuItem.Text = "E&xit";
93:            this.fileExitMenuItem.Click +=
➥ new System.EventHandler(this.fileExitMenuItem_Click);
94:                //
95:            // mdiClient1
96:                //
97:            this.mdiClient1.Dock = System.Windows.Forms.DockStyle.Fill;
98:            this.mdiClient1.Name = "mdiClient1";
99:            this.mdiClient1.TabIndex = 0;
100:                //
101:            // saveFileDialog
```

LISTING 4.11   Continued

```
102:            //
103:            this.saveFileDialog.FileName = "image";
104:            this.saveFileDialog.Filter =
➥"Bitmaps|*.bmp|Gif|*.gif|Jpeg|*.jpg|Tiff|*.tiff|Png|*.png";
105:            //
106:            // fileSep1MenuItem
107:            //
108:            this.fileSep1MenuItem.Index = 2;
109:            this.fileSep1MenuItem.Text = "-";
110:            //
111:            // fileSep2MenuItem
112:            //
113:            this.fileSep2MenuItem.Index = 4;
114:            this.fileSep2MenuItem.Text = "-";
115:            //
116:            // fileOpenMenuItem
117:            //
118:            this.fileOpenMenuItem.Index = 0;
119:            this.fileOpenMenuItem.Text = "&Open";
120:            this.fileOpenMenuItem.Click +=
➥ new System.EventHandler(this.fileOpenMenuItem_Click);
121:            //
122:            // fileCloseMenuItem
123:            //
124:            this.fileCloseMenuItem.Index = 1;
125:            this.fileCloseMenuItem.Text = "&Close";
126:            this.fileCloseMenuItem.Click +=
➥new System.EventHandler(this.fileCloseMenuItem_Click);
127:            //
128:            // mainFrameMenu
129:            //
130:        this.mainFrameMenu.MenuItems.AddRange(new MenuItem[] {
131:                                            this.fileMenuItem,
132:                                            this.windowMenuItem});
133:            //
134:            // fileMenuItem
135:            //
136:            this.fileMenuItem.Index = 0;
137:            this.fileMenuItem.MenuItems.AddRange(new MenuItem[] {
138:                                            this.fileOpenMenuItem,
139:                                            this.fileCloseMenuItem,
140:                                            this.fileSep1MenuItem,
141:                                            this.fileSaveAsMenuItem,
142:                                            this.fileSep2MenuItem,
143:                                            this.fileExitMenuItem});
```

LISTING 4.11   Continued

```
144:                this.fileMenuItem.Text = "&File";
145:                //
146:                // fileSaveAsMenuItem
147:                //
148:                this.fileSaveAsMenuItem.Index = 3;
149:                this.fileSaveAsMenuItem.Text = "Save &As...";
150:                this.fileSaveAsMenuItem.Click +=
➥new System.EventHandler(this.fileSaveAsMenuItem_Click);
151:                //
152:                // windowMenuItem
153:                //
154:                this.windowMenuItem.Index = 1;
155:                this.windowMenuItem.MdiList = true;
156:                this.windowMenuItem.Text = "Window";
157:                //
158:                // MainFrame
159:                //
160:                this.AutoScaleBaseSize = new System.Drawing.Size(5, 13);
161:                this.ClientSize = new System.Drawing.Size(592, 393);
162:                this.Controls.AddRange(new Control[] { this.mdiClient1 });
163:                this.IsMdiContainer = true;
164:                this.Menu = this.mainFrameMenu;
165:                this.Name = "MainFrame";
166:                this.Text = "ImageStudio";
167:                this.ResumeLayout(false);
168:
169:            }
170:        #endregion
171:
172:            /// <summary>
173:            /// The main entry point for the application.
174:            /// </summary>
175:            [STAThread]
176:            static void Main()
177:            {
178:                Application.Run(new MainFrame());
179:            }
180:            /////////////////////////////
181:            ///File Menu Event Handlers
182:            /////////////////////////////
183:            private void fileOpenMenuItem_Click(object sender,
➥ System.EventArgs e) {
184:
185:                if( DialogResult.OK == openFileDialog.ShowDialog( ) ) {
186:                    ImageDocument doc = new ImageDocument( );
```

LISTING 4.11   Continued

```
187:                    if( doc.Open( openFileDialog.FileName ) ) {
188:                        ImageFrameChild child = new ImageFrameChild( doc );
189:                        string[] T = openFileDialog.FileName.Split( '\\' );
190:                        child.Text = T[T.Length-1];
191:                        child.MdiParent = this;
192:                        child.Show( );
193:                    }
194:                }
195:
196:        }
197:
198:        private void fileCloseMenuItem_Click(object sender,
➥System.EventArgs e) {
199:            this.ActiveMdiChild.Close( );
200:        }
201:
202:        private void fileSaveAsMenuItem_Click(object sender,
➥System.EventArgs e) {
203:            if( DialogResult.OK == saveFileDialog.ShowDialog( ) ) {
204:                ImageDocument doc =
➥((ImageFrameChild)ActiveMdiChild).Document;
205:                doc.Save( saveFileDialog.FileName,
➥GetImageFormat( saveFileDialog.FilterIndex - 1) );
206:            }
207:        }
208:
209:        private void fileExitMenuItem_Click(object sender,
➥ System.EventArgs e) {
210:            Close( );
211:        }
212:
213:        private ImageFormat GetImageFormat( int FilterIndex ) {
214:            return (ImageFormat)fileFormats[ FilterIndex ];
215:        }
216:    }
217: }
```

The MainFrame class is certainly the largest piece of the application. However, it's important to notice that the vast majority of the code revoles around setting up and managing the user interface such as menus and the File Open dialog. The MainFrame relies on each of the previous developed classes to provide the true functionality of the application so that the MainFrame can handle the tasks associated with user interaction. The vast majority of the code within the MainFrame is acutally created during desgin-time. The only code added was to the event handlers for the various menus. As software projects grow in size and complexity, it is important to divide the responsibility amoung various smaller components as was done within the ImageStudio Demo.

> **NOTE**
>
> The subject of design patterns is an important area within software development. I suggest *Design Patterns: Elements of Object-Oriented Software*, by Erich Gamma, Richard Helm, Ralph Johnson, and John Vlissides.

The `ControlPaint` Class

Although not part of GDI+, the `ControlPaint` class offers several methods for drawing standard UI elements. In fact, the `IconButton` developed in the preceding two chapters used the `ControlPaint` class to draw the button itself. It is interesting to note that although this class exists, the base class library does not use it. The standard `Button` class, found in the `System.Windows.Forms` namespace, implements its own drawing logic. The class itself is worth mentioning because it does provide a mechanism for drawing standard controls such as buttons, check boxes, and even focus rectangles. Also because IL (Intermediate Language) is fairly readable, loading up `System.Windows.Forms.dll` into `ILDASM.exe` and peeking into the `ControlPaint` methods helps give some insight into GDI+ and basic 2D drawings.

The capability to draw the selected icon in a disabled state would enhance the `IconButton`. To accomplish this disabled image, as shown in Figure 4.8, the `ControlPaint.DrawImageDiabled` method can be used.

4

GDI+

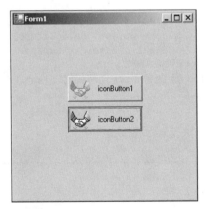

FIGURE 4.8
The `IconButton` image disabled and enabled.

The IconButton will render the icon in a disabled state, as shown in Figure 4.8, when the Enabled property is set to false. Listing 4.12 shows the changes to the IconButton.DrawIcon method to implement rendering the IconButton in a disabled state.

LISTING 4.12   IconButton Update

```
1: protected virtual void DrawIcon( Graphics g ) {
2:      System.Diagnostics.Debug.Assert( buttonIcon != null,
➥"IconButton Icon is null" );
3:
4:      int top       = ((Height/2) - (buttonIcon.Height/2));
5:      int height    = buttonIcon.Height;
6:      int width     = buttonIcon.Width;
7:
8:      if( (top + height) >= Height ) {
9:          //Scale the image to fit in (w,h) of button
10:         top = IconButton.EDGE_PADDING;
11:         int drawHeight = Height - (2*IconButton.EDGE_PADDING);
12:         float scale = ((float)drawHeight / (float)height);
13:         width = (int)((float)width*scale);
14:         height = drawHeight;
15:     }
16:     Rectangle iconRect = new Rectangle( IconButton.EDGE_PADDING, top,
➥width, height);
17:
18:     if( buttonState == ButtonState.Pushed )
19:         iconRect.Offset(1,1);
20:
21:     if( base.Enabled )
22:         g.DrawIcon( buttonIcon, iconRect );
23:     else {
24:         //Draw Image in disabled state
25:         Image disabledImage = buttonIcon.ToBitmap( );
26:         disabledImage = disabledImage.GetThumbnailImage( iconRect.Width,
➥ iconRect.Height, null, new IntPtr(0) );
27:         ControlPaint.DrawImageDisabled( g, disabledImage, iconRect.X,
➥iconRect.Y, base.BackColor );
28:     }
29:
30: this.iconDrawWidth = iconRect.Width;
31:}
```

The changes to the DrawIcon method are found between lines 21 and 28 of Listing 4.12. To use the ControlPaint.DrawImageDisabled method, the icon must be first converted to a bitmap. Then a thumbnail, or a reduced image, needs to be created based on the size of the iconRect calculated. After this is done, it's a simple matter of invoking the DrawImageDiabled method to render the grayscale image of the icon.

Summary

This concludes the brief tour of GDI+. The .NET base class libraries provide a rich set of classes and APIs for dealing with the graphical interface, fonts, and images. In addition, built-in support for translation, scaling, and rotation on GDI calls makes tasks such as rotated fonts a snap. For more in-depth information regarding GDI+, I recommend *C# and the .NET Framework: The C# Perspective*, by Robert Powell and Richard Weeks, also from Sams Publishing.

4

GDI+

Advanced Control Development

IN THIS CHAPTER

The process of building custom controls has been greatly simplified due to the richness of the base class libraries available in .NET. Already you possess the knowledge and skill necessary to create a wide assortment of controls. All that remains is learning about the services provided by the base class libraries and the VS .NET support for custom control development. In this chapter, all control and designer base classes, interfaces, events, and attributes are discussed at various levels of detail.

In this chapter, more details of the base class libraries, designers, and services are explored. Other than learning what services are available for building controls and their associated designers, an understanding of where to begin or what base class should be used is all that needs to be refined.

.NET also introduces the concept of attributes. Attributes are used to provide additional information about classes, properties, methods, and parameters. Control development makes use of various attributes, covered in this chapter, to associate controls with designers and properties with editors. Attributes provide an extremely flexible mechanism for loosely coupling components and promoting reusability.

Control Base Classes

The Windows Forms library, like custom controls, uses various base classes for both controls and designers. Often it's helpful to have a point of reference in order to proceed with a new project. A hierarchy of the class structure provides an excellent reference advantage. Figure 5.1 shows the class hierarchy starting with the `System.Windows.Forms.Control` class.

Regardless of the control you intend to build, there exists a base class from which to begin. Notice that a `Form` is in fact derived from a control base class, the `ContainerControl` class to be precise. Each level in the hierarchy provides slightly more features and modifies derived behavior to produce the desired result.

Picking the proper base class requires that the expected result and functionality of a new control is properly defined. As a guide, use the following questions to help decide what base class to derive from:

- Is it a simple control?

  Derive from the `Control` base class
- Does the content need scrolling support?

  Derive from the `Control` or `ScrollableControl` base class
- Will the control act as a parent for other controls?

  Derive from the `ContainerControl`, `Panel`, or `UserControl` base class
- Will the control act like a `Form`?

  Derive from the `UserControl` or `Form` base class

FIGURE 5.1

The control class hierarchy.

Control base classes are not the only classes that can serve as the starting point for the development of a new control. Consider the `TabPage` control that inherits from the `Panel` control class. In turn, the `Panel` control derives from the `ScrollableControl` base class. When developing a new control, give proper consideration to the base class from which to start. In addition, the same consideration should be given for the control's associated designer.

Designer Base Classes

Like controls, designers have several base classes to choose from. Each designer base class provides certain functionality that builds on the support provided by the inherited base designer class. At the root of the designer hierarchy is the `ComponentDesigner` class.

Not every control in .NET is an actual control. Rather, certain items are components that derive from `System.ComponentModel.Component`. A component has no UI of its own and is often used to hold information for part of its containing control. The Windows Forms `Menu` and `ImageList` are two such components. When a component is placed on a `Form` object, an icon for the component appears within the Component Tray of VS .NET, as shown in Figure 5.2.

5

ADVANCED
CONTROL
DEVELOPMENT

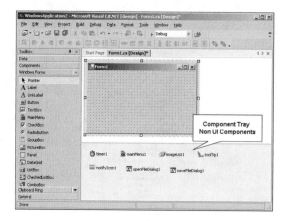

FIGURE 5.2
The VS .NET Component Tray.

In Chapter 7, "OutlookBarTab Component," the Component class serves as the base class for the OutlookBarTab that is part of the OutlookBar control. Component-derived classes use the ComponentDesigner base class to provide the necessary designer implementation. The ComponentDesigner class implements IDisposable, IDesigner, and the IDesignerFilter interfaces. As such, component designers are capable of filtering properties, events, and attributes and have the capability to expose custom verbs. In addition, components designers can shadow properties and interact with the root document designer, which is the topmost designer. The Form designer is a document designer.

Designer Services

Designer Services can be divided into three major sections: component designers, Windows Forms Designers, and drawing designers. The component designers provide the core functionality of the .NET framework designer architecture, whereas the Windows Forms Designers extend the design-time support for Windows Forms. The list of classes, interfaces, delegates, and enumerations for these three designer sections is rather extensive. They are discussed in the following sections.

System.ComponentModel.Design Namespace

The System.ComponentModel.Design namespace contains the core .NET framework designer architecture classes and interfaces that can be used to define designers and custom editors for components at design-time. Tables 5.1 through 5.4 list the classes, interfaces, delegates, and enumerations, respectively, along with a brief description of each.

TABLE 5.1   Classes

Class	Description
ActiveDesignerEventArgs	EventArgs data for the ActiveDesigner event.
ArrayEditor	UITypeEditor allows for editing arrays at design-time.
ByteViewer	Displays the content of byte arrays in hexadecimal, ANSI, and Unicode formats.
CollectionEditor	UITypeEditor provides for basic collection editing.
CollectionEditor.CollectionForm	Modal dialog for editing the collection using a UITypeEditor.
CommandID	A unique command identifier consisting of a numeric command ID and a GUID menu group identifier.
ComponentChangedEventArgs	EventArgs data for the ComponentChanged event.
ComponentChangingEventArgs	EventArgs data for the ComponentChanging event.
ComponentDesigner	Base designer class that provides support for component designer services.
ComponentDesigner.ShadowPropertyCollection	A collection of shadowed properties that should override inherited default or assigned values. Example: The Visible property is shadowed during design-time.
ComponentEventArgs	EventArgs data for the ComponentAdded, ComponentAdding, ComponentChanged, ComponentChanging, ComponentRemoved, ComponentRemoving, and ComponentRename events.
ComponentRenameEventArgs	EventArgs data for the ComponentRename Event.
DesignerCollection	Collection of designer documents.

TABLE 5.1 Continued

Class	Description
DesignerEventArgs	EventArgs data for the DesignerCreated and DesignerDisposed events.
DesignerTransaction	Provides a mechanism for undoing a series of changes during design-time.
DesignerTransactionCloseEventArgs	EventArgs data for the TransactionClosed and TransactionClosing events.
DesignerVerb	A custom verb that can be invoked by the designer.
DesignerVerbCollection	Collection of DesignerVerb objects.
DesigntimeLicenseContext	Context for supporting design-time license providers.
DesigntimeLicenseContextSerializer	Provides serialization services for license contexts.
InheritanceService	Allows for identifying inherited components.
LocalizationExtenderProvider	Design-time localization support for code generators.
MenuCommand	Menu or toolbar command item.
ServiceContainer	Implements the IServiceContainer interface.
StandardCommands	Defines the standard set of commands common to most applications.
StandardToolWindows	GUID identifiers to the set of tool windows available in the design environment.

TABLE 5.2 Interfaces

Interface	Description
IComponentChangeService	Interface to add and remove component event handlers and provides methods for raising ComponentChanged and ComponentChanging events.
IDesigner	The base designer interface for building custom component designers.

TABLE 5.2 Continued

Interface	Description
IDesignerEventService	Event notifications for the addition and removal of designers, selection changes, and provides the capability to add designers.
IDesignerFilter	Allows for Pre and Post filtering of events, properties, and attributes for a component.
IDesignerHost	Interface for mapping designer transactions and components.
IDesignerOptionService	Interface to access the designer options found on the Options submenu under the Tools menu.
IDictionaryService	Dictionary interface for a designer to store user-defined data.
IEventBindingService	Exposes events as PropertyDescriptor objects.
IExtenderListService	Provides enumeration of extender providers. A ToolTip component implements the IExtenderProvider interface.
IExtenderProviderService	Interface to add and remove extender providers at design-time.
IHelpService	Used to provide the IDE with context help information about the current task.
IInheritanceService	Used for identifying inherited components.
IMenuCommandService	Interface to add and remove commands and verbs to and from the VS .NET menu.
IReferenceService	Interface to names of and references to objects within a designer project.
IResourceService	Provides access to specific CultureInfo resources.
IRootDesigner	Support for view technologies.
ISelectionService	Used to select components at design-time.
IServiceContainer	Provides access to the various design-time services.
ITypeDescriptorFilterService	Used to filter TypeDescriptor items of a component. TypeDescriptor items include properties, attributes, and events.
ITypeResolutionService	Retrieves an assembly or type by name.

TABLE 5.3   Delegates

Delegate	Description
ActiveDesignerEventHandler	Handles the ActiveDesignerChanged event.
ComponentChangedEventHandler	Handles the ComponentChanged event.
ComponentChangingEventHandler	Handles the ComponentChanging event.
ComponentEventHandler	Handles the ComponentAdding, ComponentAdded, ComponentRemoved, and ComponentRemoving events.
ComponentRenameEventHandler	Handles the ComponentRename event.
DesignerEventHandler	Handles the DesignerCreated and DesignerDisposed events.
DesignerTransactionCloseEventHandler	Handles the TransactionClosed and TransactionClosing events.
ServiceCreatorCallback	A callback handler that can create an instance of a service on demand.

TABLE 5.4   Enumerations

Enumeration	Description
DisplayMode	Used by the ByteViewer to indicate the display type (Auto, Hex, ANSI, or Unicode).
HelpContextType	Identifiers used by the Help system.
HelpKeywordType	Identifies the type of a Help keyword.
SelectionTypes	Determines the type of selection mechanism a component supports.
ViewTechnology	Currently Passthrough and WindowsForms. Defines the view support that a designer host supports.

The granular design of the designer framework allows for fine-tuning of a component designer and supported services. The Windows Forms Designer builds on the ComponentModel design framework to extend the design-time support.

System.Windows.Forms.Design Namespace

Tables 5.5 through 5.7 list the classes, interfaces, and enumerations provided by the Windows Forms Designer framework.

TABLE 5.5   Classes

Class	Description
AnchorEditor	UITypeEditor for the Anchor layout property.
AxImporter	Imports ActiveX controls and generates a runtime callable wrapper.
AxImporter.Options	Options for the AxImporter.
AxParameterData	Design-time data for the ActiveX control.
AxWrapperGen	Generates the wrapper for ActiveX controls.
ComponentDocumentDesigner	Windows Forms Designer for designing components.
ComponentEditorForm	UI for a WindowsFormsComponentEditor.
ComponentEditorPage	An empty window that can be extended to add controls.
ComponentTray	UI for the component tray in the Forms Designer.
ControlDesigner	Base class for a designer for components that extend the Control base class.
DocumentDesigner	Extends the ScrollableControlDesigner and implements IRootDesigner. The Forms Designer is a DocumentDesigner.
EventsTab	A PropertyTab for event selection and linking. Used by the PropertyGrid.
FileNameEditor	UITypeEditor for filenames.
FolderNameEditor	UITypeEditor for folders.
MenuCommands	IDs and GUIDS that correspond to the host Command Bar menu layout.
ParentControlDesigner	Provides design-time support for selection UI handling of child controls and the capability to manipulate child controls.
PropertyTab	Base class for property tabs. Used by the PropertyGrid.
ScrollableControlDesigner	Inherits from ParentControlDesigner and provides support for scrollable controls.
WindowsFormsComponentEditor	Provides a base class for editors that use property pages similar to ActiveX control's property pages.

5

ADVANCED
CONTROL
DEVELOPMENT

TABLE 5.6   Interfaces

Interface	Description
IMenuEditorService	Provides access to the menu editing service. This service is implemented by the host designer.
IUIService	Provides interaction with the UI of the development environment that is hosting the designer.
IWindowsFormsEditorService	Used by the PropertyGrid and designers to display custom UITypeEditors.

TABLE 5.7   Enumerations

Enumeration	Description
SelectionRules	Selection rule for a component as it relates to moving and sizing.

System.Drawing.Design Namespace

The last major area of designers includes the services provided under the System.Drawing.Desing namespace. As you might expect from the name, the designers and services provided deal with UI presentation and drawing logic. In addition, interaction with the Windows Forms ToolBox is provided within this namespace. Tables 5.8 through 5.11 show the classes, interfaces, delegates, and enumerations, respectively, that are provided by the System.Drawing.Design namespace.

TABLE 5.8   Classes

Class	Description
BitmapEditor	UITypeEditor for selecting bitmaps from the Property Grid.
CategoryNameCollection	Collection of CategoryAttributes used by the PropertyGrid.
FontEditor	Editor for a Font object.
ImageEditor	UITypeEditor for selecting images.
PaintValueEventArgs	EventArgs data for the PaintEvent.
PropertyValueUIItem	Invoke handler, tool tip, and the icon for a property displayed on the properties window.

TABLE 5.8 Continued

Class	Description
ToolboxComponentsCreatedEventArgs	EventArgs data for the ComponentsCreated event when items are added to the toolbox.
ToolboxComponentsCreatingEventArgs	EventArgs data for the ComponentsCreating event of the toolbox.
ToolboxItem	Item contained within the toolbox.
ToolboxItemCollection	Collection of toolbox items.
UITypeEditor	Provides a UI for representing and editing of the values of objects (discussed in the properties section).

TABLE 5.9 Interfaces

Interface	Description
IPropertyValueUIService	Allows management of the properties list of the properties window.
IToolboxService	Allows interaction with the toolbox.
IToolboxUser	Allows testing of the toolbox for toolbox item support and selection of a toolbox item.

TABLE 5.10 Delegates

Delegate	Description
PropertyValueUIHandler	Handles the events from the IPropertyValueUIService.
PropertyValueUIItemInvokeHandler	Handles the InvokeHandler event of the PropertyValueUIItem.
ToolboxComponentsCreatedEventHandler	Handles the ComponentsCreated event.
ToolboxComponentsCreatingEventHandler	Handles the ComponentsCreating event.
ToolboxItemCreatorCallback	Handles the ToolboxComponentsCreatingEventHandler event.

TABLE 5.11   Enumerations

Enumeration	Description
`UITypeEditorEditStyle`	Indicates the value editing style for a `UITypeEditor` (`DropDown`, `Modal`, `None`).

At this point, you are likely feeling overwhelmed by the number of services available through the `System.ComponentModel.Design` namespace and the `System.Windows.Forms.Design` namespace. Fortunately, the use of all these services is rarely needed—not even for complex custom controls. It's also important to remember that each service provided is extremely granular in scope and as such its use is easier to understand. One last note: a lot of the services are already provided free; that is, you don't have to do anything to make use of them.

Note that the `IconButton` we developed has not made any explicit reference to most of the available designer services, yet the control and its associated designer are fully functional. There are times, however, when it is necessary to use the services available. During the development of the `OutlookBar` control, many of the services will be used.

Designer Attributes

Attributesplay a large role in every facet of .NET, from XML serialization to control development. The `PropertyGrid` relies heavily on custom attributes for object properties that it uses to determine the default value, determine whether the property is browsable, and make many other choices. Attributes are used to control the `PropertyGrid` and the code serializer, and for defining the `UITypeEditor` for a property, the designer for a component, and the category for a designer, among other things. The common case for attributes deals with interaction with the `PropertyGrid` and specifying the category, description, browsable, and type converter attributes. Figure 5.3 shows how attributes are used to control the `PropertyGrid`.

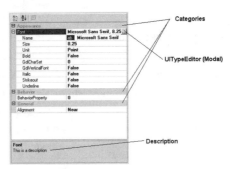

FIGURE 5.3
The `PropertyGrid`.

The use of attributes provides a powerful and expressive manner in which to decorate a component with additional functionality and services without having to inherit or write custom code. As a general rule, look for an attribute first, and then write code. Chances are there is an attribute that will accomplish that task without requiring you to write any code. The subject of attributes will continue to come up throughout this book. With each new attribute used, an explanation of its use will be covered.

Design-Time UI Clues

Now that the dry, tedious topics have been covered, it's time to get back to the fun stuff. The goal of any control designer is to provide a proper view of how the control will appear during runtime. However, it is also necessary for the designer to provide a set of hints or visual clues that facilitate the design of the control. The designer itself provides these design-time hints or UI clues by overriding the OnPaintAdornments method. Figure 5.4 shows the various UI clues provided by the TabPage designer.

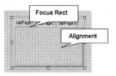

FIGURE 5.4
The TabPage designer UI clues.

Each TabPage designer draws a focus rectangle and the control alignment grid only if the grid is turned on. These subtle UI clues provide important information to the developer when he is designing the control. The focus rectangle not only shows the active tab, but also defines the client area boundary for the current TabPage. In addition, the TabPage designer draws the control alignment grid to assist the developer in aligning child controls within the boundary of the TabPage.

To see how simple it is to provide UI clues, note how the IconButtonDesigner class is extended to provide an annoying design-time adornment. The IconButton designer paints the term "DESIGN-TIME" across the top of the IconButton, as shown in Figure 5.5.

FIGURE 5.5
Providing UI clues.

Implementing the OnPaintAdornments method is similar to implementing the OnPaint method of a control. The OnPaintAdornments is called after the OnPaint method of the control has been invoked. Also, the OnPaintAdornments method is invoked only during design-time because the designer is not present during runtime. This allows for the adornments to be painted on top of the control itself. Listing 5.1 shows the updated IconButtonDesigner class source.

LISTING 5.1   IconButtonDesigner

```
 1: ////////////////////////////////////////////////////////////////////
 2: ///File          :IconButtonDesigner.cs
 3: ///Author        :Richard L. Weeks
 4: ///
 5: /// Copyright (c) 2001 by Richard L. Weeks
 6: /// This file is provided for instructional purposes only.
 7: /// No warranties.
 8: ////////////////////////////////////////////////////////////////////
 9:
10: using System;
11: using System.ComponentModel;
12: using System.ComponentModel.Design;
13: using System.Collections;
14: using System.Drawing;
15: using System.Windows.Forms;
16: using System.Windows.Forms.Design;
17:
18:
19: namespace SAMS.ToolKit.Design
20: {
21:     /// <summary>
22:     /// Simple Designer for IconButton
23:     /// </summary>
24:     public class IconButtonDesigner :
➥System.Windows.Forms.Design.ControlDesigner {
25:
26:         private enum VERBS {
27:             Red,
28:             Green,
29:             Blue
30:         }
31:
32:         private DesignerVerb[]          designerVerbs;
33:
34:     public IconButtonDesigner()    {
35:             designerVerbs = new DesignerVerb[3];
```

LISTING 5.1 Continued

```
36:                DesignerVerb[] verbs = new DesignerVerb[3];
37:                designerVerbs[(int)VERBS.Red] =
➥new DesignerVerb( "Red", new EventHandler( this.OnRedVerb ) );
38:                designerVerbs[(int)VERBS.Green] =
➥new DesignerVerb( "Green",  new EventHandler( this.OnGreenVerb ) );
39:                designerVerbs[(int)VERBS.Blue] =
➥new DesignerVerb( "Blue",  new EventHandler( this.OnBlueVerb ) );
40:            }
41:
42:        public override DesignerVerbCollection Verbs {
43:            get {
44:                return new DesignerVerbCollection( designerVerbs );
45:            }
46:        }
47:
48:
49:        //Overrides
50:
51:        /// <summary>
52:        /// Remove some basic properties that are not
➥supported by the IconButton
53:        /// </summary>
54:        /// <param name="Properties"></param>
55:        protected override void PostFilterProperties( IDictionary
➥Properties ) {
56:            Properties.Remove( "BackgroundImage" );
57:            Properties.Remove( "BackColor" );
58:        }
59:
60:
61:        //Verb Handlers
62:        protected void OnRedVerb( object sender, EventArgs e ) {
63:            this.Control.ForeColor = System.Drawing.Color.Red;
64:            UpdateCheckMarks( VERBS.Red );
65:        }
66:        protected void OnGreenVerb( object sender, EventArgs e ) {
67:            this.Control.ForeColor =  System.Drawing.Color.Green;
68:            UpdateCheckMarks( VERBS.Green );
69:        }
70:        protected void OnBlueVerb( object sender, EventArgs e ) {
71:            this.Control.ForeColor =  System.Drawing.Color.Blue;
72:            UpdateCheckMarks( VERBS.Blue );
73:    }
74:
75:
```

5

ADVANCED
CONTROL
DEVELOPMENT

LISTING 5.1   Continued

```
76:         private void UpdateCheckMarks( VERBS ActiveVerb ) {
77:             foreach( DesignerVerb dv in designerVerbs )
78:                 dv.Checked = false;
79:             designerVerbs[ (int)ActiveVerb ].Checked = true;
80:         }
81:
82:         //Provide design-time UI Clues
83:
84:         protected override void OnPaintAdornments ( PaintEventArgs e )
85:         {
86:             RectangleF layout       = e.ClipRectangle;
87:             StringFormat format       = new StringFormat( );
88:             format.Alignment      = StringAlignment.Center;
89:             format.LineAlignment      = StringAlignment.Center;
90:             Font font = new Font( "Comic Sans MS", 12f );
91:             Brush opaqueBrush = new SolidBrush(
➡ Color.FromArgb( 200, 255, 0, 0 ) );
92:
93:             e.Graphics.DrawString( "DESIGN-TIME", font, opaqueBrush,
➡layout , format );
94:         }
95:     }
96:  }
```

The `OnPaintAdornments` method found on line 84 of Listing 5.1 simply creates an opaque brush and renders the text "DESIGN-TIME" across the top of the `IconButtonControl`. Obviously, this is not the best idea for a UI clue; however, it does illustrate the ease with which UI clues or adornments can be added to a control.

Attributes

New to the .NET framework is the concept of attribute-based development. Attributes provide an extensibility mechanism for classes, properties, methods, parameters, and return values. By applying attributes to a particular entity, the default behavior can be altered to produce a new desired result. For a complete description of attributes, refer to the MSDN help.

The .NET designer architecture makes heavy use of attributes to simplify common development tasks. Examples include defining the default value for a property, assigning a category and description to properties, and indicating the default event for a control, to name a few. No discussion of the designer architecture would be complete without a list of attributes commonly used for designers, controls, serialization, licensing, and the `PropertyGrid`. Table 5.12 lists the attributes found in the `System.ComponentModel` namespace, along with descriptions.

Table 5.13 and Table 5.14 list the attributes found in the
`System.ComponentModel.Design.Serialization` and `System.Drawing` namespaces,
respectively.

TABLE 5.12 `System.ComponentModel` Attributes

Attribute	Description
AmbientValueAttribute	The value for this property originates for another source, generally the containing control.
BrowsableAttribute	Used by the `PropertyGrid` to determine whether the property should be displayed.
CategoryAttribute	Defines the category for the property or event within the `PropertyTab` of the `PropertyGrid`.
DefaultEventAttribute	Defines the default event for the component.
DefaultPropertyAttribute	Defines the default property for a component.
DefaultValueAttribute	Defines the default value for a property.
DescriptionAttribute	Defines the description for the property or event.
DesignerAttribute	Identifies the designer for the specified component.
DesignerCategoryAttribute	Defines the category for the designer.
DesignerSeralizationVisibiltyAttribute	Specifies how the designer should serialize a property.
DesignOnlyAttribute	Specifies that the property is available only at design-time.
EditorAttribute	Specifies the `UITypeEditor` for the component property.
EditorBrowsableAttribute	Specifies whether the property is available to the `UITypeEditor`.
ImmutableObjectAttribute	Specifies that the component has no editable properties.
LicenseProviderAttribute	Specifies the `LicenseProvider` for the class.

TABLE 5.12   Continued

Attribute	Description
ListBindableAttribute	Specifies a list can be used for data binding.
LocalizableAttribute	Localization for a property.
MergablePropertyAttribute	Specifies that a property can be combined with properties of other objects in the property window.
NotifyParentPropertyAttribute	Specifies that the parent property should be notified when the property is modified.
ParenthesizePropertyNameAttribute	Specifies that the property value should appear within a set of parentheses. Example: (Collection) appears next to collection-based properties such as the Tabs property of the Tab control.
PropertyTabAttribute	Identifies the property tab(s) to display for the class or classes.
ProvidePropertyAttribute	Defines the name of a property provided by the class that implements the IExtenderProvider interface. The ToolTip class is an extender provider.
ReadOnlyAttribute	Specifies that the property is read-only within the PropertyGrid.
RecommendedAsConfigurableAttribute	Specifies that the property can be used as an application setting.
RefreshPropertiesAttribute	Defines how the designer refreshes when the property is modified.
ToolboxItemAttribute	Specifies whether the component should be loaded in the toolbox.
ToolboxItemFilterAttribute	Specifies that the component will accept only other ToolboxItems belonging to the specified namespace, or type.

TABLE 5.13   `System.ComponentModel.Design.Serialization` Attributes

Attribute	Description
DesignerSerializerAttribute	Indicates the serializer for the serialization manager to use in order to serialize objects of this type.
RootDesignerSerializer	Indicates the base serializer for the root object designer.

TABLE 5.14   `System.Drawing` Attributes

Attribute	Description
ToolboxBitmapAttribute	Associates an image with the specified component. Support for small and large images.

Attributes are a prominent theme in .NET development, and custom control development is no exception.

Properties

The .NET designer architecture provides a RAD (Rapid Application Development) style environment for applications development. One of the keys to the RAD environment is the capability to modify the properties of components visually at design-time. The Windows Forms Designer provides a `PropertyGrid` that allows for modifying control properties and instantly viewing the result of those modifications.

The .NET designer base classes provide extensive support for editing various types of properties, from intrinsic types such as strings and integers to complex objects such as fonts, collections, and images. Because it is impossible to provide a property editor for types yet unknown, the `EditorAttribute` is used to define the `UITypeEditor` that the `PropertyGrid` will use to support modification of the property. Figure 5.6 shows the `UITypeEditor` for the `Nodes` collection of the `TreeView` control.

Although the `Nodes` property represents a collection, the `TreeView` control provides an alternative `UITypeEditor` rather than the standard `CollectionEditor` generally associated with collection properties.

FIGURE 5.6
Nodes *property* UITypeEditor.

UITypeEditor

Providing a custom UITypeEditor for a control or component is fairly simple, thanks in part to the existing designer architecture. The UITypeEditor base class provides four virtual methods that can be overridden to provide a custom UITypeEditor for a component. Table 5.15 lists these methods along with descriptions of each method's purpose.

TABLE 5.15   UITypeEditor Virtual Methods

Method	*Description*
EditValue	Invoked by the PropertyGrid to edit the specified property value.
GetEditStyle	Specifies the type of editor as DropDown, Modal, or None.
GetPaintValueSupported	Returns true if implementing PaintValue method; otherwise, returns false.
PaintValue	Invoked to paint a graphical representation of the edit value.

All that is required in order to associate the UITypeEditor with a particular property is the use of the EditorAttribute. The EditorAttribute specifies the type of editor to be used when editing the property at design-time. Figure 5.7 shows the UITypeEditor that will be built for the IconButton's Icon property.

FIGURE 5.7
IconEditor *for the* IconButton.

The typical coding convention for Modal style editors is to have the Form class contained within the editor class as a nested class. The drawback to this is that the designer will not allow for visual development of a nested class. When developing the UITypeEditor, you may want to create the Form class as you would any other Form and then, when finished testing, move the Form class into the editor class. This, however, creates a small issue with the resource file, the corresponding file with the resx extension. To preserve the resource information, it is necessary to include the resource file into the project. I suggest the following steps for creating nested Form classes:

1. Create a new Form class.
2. When you are finished developing the form, copy the underlying resx file somewhere safe.
3. Copy the Form class code into the target parent class, in this case the IconEditor class.
4. Delete the Form class file.
5. Add the saved resx file to the project as a resource. Adding an existing item and choosing the resx file can do this.
6. Double-click the resource file in the Solution explorer. This invokes the resource editor.
7. In the data sheet of the resource editor, modify the value of $this.name entry to be the qualified name of the dialog (see Figure 5.8). In the case of the IconEditorDialog the qualified name is IconEditor.IconEditorDialog.
8. Locate the line of code in the InitializeComponent method of the form where the resource manager is referenced. It is usually the first line. Modify the qualified name so that it matches that of the $this.name value in the resource file. The following snippet shows the line of code to modify:

```
System.Resources.ResourceManager resources =
➥new
System.Resources.ResourceManager(typeof(IconEditor.IconEditorDialog));
```

9. You are ready to build the project.

If it seems like a complex set of steps, it is. Unfortunately, the resource file support for VS .NET is not quite up to par with the way it should be in terms of ease of use. In an attempt to simplify the development process, certain tasks such as resource file management have been made overly complex.

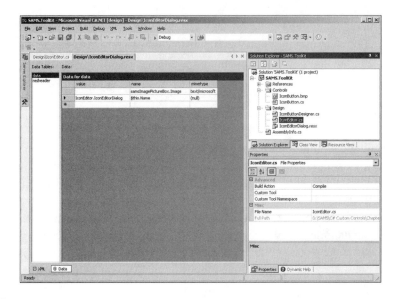

FIGURE 5.8
The resource data sheet.

Listing 5.2 contains the source for the IconEditor, along with the nested IconEditorDialog class to act as a custom UITypeEditor.

LISTING 5.2   IconEditor UITypeEditor Source

```
 1: using System;
 2: using System.Drawing;
 3: using System.Drawing.Design;
 4: using System.Collections;
 5: using System.ComponentModel;
 6: using System.Windows.Forms;
 7: using System.Windows.Forms.Design;
 8:
 9:
10: namespace SAMS.ToolKit.Design
11: {
12:
13:     public class IconEditor : System.Drawing.Design.UITypeEditor
14:     {
15:
16:         public override object EditValue(ITypeDescriptorContext context,
17:                                     IServiceProvider provider,
18:                                     object value) {
19:             IconEditorDialog dlg = new IconEditorDialog( );
```

LISTING 5.2   Continued

```
20:              IWindowsFormsEditorService winFormEditorService =
➥(IWindowsFormsEditorService)provider.GetService(
➥typeof( IWindowsFormsEditorService ) );
21:              if( DialogResult.OK == winFormEditorService.ShowDialog(dlg))
22:                  value = dlg.SelectedIcon;
23:
24:              return value;
25:          }
26:
27:     public override UITypeEditorEditStyle GetEditStyle(
➥ITypeDescriptorContext context ) {
28:              return UITypeEditorEditStyle.Modal;
29:          }
30:
31:          public override bool GetPaintValueSupported(
➥ITypeDescriptorContext context) {
32:              return true;
33:          }
34:
35:          public override void PaintValue(
➥System.Drawing.Design.PaintValueEventArgs e) {
36:              if( !(e.Value is Icon) )
37:                  return;
38:              Image img = ((Icon)e.Value).ToBitmap( );
39:              Rectangle rcBounds = e.Bounds;
40:              rcBounds.Inflate(-1,-1);
41:              Pen p = System.Drawing.SystemPens.WindowFrame;
42:              e.Graphics.DrawRectangle(p, rcBounds );
43:              if( img != null )
44:                  e.Graphics.DrawImage( img, e.Bounds );
45:          }
46:
47:
48:      protected class IconEditorDialog : System.Windows.Forms.Form
49:      {
50:          private System.Windows.Forms.PictureBox iconPreviewPictureBox;
51:          private System.Windows.Forms.Button btnOpen;
52:          private System.Windows.Forms.Button btnOK;
53:          private System.Windows.Forms.Button btnCancel;
54:          private System.Windows.Forms.PictureBox samsImagePictureBox;
55:          private System.Windows.Forms.OpenFileDialog openFileDialog;
56:
57:          private System.ComponentModel.Container components = null;
58:
59:            private System.Drawing.Icon    selectedIcon;
```

LISTING 5.2   Continued

```
60:
61:            public Icon SelectedIcon
62:            {
63:                get { return selectedIcon; }
64:                set
65:                {
66:                    selectedIcon = value;
67:                    iconPreviewPictureBox.Image =
➥ ( selectedIcon != null ? selectedIcon.ToBitmap( ) : null );
68:                }
69:        }
70:
71:
72:            public IconEditorDialog()
73:            {
74:                InitializeComponent();
75:            }
76:
77:            /// <summary>
78:            /// Clean up any resources being used.
79:            /// </summary>
80:            protected override void Dispose( bool disposing )
81:            {
82:                if( disposing )
83:                {
84:                    if (components != null)
85:                    {
86:                        components.Dispose();
87:                    }
88:                }
89:        base.Dispose( disposing );
90:            }
91:
92:            private void InitializeComponent()
93:            {
94:                System.Resources.ResourceManager resources =
➥new System.Resources.ResourceManager(typeof(IconEditor.IconEditorDialog));
95:                this.openFileDialog =
➥new System.Windows.Forms.OpenFileDialog();
96:                this.btnCancel = new System.Windows.Forms.Button();
97:                this.iconPreviewPictureBox =
➥new System.Windows.Forms.PictureBox();
98:                this.btnOpen = new System.Windows.Forms.Button();
99:                this.samsImagePictureBox =
➥new System.Windows.Forms.PictureBox();
```

LISTING 5.2 Continued

```
100:                 this.btnOK = new System.Windows.Forms.Button();
101:                 this.SuspendLayout();
102:                 //
103:                 // openFileDialog
104:                 //
105:                 this.openFileDialog.Filter = "Icon Files | *.ico";
106:                 //
107:                 // btnCancel
108:                 //
109:                 this.btnCancel.Location =
➥new System.Drawing.Point(120, 88);
110:                 this.btnCancel.Name = "btnCancel";
111:                 this.btnCancel.Size = new System.Drawing.Size(88, 24);
112:        this.btnCancel.TabIndex = 2;
113:                 this.btnCancel.Text = "Cancel";
114:                 this.btnCancel.Click +=
➥new System.EventHandler(this.btnCancel_Click);
115:                 //
116:                 // iconPreviewPictureBox
117:                 //
118:                 this.iconPreviewPictureBox.BorderStyle =
➥ System.Windows.Forms.BorderStyle.Fixed3D;
119:                 this.iconPreviewPictureBox.Location =
➥ new System.Drawing.Point(8, 8);
120:                 this.iconPreviewPictureBox.Name = "iconPreviewPictureBox";
121:                 this.iconPreviewPictureBox.Size =
➥ new System.Drawing.Size(100, 68);
122:                 this.iconPreviewPictureBox.SizeMode =
➥System.Windows.Forms.PictureBoxSizeMode.CenterImage;
123:                 this.iconPreviewPictureBox.TabIndex = 1;
124:                 this.iconPreviewPictureBox.TabStop = false;
125:                 //
126:        // btnOpen
127:                 //
128:                 this.btnOpen.Location = new System.Drawing.Point(120, 8);
129:                 this.btnOpen.Name = "btnOpen";
130:                 this.btnOpen.Size = new System.Drawing.Size(88, 24);
131:                 this.btnOpen.TabIndex = 2;
132:                 this.btnOpen.Text = "Open...";
133:        this.btnOpen.Click +=
➥new System.EventHandler(this.btnOpen_Click);
134:                 //
135:                 // samsImagePictureBox
136:                 //
```

5

ADVANCED
CONTROL
DEVELOPMENT

LISTING 5.2   Continued

```
137:                this.samsImagePictureBox.Image =
➥ ((System.Drawing.Bitmap)(resources.GetObject(
➥"samsImagePictureBox.Image")));
138:                this.samsImagePictureBox.Location =
➥new System.Drawing.Point(8, 88);
139:                this.samsImagePictureBox.Name = "samsImagePictureBox";
140:                this.samsImagePictureBox.Size =
➥new System.Drawing.Size(96, 32);
141:                this.samsImagePictureBox.SizeMode =
➥System.Windows.Forms.PictureBoxSizeMode.CenterImage;
142:                this.samsImagePictureBox.TabIndex = 3;
143:                this.samsImagePictureBox.TabStop = false;
144:                //
145:                // btnOK
146:                //
147:                this.btnOK.Location = new System.Drawing.Point(120, 48);
148:                this.btnOK.Name = "btnOK";
149:                this.btnOK.Size = new System.Drawing.Size(88, 24);
150:                this.btnOK.TabIndex = 2;
151:                this.btnOK.Text = "OK";
152:                this.btnOK.Click +=
➥new System.EventHandler(this.btnOK_Click);
153:                //
154:                // IconEditorDialog
155:          //
156:                this.AutoScaleBaseSize = new System.Drawing.Size(5, 13);
157:                this.ClientSize = new System.Drawing.Size(228, 129);
158:            this.Controls.AddRange(new System.Windows.Forms.Control[]{
159:                                        this.samsImagePictureBox,
160:                                        this.btnCancel,
161:                                        this.btnOK,
162:                                        this.btnOpen,
163:                                    this.iconPreviewPictureBox});
164:                this.FormBorderStyle =
➥System.Windows.Forms.FormBorderStyle.FixedDialog;
165:                this.Name = "IconEditorDialog";
166:                this.Text = "IconButton UITypeEditor";
167:                this.ResumeLayout(false);
168:
169:            }
170:
171:        private void btnOpen_Click(object sender, System.EventArgs e)
172:        {
173:            if( DialogResult.OK == openFileDialog.ShowDialog( ) ) {
174:                try {
```

LISTING 5.2 Continued

```
175:                        selectedIcon =
➥new Icon( openFileDialog.FileName );
176:                    } catch( Exception exception ) {
177:                        MessageBox.Show( this, exception.Message );
178:                    } finally {
179:                        iconPreviewPictureBox.Image =
➥ ( selectedIcon != null ? selectedIcon.ToBitmap( ) : null );
180:                    }
181:                }
182:            }
183:
184:            private void btnOK_Click(object sender, System.EventArgs e)
185:            {
186:                DialogResult = DialogResult.OK;
187:                Close( );
188:            }
189:
190:             private void btnCancel_Click(object sender, System.EventArgs e)
191:            {
192:                DialogResult = DialogResult.Cancel;
193:                Close( );
194:        }
195:        }
196:  }
197: }
```

The code in Listing 5.2 consists of two major components: the dialog for selecting and previewing the icon image, and the code necessary to paint the icon image within the PropertyGrid.

The nested IconEditorDialog is a basic Form-derived class that is used to display an OpenFileDialog for selecting an icon. In addition, the IconEditDialog creates an instance of an IconButton to allow for a simple preview mechanism. After an icon is selected, the IconEditDialog is closed and the IconEditor class is responsible for providing the necessary code to update the PropertyGrid.

The IconEditor class provides the implementation necessary to interact with the PropertyGrid. The first task is to return the type of editor that will be provided. For the IconEditor, the type of Modal is returned, as a nested Form will be used. Other types are DropDown and None. When the EditValue method is invoked, the IconEditor creates and displays the nested IconEditorDialog to allow for the selection of an icon image. When the value of the icon is modified, the PropertyGrid will invoke the GetPaintValueSupported method to determine whether the editor will handle displaying some representation of the property within the PropertyGrid.

Next, the `PaintValue` method is invoked if the `GetPaintValueSupported` method returns `true`. The `PaintValue` method is responsible for painting within the `PropertyGrid` for the associated property. The `IconEditor` renders a miniature image of the icon within0 the `PropertyGrid`.

To associate the `IconEditor` with the `Icon` property, modify the `IconButton` source and add the `EditorAttribute` to the `Icon` property as shown in Listing 5.3.

LISTING 5.3   Applying the `EditorAttribute`

```
1: [
2: System.ComponentModel.Description("The Icon to be displayed in the button"),
3: System.ComponentModel.Category( "Appearance" ),
4: System.ComponentModel.DefaultValue( null ),
5: System.ComponentModel.Editor( typeof( SAMS.ToolKit.Design.IconEditor ),
➥typeof( System.Drawing.Design.UITypeEditor ) )
6: ]
7: public Icon Icon { /* omitted */ }
```

Basic Control Debugging

By now you may be wondering how to debug controls, designers, and editors. As with any class library project, there needs to be an application that will use the library. This application can be set as the startup program for debugging purposes. In the case of designers and editors, VS .NET provides the solution. In the project properties, set the Start Application to `devenv.exe`, as shown in Figure 5.9.

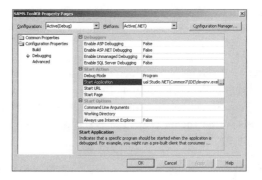

FIGURE 5.9
Debugging setup.

Now when the project is executed, a new instance of VS .NET will be launched. This will allow for setting break points within the control, designer, and editor.

Summary

This chapter certainly covered a lot of ground and provides a point of reference for the entire book. With the designer architecture and services detailed in this chapter, you have all the basic information you'll need in order to create advanced controls. I suggest reviewing the various base classes and interfaces presented here before moving on to the remainder of the chapters.

The next four chapters are dedicated to building a fairly complex control, along with designers and custom editors. Many of the designer services, classes, interfaces, and attributes listed in this chapter will be used during the construction of the OutlookBar, aka the Shortcut Control.

Control Design Concepts

IN THIS CHAPTER

Building quality custom controls requires knowledge and practice. During the development process, there is a time of discovery. This discovery process includes learning the underlying system, the framework, and the most practical design for the control in order to provide a clear strategy for moving the project forward. To grow knowledge, there must be a starting point from which to begin. The Windows Forms base class library can be used as such a starting point.

By studying the current set of controls and their associated designers and UITypeEditors (see Chapter 5, "Advanced Control Development," for more information on UITypeEditors), you can glean lessons and apply them to new endeavors.

Before this chapter delves into designing and building the OutlookBar control, its subcomponents, and related designers, a tour of the existing set of Windows Forms controls will provide some insight that can be applied to the construction of the OutlookBar control to be built in chapters 7, 8, and 9.

It is necessary to understand how the common controls shipped with VS .NET are constructed so that the principles behind their design and implementation can be applied to new custom controls. The remainder of this chapter is spent exploring the concepts behind the implementation of the current common controls. In addition, we explore how to use the current set of controls to gain a better understanding of how to create custom controls.

Control Design

All Windows-based applications provide several well-known UI elements, such as menus, toolbars, and status bars. Beyond these basic UI elements, most modern applications provide their own custom set of controls and/or extend common UI elements to add some flair to the application. The leader and most-often-imitated UI elements are Microsoft's. MS Office has been a constant source of new UI elements and ideas for third-party control vendors. Advanced docking toolbars, custom menus, and windows are now available from several different vendors.

Users of Visual C++ and MFC (Microsoft Foundation Classes) have some basic UI elements afforded to them, such as simple docking toolbars. However, advanced UI elements such as those found in the latest edition of MS Office and VS .NET are not to be found within any provided framework or .NET classes. If you want your application to resemble a Microsoft application, you will have to purchase a set of libraries from a third-party vendor or create your own set of UI classes.

As with any type of project, certain criteria should be followed when creating custom UI elements. These are the criteria:

- Looks cool
- Looks really cool
- Concise usage
- Design-time support

Did I mention that it needs to look cool? After all, if you want your control to be noticed, it has to have a sexy wrapper. Consider the menus in VS .NET verses the standard menus available as part of Windows Forms development. Figure 6.1 shows a side-by-side comparison of these two menus.

FIGURE 6.1
A menu comparison—VS .NET on the left, boring on the right.

Both menus shown in Figure 6.1 provide the same functionality; however, users looking at the two will believe that somehow, in some way, the cooler-looking menus translate into a more powerful application. When building a control, make sure that it (a) looks cool and (b) looks really cool.

Of course, if the control only looks cool but does not offer any functionality, it is useless. Creating a nice-looking control will get a developer's attention, and providing a useful control will get developers to actually use the control.

Control Internals

The .NET SDK ships with the tool ILDASM (IL Disassembler). IL is the Intermediate Language to which all .NET languages are compiled. By now, most of you are probably familiar with this tool. ILDASM displays the contents of a managed assembly, including the manifest, value types, interfaces, classes, enums, and delegates. In addition, ILDASM displays the IL code for all class methods and properties. This IL code is fairly readable and can be translated into C# with little effort. Producing the exact original C# code should not be expected because IL is not a one-to-one mapping tool as far as code is concerned.

Examples are often the best way to learn a new task, and with ILDASM you essentially have a huge set of examples just waiting to be explored. Every control, designer, and UITypeEditor for the controls shipped with .NET is located within one of three assemblies: System.Windows.Forms.dll, System.Design.dll, or System.Drawing.Design.dll. These three assemblies contain all the code you could ever need to use as examples. However, there is one drawback: the only way to view the code is with ILDASM and the code shows as IL. This does not represent an insurmountable obstacle because IL is not very hard to understand even if you don't know how to program in it. You can figure out most of what you need to know by looking at the IL code itself.

Hand Translation

The easiest path for translating IL code to C# is to do it by hand. Given the readability of IL, such a task is not difficult. Consider the UITypeEditor ImageEditor found in the System.Drawing.Design namespace. The Image object uses this editor during design-time as the UITypeEditor. The ImageEditor class displays an Open File dialog and draws the selected image within the property grid, as shown in Figure 6.2.

FIGURE 6.2
ImageEditor *at work.*

UITypeEditors can provide the implementation of the virtual PaintValue method. The ImageEditor overrides this method to draw the selected image within the property grid cell, as shown in Figure 6.2. Remember the UITypeEditor for the IconButton control? The PaintValue method is a basic C# translation of the IL code for the ImageEditor's PaintValue method. Listing 6.1 shows the IL code from the ImageEditor.PaintValue method. This IL code was copied from the code window of ILDASM.

LISTING 6.1   IL Code for ImageEditor.PaintValue

```
1: .method public hidebysig virtual instance void
2:         PaintValue(class [System.Drawing]
➥System.Drawing.Design.PaintValueEventArgs e) cil managed
3: {
4:   // Code size       98 (0x62)
5:   .maxstack  4
6:   .locals (class [System.Drawing]System.Drawing.Image V_0,
7:           valuetype [System.Drawing]System.Drawing.Rectangle V_1)
```

LISTING 6.1 Continued

```
 8:    IL_0000:  ldarg.1
 9:    IL_0001:  callvirt    instance object
➥[System.Drawing]System.Drawing.Design.PaintValueEventArgs::get_Value()
10:    IL_0006:  isinst      [System.Drawing]System.Drawing.Image
11:    IL_000b:  brfalse.s   IL_0061
12:    IL_000d:  ldarg.1
13:    IL_000e:  callvirt    instance object
➥[System.Drawing]System.Drawing.Design.PaintValueEventArgs::get_Value()
14:    IL_0013:  castclass   [System.Drawing]System.Drawing.Image
15:    IL_0018:  stloc.0
16:    IL_0019:  ldarg.1
17:    IL_001a:  callvirt    instance valuetype
➥ [System.Drawing]System.Drawing.Rectangle
➥ [System.Drawing]System.Drawing.Design.PaintValueEventArgs::get_Bounds()
18:    IL_001f:  stloc.1
19:    IL_0020:  ldloca.s    V_1
20:    IL_0022:  dup
21:    IL_0023:  call        instance int32
➥[System.Drawing]System.Drawing.Rectangle::get_Width()
22:    IL_0028:  ldc.i4.1
23:    IL_0029:  sub
24:    IL_002a:  call        instance void
➥ [System.Drawing]System.Drawing.Rectangle::set_Width(int32)
25:    IL_002f:  ldloca.s    V_1
26:    IL_0031:  dup
27:    IL_0032:  call        instance int32
➥ [System.Drawing]System.Drawing.Rectangle::get_Height()
28:    IL_0037:  ldc.i4.1
29:    IL_0038:  sub
30:    IL_0039:  call        instance void
➥ [System.Drawing]System.Drawing.Rectangle::set_Height(int32)
31:    IL_003e:  ldarg.1
32:    IL_003f:  callvirt    instance class
➥ [System.Drawing]System.Drawing.Graphics
➥ [System.Drawing]System.Drawing.Design.PaintValueEventArgs::
➥get_Graphics()
33:    IL_0044:  call        class [System.Drawing]System.Drawing.Pen
➥ [System.Drawing]System.Drawing.SystemPens::get_WindowFrame()
34:    IL_0049:  ldloc.1
35:    IL_004a:  callvirt    instance void [System.Drawing]System.Drawing.
➥Graphics::DrawRectangle(class [System.Drawing]System.Drawing.Pen,
36:                        valuetype [System.Drawing]System.Drawing.Rectangle)
37:    IL_004f:  ldarg.1
38:    IL_0050:  callvirt    instance class [System.Drawing]System.Drawing.
➥Graphics [System.Drawing]System.Drawing.Design.PaintValueEventArgs::
➥get_Graphics()
```

LISTING 6.1   Continued

```
39:    IL_0055:  ldloc.0
40:    IL_0056:  ldarg.1
41:    IL_0057:  callvirt   instance valuetype [System.Drawing]System.Drawing.
➥Rectangle [System.Drawing]System.Drawing.Design.PaintValueEventArgs::
➥get_Bounds()
42:    IL_005c:  callvirt   instance void [System.Drawing]System.Drawing.
➥Graphics::DrawImage(class [System.Drawing]System.Drawing.Image,
43:                       valuetype [System.Drawing]System.Drawing.Rectangle)
44:    IL_0061:  ret
45: } // end of method ImageEditor::PaintValue
```

The 45 lines of code in Listing 6.1 translate into about 12 lines of C# code. Listing 6.2 shows the approximate translation from the original IL code to the C# equivalent.

LISTING 6.2   C# Translation from the Original IL Method

```
 1: public override void PaintValue(
➥System.Drawing.Design.PaintValueEventArgs e) {
 2:      if( !(e.Value is Icon) )
 3:          return;
 4:
 5:      Image img = ((Icon)e.Value).ToBitmap( );
 6:      Rectangle rcBounds = e.Bounds;
 7:      rcBounds.Inflate(-1,-1);
 8:      Pen p = System.Drawing.SystemPens.WindowFrame;
 9:      e.Graphics.DrawRectangle(p, rcBounds );
10:      if( img != null )
11:      e.Graphics.DrawImage( img, e.Bounds );
12: }
```

I translated the IL code to C# in just a few short minutes. Again, it is important to note that the translation is not exact, but rather an approximation of the original C# code. The main reason for showing the IL is so that you can compare the IL statements to the C# code.

IL is somewhat verbose when it comes to the code listing. This is due to the low-level nature of IL, and it serves as a good example of the level of abstraction provided by languages such as C#. When you need to know how a control, editor, type converter, or designer is functioning, make use of ILDASM to view its implementation.

Control Relationships

Every Windows Form control derives from the `Control` base class. This includes the `Form` class. Because controls are capable of hosting or parenting other controls, it's possible to have a `Form` as the child of a `Panel` control. Strange as this may sound, Figure 6.3 shows a child `Form` being parented by a `Panel` control.

FIGURE 6.3
A form within a panel.

Not only is the `Form` in Figure 6.3 a child of the `Panel`, but also the `Panel`, true to form, will clip child controls. This means that dragging around the `Form` will cause it to be clipped to the bounding area of the `Panel`. Figure 6.4 shows the child `Form` being clipped by the `Panel`.

FIGURE 6.4
An example of clipping.

Even stranger than hosting a `Form` within a `Panel` is the capability to host a `Form` within a `Button`. Although there is no practical reason to host a form in a button, it's important that you understand the relationship of controls and windows and how that relationship affects behavior.

This begs the question of why you would want to use this design. Why allow a `Form`, which should be a `TopLevel` component, be the child of a `Panel` or `Button`? Everything is a window, regardless of what shape or functionality it takes on. Because the `Control` class offers the basic framework, everything is now considered a control.

The `Control` base class implements all necessary ActiveX control interfaces, basic drag-and-drop, and the all important `IWin32Window` interface. The `IWin32Window` interface provides access to the underlying window handle. This window handle can be used to call Win32 functions that require a handle to the current window.

Most of the controls and classes provided with Windows Forms are available for your own use when developing controls or applications. However, several classes are private to the `Windows.Forms` and `Windows.Forms.Design` namespace. One of the more interesting classes is the `UnsafeNativeMethods` class. This is, of course, just one of many private classes found within the .NET base class library. Even though the classes are private and cannot be used to create new controls, nothing prevents your peeking at their implementation with ILDASM to see what functionality they provide and how they are used.

Designer Internals

Designers represent one of the most critical aspects of custom control development; however, the documentation surrounding their implementation is somewhat lacking, to say the least. Without a proper designer, a newly developed custom control will not respond to the design-time actions of a developer or the development environment. Even though the documentation for designers is rather light, the openness of .NET and the capability to peek inside the internals of other designers provides some insight as to the design and development of control designers.

There Can Be Only One Designer

One of the most important things to note about a designer is the fact that there is only one instance of a designer. Let's use the `IconButton` as an example. If there are three `IconButtons` on the form, there exists only a single `IconButtonDesigner`. Figure 6.5 shows this basic relationship between a control and its designer.

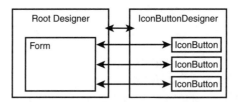

FIGURE 6.5
The designer relationship.

Just before the designer is to be utilized, the context information for the designer is updated. When a different `IconButton` is selected, the designer's `Control` property is set to the currently selected control.

IComponentChangeService

Whenever an action such as a component being added or removed takes place, all active designers that have subscribed to the ComponentChangeService are notified. Remember that a designer subscribes to the ComponentChangeService by overriding the Initialize method. During initialization, the designer can choose to subscribe to the events listed in Table 6.1.

TABLE 6.1   IComponentChangeService Events

Event	Description
ComponentAdded	A component has been added.
ComponentAdding	A component is about to be added.
ComponentChanged	A component has been changed.
ComponentChanging	A component is in the process of being changed.
ComponentRemoved	A component has been removed.
ComponentRemoving	A component is about to be removed.
ComponentRename	A component has been renamed.

Because there is only a single designer for the IconButton, each time an IconButton is added, the IconButtonDesigner's Initialize method is invoked. This means that the designer will receive one notification for each control it is responsible for designing when a subscribed change event occurs. If there are three IconButtons on the form, then three notifications will be sent to the designer. It is important to note that anytime a control or component changes, all designers are notified of the change. This is true even if the designer does not manage the control being changed.

The delegate parameters for a change event specify a parameter: ComponentChangeEventArgs. The ComponentChangeEventArgs provides a property, Component, that specifies the component associated with the event. This allows for the receiver of the event, in this case the designer, to determine the context of the event and to determine whether the change event should be responded to. In Chapter 8, "OutlookBar Control," the designer uses the IComponentChangeService to track which controls it is parenting within the individual tabs.

A Preview of the OutlookBar Control

The OutlookBar control will be designed and implemented in a manner that encompasses much of the material covered so far. In addition, some basic design patterns and guides will be offered during the development process. Learning by example has always been an effective way to teach and learn new material. I also encourage you to extend what you learn by enhancing the projects discussed in the following chapters.

Chapter 6

One key point to understand about control development is that the presentation of the control—that is, the rendering of the look and feel—is the most time-consuming aspect of control development. Creating the underlying logic and designer is often very easy in comparison to the requirements of generating the proper UI and usability of a control. Figure 6.6 shows the completed OutlookBar control.

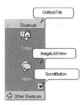

FIGURE 6.6
The completed OutlookBar *control.*

The OutlookBar control project spans three chapters. The first step in building the OutlookBar consists of designing and building the individual tabs found within the control. These tabs will be built as components and not as actual controls. This approach provides designer support for the tabs and lessens the overall weight of the control.

This brings us back to the subject of soft controls. Remember that soft controls look and act like regular controls to an end user but in fact are not controls. Soft controls have no corresponding HWND, window handle, and require some parent control to pass messages to them for processing. This approach saves valuable system resources and is often a more simple way to build complex controls.

As far as designer support for soft controls is concerned, deriving a soft control from the Component base class enables a default designer to be assigned to the soft control. In addition, a custom designer can be created for the soft control. The VS .NET IDE will also handle the basic process of code serialization for the soft control, thus removing the burden of creating a custom code serializer for the control.

NOTE

Creating custom code serialization is not a task you'll likely encounter when developing custom controls and as such is not covered here. However, information about creating custom code serialization can be found within MSDN.

Here's how the `OutlookBar` control will be developed:

- Chapter 7, "`OutlookBarTab` Component," shows how the tabs are built as components.
- Chapter 8, "`OutlookBar` Control," develops the `OutlookBar` control to host one or more of the `OutlookBarTab` components.
- Chapter 9, "`ImageListView` Control," shows you how the `ImageListView` control is developed. This is a standalone control that can be hosted by the `OutlookBar` control.

Summary

The next few chapters are geared toward applying the knowledge gained so far. Each successive chapter moves closer to providing the final goal, a working `OutlookBar`-style control. The final result should be considered a starting point, a control from which to expand its functionality, appearance, and design-time support.

OutlookBarTab Component

IN THIS CHAPTER

All projects, no matter how small or large, must start somewhere. Ideally, you should build the core components of a system and gradually expand outward until such time as the outer layers can be built in parallel. The OutlookBar control will be developed using this same process. First, the OutlookBarTab is created. The OutlookBarTab provides a simple starting point for the overall project. In Chapter 8, "OutlookBar Control," the OutlookBarTab is used within the main OutlookBar control. The OutlookBar control is then further extended in Chapter 9, "ImageListView Control," to provide for image support.

Detailed Design

Before diving into the code for the OutlookBarTab, its design must be fully specified. The design details include the following:

- Base class
- Interfaces
- Properties
- Events
- Public methods
- User interface
- Control/Component designer

After the design criteria have been established, it's merely a matter of realizing the design in code. The first question, of course, is where to start.

Base Class

Deciding on the base class for the OutlookBarTab requires determining what role the component plays, the needs of the component, and its interaction with its eventual container. Because the OutlookBarTab represents a graphical entity on the screen, it might seem necessary for it to derive from the Control base class. The Control base class would allow for the OutlookBarTab to receive Windows messages, such as keystrokes and mouse events. However, there is no requirement which states that only controls can draw on the screen. All that is required to draw on the screen is a device context, such as the Graphics object.

In fact, the OutlookBarTab mostly serves to hold information about a particular tab within the OutlookBar control. The individual tabs are not full-blown controls, but rather a means for the user to choose which tab within the control to activate. These types of controls are known as soft-controls. Remember that soft-controls do not have an associated window handle or message loop and therefore do not require any real resources. This design allows for a light and efficient control design.

In contrast, if the OutlookBarTab were to be derived from the Control base class, each individual tab would have an associated window handle and the extra weight of the Control base class. The upside to this is that each OutlookBarTab would be capable of processing Windows messages on its own.

In processing the messages, the OutlookBarTab control would then need to notify its parent container, in this case the OutlookBar control, of relevant events such as activation via a mouse click. Exposing events from the control to which the OutlookBar control would subscribe would develop this interaction.

Deciding on the base class for any control requires careful consideration of the intended use and the requirements of the control. The reason for creating the OutlookBarTab as a soft-control is to provide an example of soft-control creation and use. After all, the purpose of this book is to demonstrate various techniques for creating custom controls.

Interfaces

As seen in Chapter 5, "Advanced Control Development," the .NET BCL, base class library, provides several interfaces geared toward control development. The various control base classes implement these interfaces to provide a default implementation. During the development of a custom control, it may be necessary to override the implementation of one or more interface methods or properties. In the next chapter, a custom control collection is constructed to maintain a collection of OutlookBarTabs. This custom collection is constructed by implementing the necessary collection interfaces: ICollection, IList, and IEnumerable.

Properties and Events

Defining the OutlookBarTab properties is relatively easy. Consider what information the component needs to contain, and chances are most of that information will need to be available to users of the component. In addition to these properties, there needs to exist an event to notify observers of the component when a particular property has changed. The event name should coincide with the name of the property. For example, the Text property should have a corresponding event named OnTextChanged. This property/event pair holds true for all properties.

Beginning with properties, the purpose of the OutlookBarTab is to hold a child control, such as a panel or list box. The OutlookBarTab also provides a text caption and an associated icon. In addition, the text color and text alignment of the tab can be changed during design-time and at runtime. The properties for the OutlookBarTab are listed in Table 7.1.

TABLE 7.1   Basic Properties for the `OutlookBarTab` Component

Property	Description
Text	The text or caption to be displayed
ForeColor	The text color for the component
Alignment	The text alignment for the component
Icon	The associated icon image for the component
Child	The associated child control to be contained within the `OutlookBarTab`

The properties listed in Table 7.1 are used to define the appearance of the `OutlookBarTab`. In addition, each property has a corresponding event that is used to notify the `OutlookBar` control that a property has been modified. The property/event pairing is suggested by the design guidelines provided by Microsoft for control development. Table 7.2 lists the matching events for the properties in Table 7.1.

TABLE 7.2   Property Changed Events

Event	Description
TextChanged	Raised when the `Text` property has been modified.
ForeColorChanged	Raised when the `ForeColor` property has been modified.
TextAlignmentChanged	Raised when the `Alignment` property has been modified.
IconChanged	Raised when the associated icon image has been modified.
ChildChanged	Raised when the child control has been replaced with a new child control.

Each of the events from Table 7.2 has a corresponding protected member method associated with it. The corresponding member methods have the method signature

```
protected virtual OnEventName( object sender, EventArgs e )
```

where the *EventName* is replaced with the name of the corresponding event. Again, this is according to the development guidelines proposed by Microsoft. This is done so that any derived classes have the first opportunity to handle the various events. This is accomplished by overriding the protected event methods.

Public Methods

To keep the OutlookBarTab component simple, only two public methods are provided for the soft-control. Based on previous discussions of soft-controls, you have probably guessed that the two public methods relate to drawing and hit-testing. Table 7.3 lists the public methods for the OutlookBarTab component.

TABLE 7.3   OutlookBarTab Public Methods

Method	Description
HitTest	Determines whether the point passed in lies within the bounding rectangle of the component.
Draw	Renders the component using the passed-in Graphics object.

When you're building soft-controls, the methods listed in Table 7.3 are the usual starting point. Of the two methods, the Draw method is often subdivided into several smaller methods, with each method handling a different aspect of the drawing logic.

User Interface

Even though the OutlookBarTab is not a control, it will still be responsible for rendering its own UI within the OutlookBar control. The reason for this is to keep the drawing code contained within the OutlookBarTab. This frees the parent control from having to perform the drawing of the soft-control and helps segment the code. In addition, the OutlookBarTab component could then serve as a base class, and the derived class could in turn provide its own custom drawing logic.

Rendering of the tab component includes a normal look with and without an image, and a pushed look, such as when a mouse has been clicked over the tab. In addition, the OutlookBarTab will trim its text with an ellipsis (...) set of characters when the text length exceeds the size of the tab. Figure 7.1 shows the various looks of the tab component.

FIGURE 7.1
The OutlookBarTab look and feel.

7

OUTLOOKBARTAB
COMPONENT

In addition, the `OutlookBarTab` will keep track of its own bounding rectangle and provide hit-testing, determining whether a mouse click point is contained within its bounding region. The bounding rectangle is the physical size of the component and is used when determining whether a mouse click has occurred within the component. This is known as hit-testing.

Designer

One of the most critical aspects of a control from a developer's point of view is the design-time experience. When end users of an application see the runtime behavior, a developer requires that the control be rich in design-time functionality. The need to provide an easy-to-design control with custom editing features requires careful attention to be given to the designer for a control.

Sometimes the default designer provides the necessary support, as is the case with the `OutlookBarTab` component. For a `Component`-derived class the `ComponentDesigner` class represents the default designer. For classes derived from the `Control` base class, the default designer is the `ControlDesigner` class.

The basic support derived from the `ComponentDesigner` consists of placing an icon within the Icon Tray area of the VS .NET IDE and property browser support. In addition, basic code serialization services are provided.

During the development of the `OutlookBar` control in Chapter 8, a custom designer will be required to provide features such as drag-and-drop at design-time for child controls.

Implementation

Now that the responsibilities and expected functionality of the `OutlookBarTab` have been defined, it's time to realize the design in code. Listing 7.1 provides the complete listing for the `OutlookBarTab` component.

LISTING 7.1 OutlookBarTab

```
 1: using System;
 2: using System.ComponentModel;
 3: using System.Drawing;
 4: using System.Windows.Forms;
 5:
 6: namespace SAMS.ToolKit.Controls
 7: {
 8:
 9:     [
10:     Description( "OutlookBarTab Component" ),
11:     ToolboxItem( false )
```

LISTING 7.1 Continued

```
12:      ]
13:      public class OutlookBarTab     : System.ComponentModel.Component {
14:
15:          #region STATIC FIELDS
16:          internal static int        EDGE_PADDING = 4;
17:          #endregion
18:
19:          #region Protected Instance Members
20:          protected string           text;
21:          protected StringAlignment   textAlignment;
22:          protected Color                 foreColor;
23:          protected Icon               tabIcon;
24:          protected Control           child;
25:
26:          protected Rectangle            tabRect;
27:          protected Rectangle            iconRect;
28:          protected ButtonState        buttonState;
29:          #endregion
30:
31:
32:          #region Internal Events
33:
34:          [Description( "Event rasied when the Text property has
➥ been modified" )]
35:          public event EventHandler    TextChanged;
36:
37:          [Description( "Event rasied when the TextAlignment property
➥ has been modified" )]
38:          public event EventHandler    TextAlignmentChanged;
39:
40:          [Description( "Event rasied when the ForeColor property
➥has been modified" )]
41:          public event EventHandler    ForeColorChanged;
42:
43:          [Description( "Event rasied when the Icon property has
➥ been modified" )]
44:          public event EventHandler    IconChanged;
45:
46:          [Description( "Event rasied when the Child property has
➥ been modified" )]
47:          public event EventHandler    ChildChanged;
48:
49:          #endregion
50:
51:
```

LISTING 7.1   Continued

```
52:          #region Properties
53:
54:          [
55:          Description( "The text displayed on the control tab" ),
56:          Category( "Appearance" )
57:          ]
58:          public string Text {
59:              get { return text; }
60:              set {
61:                  if( !text.Equals( (string)value ) ) {
62:                      text = value;
63:                      OnTextChanged( new EventArgs( ) );
64:                  }
65:              }
66:          }
67:
68:          [
69:          Description( "Specifies the alignment of the text within the
➥ control tab" ),
70:          Category( "Appearance" )
71:          ]
72:          public StringAlignment Alignment {
73:              get { return textAlignment; }
74:              set {
75:                  if( textAlignment != value ) {
76:                      textAlignment = value;
77:                      OnTextAlignmentChanged( new EventArgs( ) );
78:                  }
79:              }
80:          }
81:
82:          [
83:          Description( "Specifies the color used to render the text
➥ on the tab control" ),
84:          Category( "Appearance" )
85:          ]
86:          public Color ForeColor {
87:              get { return foreColor; }
88:              set {
89:                  if( foreColor != value ) {
90:                      foreColor = value;
91:                      OnForeColorChanged( new EventArgs( ) );
92:                  }
93:              }
94:          }
```

LISTING 7.1   Continued

```
 95:
 96:        [
 97:        Description( "Specifies the Icon to drawn on the control tab" ),
 98:        Category( "Appearance" ),
 99:        DefaultValue( null )
100:        ]
101:        public Icon Icon {
102:            get { return tabIcon; }
103:            set {
104:                if( tabIcon != value ) {
105:                    tabIcon = value;
106:                    OnIconChanged( new EventArgs( ) );
107:                }
108:            }
109:        }
110:
111:        [
112:        Description( "Child control hosted within the control tab" ),
113:        Category( "Behavior" )
114:        ]
115:        public Control Child {
116:            get { return child; }
117:            set {
118:                if( child != value ) {
119:                    child = value;
120:                    OnChildChanged( new EventArgs( ) );
121:                }
122:            }
123:        }
124:
125:        [ Browsable( false ) ]
126:        internal ButtonState ButtonState {
127:            get { return buttonState; }
128:        }
129:
130:        [ Browsable( false ) ]
131:        internal Rectangle TabRect {
132:            get { return tabRect; }
133:        }
134:
135:        #endregion
136:
137:        public OutlookBarTab()
138:        {
139:            text = "";
```

LISTING 7.1 Continued

```
140:                foreColor = System.Drawing.SystemColors.ControlText;
141:                child = null;
142:                tabIcon = null;
143:                textAlignment = StringAlignment.Center;
144:            }
145:
146:        public virtual void Draw( Graphics g,
147:                                  Rectangle destRect,
148:                                  Font font,
149:    ButtonState buttonState ) {
150:
151:                tabRect = destRect;
152:                this.buttonState = buttonState;
153:
154:            DrawButton( g );
155:            if( tabIcon != null )
156:                DrawIcon( g );
157:            DrawText( g, font );
158:        }
159:
160:        public bool HitTest( Point pt ) {
161:            return tabRect.Contains( pt );
162:        }
163:
164:        #region Protected Instance Methods
165:
166:
167:
168:        protected virtual void DrawButton( Graphics g ) {
169:            ControlPaint.DrawButton( g, tabRect, buttonState );
170:        }
171:
172:
173:    protected virtual void DrawIcon( Graphics g ) {
174:            int top = tabRect.Top + EDGE_PADDING;
175:            int left = tabRect.Left + EDGE_PADDING;
176:            int width = tabIcon.Width;
177:            int height = tabIcon.Height;
178:
179:            //Does the Icon need scaled?
180:            if( (top+height) >= (tabRect.Height - (2*EDGE_PADDING))) {
181:                float maxHeight = (tabRect.Height - (2*EDGE_PADDING));
182:                float scaleFactor = maxHeight / (float)height;
183:                height = (int)((float)height*scaleFactor);
184:                width = (int)((float)width*scaleFactor);
```

LISTING 7.1   Continued

```
185:                 }
186:
187:                 iconRect = new Rectangle( left, top, width, height );
188:                 if( buttonState == ButtonState.Pushed )
189:                     iconRect.Offset(1,1);
190:
191:                 g.DrawIcon( tabIcon, iconRect );
192:             }
193:
194:         protected virtual void DrawText( Graphics g, Font font ) {
195:             Rectangle textRect = tabRect;
196:
197:    textRect.X += EDGE_PADDING;
198:             textRect.Width -= EDGE_PADDING;
199:             textRect.Y += EDGE_PADDING;
200:             textRect.Height -= EDGE_PADDING;
201:
202:             //Adjust for possible icon
203:             if( tabIcon != null ) {
204:                 textRect.X += iconRect.Width;
205:                 textRect.Width -= iconRect.Width;
206:             }
207:
208:             //Adjust for button state
209:             if( buttonState == ButtonState.Pushed )
210:                 textRect.Offset(1,1);
211:
212:             //Render the Text
213:             StringFormat fmt     = new StringFormat( );
214:             fmt.Alignment        = textAlignment;
215:             fmt.LineAlignment    = StringAlignment.Center;
216:             fmt.Trimming         = StringTrimming.EllipsisCharacter;
217:             fmt.FormatFlags         = StringFormatFlags.NoWrap |
➥StringFormatFlags.LineLimit;
218:
219:             Brush textBrush = new SolidBrush( foreColor );
220:
221:             g.DrawString( text,  font, textBrush, textRect, fmt );
222:
223:             textBrush.Dispose( );
224:         }
225:
226:
227:         protected virtual void OnTextChanged( EventArgs e ) {
228:             if( TextChanged != null )
```

LISTING 7.1   Continued

```
229:                    TextChanged( this, e );
230:            }
231:            protected virtual void OnTextAlignmentChanged( EventArgs e ) {
232:                if( TextAlignmentChanged != null )
233:                    TextAlignmentChanged( this, e );
234:            }
235:            protected virtual void OnForeColorChanged( EventArgs e ) {
236:                if( ForeColorChanged != null )
237:                    ForeColorChanged( this, e );
238:            }
239:            protected virtual void OnIconChanged( EventArgs e ) {
240:                if( IconChanged != null )
241:                    IconChanged( this, e );
242:            }
243:            protected virtual void OnChildChanged( EventArgs e ) {
244:                if( ChildChanged != null )
245:                    ChildChanged( this, e );
246:            }
247:    #endregion
248:        }
249: }
```

The implementation of the OutlookBarTab follows the general layout of the topics discussed within this chapter. Each of the outlined properties, events, and public methods has been implemented. In addition, the Draw method delegates various drawing tasks to specific protected methods within the component.

As expected, the drawing of the components represents most of the component's logic. The OutlookBarTab must determine how to draw itself based on the properties, size, and state of the tab. Drawing of the tab is broken down into three areas: DrawButton, DrawIcon, and DrawText.

The DrawButton method uses the familiar ControlPaint class to render a basic button-style control. Next, the DrawIcon method draws a properly scaled version of the icon image associated with the tab component. Finally, the DrawText method is called to draw the text for the component, taking into consideration the icon and text length.

It's important to note the use of the ToolboxItem attribute used on the OutlookBarTab class. The ToolboxItem attribute specifies whether the toolbox should create a toolbox item. In addition, it can be used to specify the type of toolbox item to create. In the case of the OutlookBarTab, the component should not be available on the toolbar. This will prevent the component from being available for use as a toolbox control. After all, the OutlookBarTab is really a subcomponent of the OutlookBar control.

Testing the Component

Without having the `OutlookBar` control implemented, testing the `OutlookBarTab` requires creating a custom test-bed application. One thing to keep in mind when building custom controls is that most of the time you are left to your own devices when it comes to testing the control. Although VS .NET provides a rich infrastructure for control development, many times your own creativity and necessity will spawn new tools for testing.

As with many of the applications built so far for testing, the property grid will serve as a means to interact with the properties provided by the `OutlookBarTab` component. Figure 7.2 shows the test-bed application.

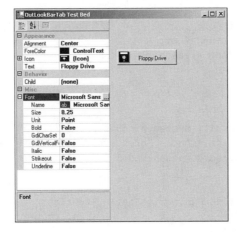

FIGURE 7.2
The `OutlookBarTab` *test-bed demo*

Before diving into the source for the test bed, you should have noticed the `Font` property being displayed within the property grid. The `OutlookBarTab` component has no `Font` property, yet a grid item appears. When the `OutlookBar` control is built, its own `Font` property will be used when rendering the child tabs, and as such this functionality should be tested as well. To provide the `Font` property, the `OutlookBarTab` will serve as a base class from which a derived class will provide a single property: `Font`.

Listing 7.2 shows the source listing for the test-bed application.

LISTING 7.2   Testing the `OutlookBarTab` Component

```
1: using System;
2: using System.Drawing;
3: using System.Collections;
```

LISTING 7.2   Continued

```
4: using System.ComponentModel;
5: using System.Windows.Forms;
6: using System.Data;
7:
8: namespace OutlookBarTabTest
9: {
10:
11:     public class OutlookBarTabWithFont :
➥SAMS.ToolKit.Controls.OutlookBarTab {
12:
13:         private Font font;
14:
15:         public Font Font {
16:             get { return font; }
17:             set { font = value; }
18:         }
19:     }
20:
21:
22:     public class Form1 : System.Windows.Forms.Form {
23:         private System.Windows.Forms.PropertyGrid propertyGrid1;
24:         private System.ComponentModel.Container components = null;
25:
26:
27:         private OutlookBarTabWithFont    testTab;
28:
29:         public Form1() {
30:             //
31:             // Required for Windows Form Designer support
32:             //
33:             InitializeComponent();
34:
35:             testTab = new OutlookBarTabWithFont( );
36:             testTab.Font = this.Font;
37:             this.propertyGrid1.SelectedObject = testTab;
38:             this.propertyGrid1.PropertyValueChanged +=
➥new PropertyValueChangedEventHandler( OnPropertyValueChanged );
39:
40:         }
41:
42:         protected void OnPropertyValueChanged( object sender,
➥PropertyValueChangedEventArgs e ) {
43:             this.Invalidate( );
44:         }
45:
```

LISTING 7.2   Continued

```
46:          protected override void OnPaint( PaintEventArgs e ) {
47:             base.OnPaint( e );
48:
49:             testTab.Draw( e.Graphics, new Rectangle(216,64,128,32 ),
➥testTab.Font, ButtonState.Normal );
50:          }
51:
52:          protected override void OnMouseDown( MouseEventArgs e ) {
53:             if( e.Button == MouseButtons.Left &&
➥ testTab.HitTest( new Point( e.X, e.Y ) ) )
54:                testTab.Draw( CreateGraphics( ),
➥new Rectangle(216,64,128,32 ),  testTab.Font, ButtonState.Pushed );
55:          }
56:
57:          protected override void OnMouseUp( MouseEventArgs e ) {
58:                testTab.Draw( CreateGraphics( ),
➥new Rectangle(216,64,128,32 ), testTab.Font, ButtonState.Normal );
59:          }
60:
61:
62:
63:          protected override void Dispose( bool disposing )
64:          {
65:             if( disposing )
66:             {
67:                if (components != null)
68:                {
69:                   components.Dispose();
70:                }
71:             }
72:             base.Dispose( disposing );
73:          }
74:
75:          #region Windows Form Designer generated code
76:          /// <summary>
77:          /// Required method for Designer support - do not modify
78:          /// the contents of this method with the code editor.
79:          /// </summary>
80:          private void InitializeComponent()
81:          {
82:             this.propertyGrid1 = new System.Windows.Forms.PropertyGrid();
83:             this.SuspendLayout();
84:             //
85:             // propertyGrid1
86:             //
```

LISTING 7.2   Continued

```
 87:              this.propertyGrid1.CommandsVisibleIfAvailable = true;
 88:              this.propertyGrid1.Dock = System.Windows.Forms.DockStyle.Left;
 89:              this.propertyGrid1.LargeButtons = false;
 90:              this.propertyGrid1.LineColor =
➥System.Drawing.SystemColors.ScrollBar;
 91:              this.propertyGrid1.Name = "propertyGrid1";
 92:              this.propertyGrid1.Size = new System.Drawing.Size(200, 273);
 93:              this.propertyGrid1.TabIndex = 0;
 94:              this.propertyGrid1.Text = "propertyGrid1";
 95:              this.propertyGrid1.ViewBackColor =
➥ System.Drawing.SystemColors.Window;
 96:              this.propertyGrid1.ViewForeColor =
➥System.Drawing.SystemColors.WindowText;
 97:              //
 98:              // Form1
 99:              //
100:              this.AutoScaleBaseSize = new System.Drawing.Size(5, 13);
101:              this.ClientSize = new System.Drawing.Size(360, 273);
102:              this.Controls.AddRange(new System.Windows.Forms.Control[] {
103:     this.propertyGrid1});
104:              this.Name = "Form1";
105:              this.Text = "OutoolBarTab Test Bed";
106:              this.ResumeLayout(false);
107:
108:          }
109:          #endregion
110:
111:          /// <summary>
112:          /// The main entry point for the application.
113:          /// </summary>
114:          [STAThread]
115:          static void Main()
116:          {
117:              Application.Run(new Form1());
118:          }
119:  }
120: }
```

By deriving the class OutlookBarTabWithFont from the OutlookBarTab component, a Font property can be added for the property grid support. At the same time, this technique does not disturb the OutlookBarTab component in any way that would alter its behavior.

The test-bed application is a standard Windows Forms–based application. To test the OutlookBarTab component, the form will act as the parent and handle managing the component. The major areas of the test bed revolve around mouse events and painting. When a mouse click occurs on the parent form, the x and y coordinates of the mouse click are passed to the OutlookBarTab for hit-testing. Again, hit-testing is used to determine whether a point is located within the soft-control.

Depending on the result of the hit-testing for the OutlookBarTab, the appropriate parameters are passed to the Draw method of the component. Again, the Draw method handles all the drawing logic for the component.

In addition to mouse events and drawing, the main form subscribes or listens to the events of the component. These events include TextChanged, ForeColorChanged, and so on. When a property of the component has changed, it is necessary for the parent form to provide a Graphics object that the OutlookBarTab can use to redraw itself to reflect the changed properties. All the necessary testing code is found between lines 42 and 59 of Listing 7.2.

Using the PropertyGrid control gives a pseudo design-time feeling to the component being tested. The VS .NET IDE provides no support for testing soft-controls such as the OutlookBarTab, and a simple test application such as that developed in Listing 7.2 could easily be extended and reused to test and develop other soft-controls.

Summary

The journey toward a functional and popular control, the OutlookBar, is now underway. In the next two chapters control development is the primary focus. The OutlookBarTab component serves as the basis for building the larger control. Developing controls requires defining the various components and building small blocks from which the main control will be constructed. In this chapter several ideas have been re-enforced, and some new ideas have been introduced. The process of building controls is a fantastic journey, and it has just begun.

OutlookBar Control

IN THIS CHAPTER

Building on the knowledge gained thus far, it's time to begin developing a more advanced control. The OutlookBar control is one of the most common custom controls used by applications. In fact, there are many Toolkits, providers of custom controls, which are companies that offer the OutlookBar as part of the standard offering of controls. At the end of this chapter, you will have created your own functional OutlookBar control to use in your projects.

The process of building the OutlookBar control is divided into three major sections: The OutlookBar control, a custom collection for managing OutlookBarTab components, and the control's designer. As with the other controls developed so far, the process will begin by first defining the requirements for the control, including the listing of properties, events, and public methods. In addition, the topic of custom events and custom event parameters will also be discussed.

As with the OutlookBarTab component developed in the preceding chapter, a test application will be created to aid in the development of the OutlookBar control. Remember, you'll need to get creative to test controls during their development rather than relying on the VS .NET IDE. The reasoning for this is that in the early stages of control development, the control will more than likely lack full support for interacting with the IDE. As such, creating small test applications will allow for basic testing and debugging until such time as the control provides the necessary support for the VS .NET IDE.

Control Design

The main functional requirement of the OutlookBar control is that the control will host other controls within the OutlookBarTab components. Each new child control will be associated with a particular tab within the OutLookBar, and that child control will be activated when its parent tab is selected. Figure 8.1 shows the OutlookBar control hosting a TreeView control and a Panel control.

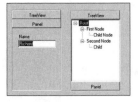

Figure 8.1
The OutlookBar control in action.

Because the OutlookBar control will act as a container control for other .NET controls, the emphasis of this chapter is to demonstrate the implementation of this particular requirement. Extending the OutlookBar controls feature set will be left to you as an exercise.

Before the discussion dives into the code for the control, the subject of defining custom events needs to be discussed. The following section discusses custom events.

Custom Events

The `OutlookBar` control defines a custom event and an associated event handler. In Windows Forms development, controls raise events to notify the observer either of some change in the state of the control or that an action has occurred that should be responded to. Generally, event handlers for such events take the following form:

access-modifier void On*Control-Name_Event*(object sender, EventArgs e)

The `EventArgs` parameter can be the `System.EventArgs` class or a class that derives from `EventArgs`, such as `PaintEventArgs` or `MouseEventArgs`.

Defining custom events and event handlers, known as delegates, provides a clear message to the user of the control as to the event type and the expected event arguments that pertain to the event. Listing 8.1 shows the proper semantic for defining custom events.

LISTING 8.1 Custom Events

```
1: using System;
2:
3: namespace CustomEvents
4: {
5:
6:
7:     public class MyCustomEventArgs : System.EventArgs {
8:
9:         private string    msg;
10:
11:         public string Message {
12:             get { return msg; }
13:         }
14:
15:
16:         public MyCustomEventArgs( string Message ) {
17:             msg = Message;
18:         }
19:     }
20:
21:     public delegate void MyCustomEventHandler( object sender,
➥MyCustomEventArgs e );
22:
23:
24:     public class MyControl {
```

LISTING 8.1   Continued

```
25:
26:         public event MyCustomEventHandler    CustomEvent;
27:
28:
29:         public void RaiseEvent( string Message ) {
30:             OnMyCustomEvent( new MyCustomEventArgs( Message ) );
31:         }
32:
33:         protected virtual void OnMyCustomEvent( MyCustomEventArgs e ) {
34:             if( CustomEvent != null )
35:                 CustomEvent( this, e );
36:         }
37:
38:     }
39:
40:
41:
42:
43:     public class EventTest {
44:
45:         public static void OnMyControl_CustomEvent( object sender,
➥ MyCustomEventArgs e ) {
46:             Console.WriteLine( string.Format( "Caught custom event :
➥{0}", e.Message ) );
47:         }
48:
49:         public static void Main( ) {
50:
51:             MyControl ctrl = new MyControl( );
52:
53:             ctrl.CustomEvent += new MyCustomEventHandler(
➥EventTest.OnMyControl_CustomEvent );
54:
55:             ctrl.RaiseEvent( "Raising Event" );
56:  }
57:     }
58: }
```

The process of creating custom events generally begins by defining the event and the event parameters. According to the development guidelines provided by Microsoft, event handlers should define two parameters. The first parameter for an event is the sender or originator of the event. The second parameter is the necessary information about the event, and it should be an EventArgs derived class.

Delegates are the basic mechanism for handling events and notifications within the .NET framework. Extending the basic set of events and defining custom events is a programming task that all .NET developers should become proficient in.

Notice the method `OnMyCustomEvent` on line 33 of Listing 8.1. Defining a protected virtual event handler within the class allows for derived classes to override the event handler to perform any custom processing before allowing the event to propagate to the registered observers of the event.

`OutlookBar` Control Implementation

The implementation for the `OutlookBar` control is divided into three parts:

- The `OutlookBar` control
- Custom `OutlookBarTab` collection
- `OutlookBarDesigner`

The `OutlookBar` control provides a custom event for notification when the selected `OutlookBarTab` changes. In addition, some basic properties are provided, such as the active tab, the index of the active tab, and a collection of `OutlookBarTab` objects.

The `OutlookBarTab` collection provides a means to add new tabs to the `OutlookBar` at design-time or runtime. This collection is discussed later in the chapter.

The `OutlookBarDesigner` adds support for drag-and-drop during design-time, as well as the capability to activate the hosted tabs within the control similar to the Windows Forms `TabControl`. This designer is discussed later in the chapter.

To keep the code to a minimum while still providing a useful control, the `OutlookBar` control will provide only a bare minimum set of properties and only a single event. Table 8.1 lists the properties exposed by the `OutlookBar` control.

TABLE 8.1 `OutlookBar` Control Properties and Descriptions

Property	Description
Tabs	Exposes a custom collection of `OutlookBarTab` components.
ActiveTabIndex	Provides a quick index into the `Tabs` collection.
ActiveTab	Provides access to the currently selected or active tab within the `OutlookBar` control. This property is read-only.

As stated previously, the `OutlookBar` control provides only a single event. In addition to the event, a custom event argument is defined as well. Table 8.2 lists the properties of the custom event: `OutlookBarSelectedTabChangedEventArgs`. (That name alone can cause carpal tunnel syndrome.)

TABLE 8.2   Properties of the `OutlookBarSelectedTabChangedEventArgs` Class

Property	Description
ActiveTab	The currently active `OutlookBarTab` component.
PreviousTab	The formerly active `OutlookBarTab` component.

The custom event is exposed via the following delegate:

```
public delegate void OutlookBarSelectedTabChangedEventHandler( object sender,
➥ OutlookBarSelectedTabChangedEventArgs e );
```

Most of the `OutlookBar` control code, excluding the custom nested collection, deals with drawing and child control management. Listing 8.2 provides the core implementation of the `OutlookBar` control. The implementation is discussed in more detail following this code listing.

LISTING 8.2   `OutlookBar` Control

```
 1: using System;
 2: using System.Drawing;
 3: using System.Drawing.Drawing2D;
 4: using System.ComponentModel;
 5: using System.Windows.Forms;
 6: using System.Collections;
 7:
 8: namespace SAMS.ToolKit.Controls
 9: {
10:
11:     public enum HitTestType {
12:         TABS,
13:         CLIENT
14:     }
15:
16:     #region OutlookBar EventArgs
17:
18:     public class OutlookBarSelectedTabChangedEventArgs : EventArgs {
19:         private OutlookBarTab        activeTab;
20:         private OutlookBarTab        prevTab;
21:
```

LISTING 8.2   Continued

```
22:
23:          public OutlookBarTab ActiveTab {
24:              get { return activeTab; }
25:          }
26:
27:          public OutlookBarTab PreviousTab {
28:              get { return prevTab; }
29:          }
30:
31:          public OutlookBarSelectedTabChangedEventArgs(
➥OutlookBarTab active, OutlookBarTab prev ) {
32:              activeTab    = active;
33:              prevTab      = prev;
34:          }
35:      }
36:
37:      public delegate void OutlookBarSelectedTabChangedEventHandler(
➥object sender, OutlookBarSelectedTabChangedEventArgs e );
38:      #endregion
39:
40:      #region OutlookBar Control
41:
42:      [
43:      Description( "The OutlookBar Control aka Shortcut Bar" ),
44:      DefaultEvent( "SelectedTabChanged" ),
45:      DefaultProperty( "Tabs" ),
46:      Designer( typeof( SAMS.ToolKit.Design.OutlookBarDesigner ) )
47:      ]
48:      public class OutlookBar : System.Windows.Forms.ContainerControl {
49:
50:          #region Instance Members, Properties and Events
51:
52:          private System.ComponentModel.Container   components    = null;
53:          private TabCollection                     tabCollection;
54:          private int                               activeTabIndex;
55:          private int                               hitTabIndex;
56:          private Rectangle                         activeClientRect;
57:          private int                               tabHeight;
58:
59:
60:          [
61:          Description( "Raised when the active outlooktab changes" ),
62:          Category( "Behavior" )
63:          ]
```

LISTING 8.2   Continued

```
64:        public event OutlookBarSelectedTabChangedEventHandler
➥ SelectedTabChanged;
65:
66:
67:        [
68:        Description( "The collection of OutlookTabs" ),
69:        Category( "Appearance" ),
70:        DesignerSerializationVisibility(
➥ DesignerSerializationVisibility.Content )
71:        ]
72:        public TabCollection Tabs {
73:            get { return tabCollection; }
74:            set {
75:                tabCollection.Clear( );
76:                tabCollection = value;
77:            }
78:        }
79:
80:        [
81:   Browsable( false ),
82:        DesignerSerializationVisibility(
➥ DesignerSerializationVisibility.Hidden )
83:        ]
84:        public int ActiveTabIndex {
85:            get {
86:                return activeTabIndex;
87:            }
88:            set {
89:                ActivateTab( (int)value );
90:            }
91:        }
92:
93:        [
94:        Browsable( false ),
95:        DesignerSerializationVisibility(
➥ DesignerSerializationVisibility.Hidden )
96:        ]
97:        public OutlookBarTab ActiveTab {
98:            get { return tabCollection[ activeTabIndex ]; }
99:        }
100:
101:        [ DesignerSerializationVisibility(
➥ DesignerSerializationVisibility.Hidden ) ]
102:        public new ControlCollection Controls {
```

LISTING 8.2 Continued

```
103:                    get { return base.Controls; }
104:            }
105:
106:
107:        #endregion
108:
109:    #region Construction, Initialization and Public Instance Methods
110:
111:        public OutlookBar( ) {
112:            InitializeComponent( );
113:
114:            //Set default values
115:            tabCollection        = new TabCollection( this );
116:            activeTabIndex       = -1;
117:            hitTabIndex          = -1;
118:            activeClientRect     = new Rectangle(0,0,0,0);
119:            tabHeight            = 24;
120:        }
121:
122:        //Required for Designer Support
123:        private void InitializeComponent( ) {
124:        }
125:
126:        public bool HitTest( HitTestType testType, Point pt,
➡ out int TabIndex ) {
127:            bool bResult = false;
128:            TabIndex = -1;
129:
130:            if( testType == HitTestType.CLIENT ) {
131:                bResult = this.activeClientRect.Contains( pt );
132:            } else {
133:                int hitTabCache = this.hitTabIndex;
134:                bResult = HitTestTabs( pt );
135:                if( bResult )
136:                    TabIndex = hitTabIndex;
137: hitTabIndex = hitTabCache;
138:            }
139:            return bResult;
140:        }
141:
142:        #endregion
143:
144:        #region ContainerControl Overrides
145:
146:        protected override void Dispose( bool disposing ) {
```

8

LISTING 8.2   Continued

```
147:                if( disposing ) {
148:                    if (components != null) {
149:                        components.Dispose();
150:                    }
151:                }
152:                base.Dispose( disposing );
153:            }
154:
155:            protected override void OnFontChanged( EventArgs e ) {
156:                base.OnFontChanged( e );
157:                ReCalctabHeight( );
158:                Invalidate( );
159:            }
160:
161:            protected override void OnSizeChanged( EventArgs e ) {
162:                base.OnSizeChanged( e );
163:                ReCalcClientRect( );
164:                Invalidate( );
165:            }
166:
167:            protected override void OnMouseDown( MouseEventArgs e ) {
168:                if( e.Button == MouseButtons.Left ) {
169:                    if( HitTestTabs( new Point( e.X, e.Y ) ) ) {
170:        Graphics g        = CreateGraphics( );
171:                        DrawTab( g, hitTabIndex, ButtonState.Pushed );
172:                        g.Dispose( );
173:                    } else
174:                        base.OnMouseDown( e );
175:                } else
176:                    base.OnMouseDown( e );
177:            }
178:
179:            protected override void OnMouseUp( MouseEventArgs e ) {
180:                if( (e.Button == MouseButtons.Left) &&
➡ (hitTabIndex != -1) ) {
181:
182:                    Graphics g = CreateGraphics( );
183:                    DrawTab( g, hitTabIndex, ButtonState.Normal );
184:                    g.Dispose( );
185:
186:                    if( tabCollection[ hitTabIndex ].HitTest(
➡new Point( e.X, e.Y ) ) ) {
187:                        int activeIndex = hitTabIndex;
188:                        hitTabIndex = -1;
```

LISTING 8.2   Continued

```
189:                         ActivateTab( activeIndex );
190:                    }
191:
192:              } else
193:        base.OnMouseUp( e );
194:          }
195:
196:        protected override void OnPaint( PaintEventArgs e ) {
197:            base.OnPaint( e );
198:            DrawBorder( e.Graphics );
199:            DrawTabs( e.Graphics );
200:            ActivateChildControl( );
201:        }
202:        #endregion
203:
204:        #region Protected/Internal/Private Instance Methods
205:
206:        protected virtual bool HitTestTabs( Point pt ) {
207:
208:            for( int tabIndex = 0; tabIndex < tabCollection.Count;
➥ tabIndex++ ) {
209:                if( tabCollection[ tabIndex ].HitTest( pt ) ) {
210:                    hitTabIndex = tabIndex;
211:                    return true;
212:                }
213:            }
214:            hitTabIndex = -1;
215:            return false;
216:        }
217:
218:        protected virtual void ActivateTab( int tabIndex ) {
219:
220:            if( (tabIndex == activeTabIndex) ||
➥ (tabIndex >= tabCollection.Count))
221:                return;
222:
223:            OutlookBarTab prevTab   = tabCollection[ activeTabIndex ];
224:            OutlookBarTab activeTab = tabCollection[ tabIndex ];
225:
226:            DeActivateTab( activeTabIndex );
227:
228:            activeTabIndex = tabIndex;
229:
230:            ReCalcClientRect( );
```

LISTING 8.2   Continued

```
231:
232:             Invalidate( );
233:             Update( );
234:             ActivateChildControl( );
235:
236:             OnSelectedTabIndexChanged( new
➥ OutlookBarSelectedTabChangedEventArgs( activeTab, prevTab ) );
237:         }
238:
239:      protected virtual void DeActivateTab( int tabIndex ) {
240:          OutlookBarTab T = tabCollection[ tabIndex ];
241:          if( (T != null) && (T.Child != null) )
242:    T.Child.Visible = false;
243:         }
244:
245:      protected virtual void ActivateChildControl( ) {
246:          OutlookBarTab T = tabCollection[ activeTabIndex ];
247:          if( (T != null ) && (T.Child != null) ) {
248:             T.Child.Visible      = true;
249:             T.Child.Size         = new Size( activeClientRect.Width,
➥activeClientRect.Height );
250:             T.Child.Location     = new Point( activeClientRect.Left,
➥activeClientRect.Top );
251:             T.Child.BringToFront( );
252:          }
253:      }
254:
255:      protected virtual void ReCalctabHeight( ) {
256:          Graphics g = CreateGraphics( );
257:          tabHeight =    (int)(Font.GetHeight( g ) +
➥ (float)(2*OutlookBarTab.EDGE_PADDING));
258:          g.Dispose( );
259:      }
260:
261:      protected virtual void ReCalcClientRect( ) {
262:          activeClientRect = new Rectangle( 1,1,Width - 2,Height - 2);
263:          activeClientRect.Y += tabHeight * ( activeTabIndex + 1 );
264:    activeClientRect.Height -= tabCollection.Count * tabHeight;
265:      }
266:
267:      protected virtual void DrawBorder( Graphics g ) {
268:          ControlPaint.DrawBorder3D( g, new Rectangle(0,0,Width,Height),
➥ Border3DStyle.Etched, Border3DSide.All );
269:      }
```

LISTING 8.2   Continued

```
270:
271:          protected virtual void DrawTabs( Graphics g ) {
272:
273:               if( tabCollection.Count == 0 )
274:                   return;
275:
276:               Rectangle tabRect = new Rectangle( 1, 1, Width - 2,
➥tabHeight );
277:               for( int tabIndex = 0; tabIndex < tabCollection.Count;
➥ tabIndex++ ) {
278:                   OutlookBarTab T = tabCollection[ tabIndex ];
279:                   DrawTab( g, T, tabRect, (tabIndex == hitTabIndex ?
➥ ButtonState.Pushed : ButtonState.Normal) );
280:
281:     if( tabIndex == activeTabIndex )
282:                       tabRect.Y = activeClientRect.Bottom;
283:                   else
284:                       tabRect.Y += tabHeight;
285:               }
286:           }
287:
288:          protected virtual void DrawTab( Graphics g, int tabIndex ) {
289:               OutlookBarTab T = tabCollection[ tabIndex ];
290:               DrawTab( g, T, T.TabRect, T.ButtonState );
291:           }
292:
293:          protected virtual void DrawTab( Graphics g, int tabIndex,
➥ ButtonState buttonState ) {
294:               OutlookBarTab T = tabCollection[ tabIndex ];
295:               DrawTab( g, T, T.TabRect, buttonState );
296:           }
297:          protected virtual void DrawTab( Graphics g, int tabIndex,
➥Rectangle tabRect, ButtonState buttonState ) {
298:               DrawTab( g, tabCollection[ tabIndex ], tabRect, buttonState );
299:           }
300:
301:          protected virtual void DrawTab( Graphics g,
➥OutlookBarTab outlookTab, Rectangle tabRect, ButtonState buttonState ) {
302:               outlookTab.Draw( g, tabRect, Font, buttonState );
303:           }
304:
305:   protected virtual void SubscribeToTabEvents( OutlookBarTab tab ) {
306:               System.Reflection.EventInfo[] events =
➥tab.GetType( ).GetEvents(   );
```

LISTING 8.2   Continued

```
307:
308:              foreach( System.Reflection.EventInfo ei in events )
309:                  ei.AddEventHandler( tab, new EventHandler(
➥ this.OnTabPropertyChanged ) );
310:          }
311:
312:      protected virtual void UnSubscribeToTabEvents(
➥OutlookBarTab tab ) {
313:              System.Reflection.EventInfo[] events =
➥ tab.GetType( ).GetEvents( );
314:
315:              foreach( System.Reflection.EventInfo ei in events )
316:                  ei.RemoveEventHandler( tab, new EventHandler(
➥this.OnTabPropertyChanged ) );
317:          }
318:
319:      protected virtual void OnTabPropertyChanged( object sender,
➥ EventArgs e ) {
320:              Control ctrl = ((OutlookBarTab)sender).Child;
321:
322:          f( ctrl != null && !Controls.Conatins( ctrl ) ) {
323:              ctrl.Visible = false;
324:              this.Controls.Add( ctrl );
325:          }
326:          Invalidate( );
327:          }
328:
329:      protected virtual void OnSelectedTabIndexChanged(
➥OutlookBarSelectedTabChangedEventArgs e ) {
330:              if( SelectedTabChanged != null )
331:                  SelectedTabChanged( this, e );
332:          }
333:
334:      #endregion
335:
336:
337:
338:
339:      #region TabCollection
340:      public class TabCollection : ICollection, IEnumerable, IList {
341:
342:          private OutlookBar       owner              = null;
343:          private ArrayList        internalArrayList   = null;
344:
345:
```

LISTING 8.2   Continued

```
346:            public TabCollection( OutlookBar parent ) {
347:                owner = parent;
348:                internalArrayList = new ArrayList( );
349:            }
350:
351:            //ICollection Interface implementation
352:            public int Count {
353:                get { return internalArrayList.Count; }
354:            }
355:            public bool IsSynchronized {
356:                get { return internalArrayList.IsSynchronized; }
357:            }
358:            public object SyncRoot {
359:                get { return internalArrayList.SyncRoot; }
360:            }
361:
362:            public void CopyTo( Array array, int arrayIndex ) {
363:                internalArrayList.CopyTo( array, arrayIndex );
364:            }
365:
366:    //IList interface implementation
367:            public bool IsFixedSize {
368:                get { return false; }
369:            }
370:
371:            public bool IsReadOnly {
372:                get { return false; }
373:            }
374:
375:            //Only used when Interface IList is acquired.
376:            //IList iList = (IList)TabCollection;
377:            object IList.this[ int index ] {
378:                get { return this[ index ]; }
379:                set { this[ index ] = (OutlookBarTab)value; }
380:            }
381:
382:            int IList.Add( object o ) {
383:                return this.Add( (OutlookBarTab)o );
384:            }
385:
386:            void IList.Clear( ) {
387:                this.Clear( );
388:            }
389:
390:            public bool Contains( object o ) {
```

LISTING 8.2   Continued

```
391:                    return internalArrayList.Contains( o );
392:            }
393:
394:            public int IndexOf( object o ) {
395: return internalArrayList.IndexOf( o );
396:            }
397:
398:            void IList.Insert( int index, object o ) {
399:                this.Insert( index, (OutlookBarTab)o );
400:            }
401:
402:            void IList.Remove( object o ) {
403:                this.Remove( (OutlookBarTab)o );
404:            }
405:
406:            void IList.RemoveAt( int index ) {
407:                this.RemoveAt( index );
408:            }
409:
410:            //IEnumerable interface implementation
411:            public IEnumerator GetEnumerator( ) {
412:                return internalArrayList.GetEnumerator( );
413:            }
414:
415:            //TabCollection implementation
416:            public int Add( OutlookBarTab tab ) {
417:                owner.SubscribeToTabEvents( tab );
418:                int idx = internalArrayList.Add( tab );
419:                if( tab.Child != null )
420:        owner.Controls.Add( tab.Child );
421:                owner.ActivateTab( idx );
422:                return idx;
423:            }
424:
425:            public void AddRange( OutlookBarTab[] tabs ) {
426:                foreach( OutlookBarTab T in tabs )
427:                    Add( T );
428:            }
429:
430:            public void Remove( OutlookBarTab tab ) {
431:                RemoveAt( IndexOf( tab ) );
432:            }
433:
434:            public void RemoveAt( int index ) {
435:                OutlookBarTab T = this[index];
```

LISTING 8.2   Continued

```
436:                    owner.Controls.Remove( T.Child );
437:                    internalArrayList.Remove( T );
438:                    owner.UnSubscribeToTabEvents( T );
439:
440:                    if( internalArrayList.Count > 0 ) {
441:                        //Was this the active Tab?
442:                        if( index == owner.activeTabIndex ) {
443:                            index++; index %=( Count+1 );
444:                        }
445:                    }
446:        owner.Invalidate( );
447:                }
448:
449:            public void Insert( int index, OutlookBarTab tab ) {
450:                internalArrayList.Insert( index, tab );
451:                if( tab.Child != null )
452:                    owner.Controls.Add( tab.Child );
453:                owner.SubscribeToTabEvents( tab );
454:                //is the new tab before or after the current tab?
455:                if( index <= owner.activeTabIndex )
456:                    owner.activeTabIndex++;
457:                owner.Invalidate( );
458:            }
459:
460:            public void Clear( ) {
461:                foreach( OutlookBarTab tab in internalArrayList )
462:                    owner.UnSubscribeToTabEvents( tab );
463:
464:                owner.Controls.Clear( );
465:                internalArrayList.Clear( );
466:                owner.activeTabIndex = -1;
467:                owner.Invalidate( );
468:            }
469:
470:            public OutlookBarTab this[ int index ] {
471:                get {
472:                    // The CollectionEditor is famous for passing the
473:                    // index value of -1. For what reason, I have no idea.
474:                    try {
475:            return (OutlookBarTab)internalArrayList[index];
476:                    } catch( Exception e ) {
477:                        System.Diagnostics.Debug.WriteLine( e.Message );
478:                        System.Diagnostics.Debug.WriteLine(
➥string.Format( "TabCollection[{0}] invalid index", index ) );
```

8

OUTLOOKBAR
CONTROL

LISTING 8.2   Continued

```
479:                          }
480:                              return null;
481:                  }
482:              set {
483:                      internalArrayList[index] = value;
484:              }
485:          }
486:      }
487:      #endregion
488:
489:  }
490:  //TabCollection Goes here
}
```

The code listing in 8.2 represents all the code for the `OutlookBar` control, including the implementation of the custom collection. The custom collection is covered later in the chapter.

The purpose of the `OutlookBar` control is to host other controls. Most of the code for the `OutlookBar` control deals with the management of the child controls. When an `OutlookBar` tab becomes active, the `OutlookBar` control must calculate the area that represents the child control's size and position. The purpose behind this calculation is so that the child control can be properly positioned within the active tab. When this is done, it appears that the child control is connected to the tab. When a different tab is activated, a new child control rectangle is calculated and the current tab's child control is repositioned and made visible.

Calculating the active child control's position requires knowing the number of tabs, the height of a tab, and the active tab index. The active tab represents the top of the child control's position, and the height of the child control is determined by subtracting the height of any tabs below the child control. The method `ReCalcClientRect`, on line 261 of Listing 8.2, provides the logic necessary to determine the position of an active child control.

Again, the main job or function of the `OutlookBar` control is the management of `OutlookBarTabs` and the associated child controls. Managing the various `OutlookBarTabs` requires tracking mouse events, just as in the test application from the preceding chapter, and providing a custom collection to track the `OutlookBarTabs`. Tracking mouse events occurs in the methods `OnMouseDown` and `OnMouseUp`. Each of these methods uses the `HitTest` method provided by the `OutlookBarTab` component to determine whether the mouse click has occurred on a tab component.

In addition, the base class `Controls` property required an attribute that prevents the `ControlCollection` from being persisted in generated code. By default, any exposed collection automatically has its contents saved, or generated, by the code generator during design-time. The reason for not wanting this collection to be generated is that child controls are added to this collection when new `OutlookBarTab` objects are added to the `Tabs` collection. If the `OutlookBar` control persisted both the `Tabs` collection and the `Controls` collection, this would cause double the references to controls contained with the `OutlookBar` control.

The design of the `OutlookBar` control was driven by the functional requirements and expected runtime behavior to be provided. Determining the base class from which they derived came down to two possible choices: `ContainerControl` or `UserControl`. Each of these base classes provides the necessary functionality needed by the `OutlookBar` control. Such functionality includes the capability to host child controls and provide focus management. The decision to use `ContainerControl` as the base class was the result of realizing that the `UserControl` class provides no extra functionality required by the `OutlookBar` control than does the `ContainerControl`. Therefore, the `ContainerControl` provided the proper level of support without any additional overhead, as would be introduced by the `UserControl` base class with its extra level of inheritance.

Among the more interesting implementation parts of the `OutlookBar` control are the methods `SubscribeToTabEvents` and `UnSubscribeToTabEvents`. Using the `Reflection` API makes it possible to subscribe to all available events without having to know all the events being exposed by the `OutlookBarTab` component. Whenever the `OutlookBarTab` raises an event, the `OutlookBar` control will invalidate itself to reflect the changes in its child components.

Custom Collections

Following the design of the Windows Forms `Tab` control, the `OutlookBar` provides a custom collection for the `OutlookBarTab` objects to be managed by the control. This custom collection provides a means to add new tabs to the `OutlookBar` at both design-time and runtime. The `TabCollection` is then serialized during design-time by the code generated. Providing a custom collection requires implementing the `ICollection`, `IEnumerable`, and `IList` interfaces. Tables 8.3 through 8.7 describe the properties and methods for these interfaces.

TABLE 8.3 Properties of `ICollection`

Property	Description
Count	Returns the number of objects within the collection.
IsSynchronized	Used to determined whether access to the collection is thread-safe.
SyncRoot	Object used to synchronize access to the collection.

8

OUTLOOKBAR
CONTROL

TABLE 8.4   Methods of `ICollection`

Method	Description
CopyTo	Copies the current contents of the collection to an array starting at the supplied index.

TABLE 8.5   Method of `IEnumerable`

Method	Description
GetEnumerator	Returns an enumerator that can be used to iterate through the items within a collection.

TABLE 8.6   Properties of `IList`

Property	Description
IsFixedSize	Returns `true` if the collection size is static or fixed.
IsReadOnly	Return `true` if the collection is read-only in nature.
Item	(Indexer) Provides direct access to an item within the collection.

TABLE 8.7   Methods of `IList`

Method	Description
Add	Adds a new item to the collection.
Clear	Removes all items from the collection.
Contains	Determines whether the collection contains the specified item.
IndexOf	Retrieves the index of a specified item.
Insert	Inserts an item into the collection at a specified index.
Remove	Removes the specified item from the collection.
RemoveAt	Removes the item at the specified index.

In addition to the methods required by the implemented interfaces, the `TabCollection` also implements the method `AddRange`. The code generator, when adding child components to a parent container, uses the `AddRange` method. Also, the `TabCollection` is a nested class within the `OutlookBar` control itself, because it is dependant on the services provided by the `OutlookBar` control. As such, the `TabCollection` class cannot stand on its own because its implementation requires access to protected methods within the `OutlookBar` control. Listing 8.3 provides the source for the `TabCollection` implementation.

LISTING 8.3   TabCollection

```
 1:
 2:
 3: public class TabCollection : ICollection, IEnumerable, IList {
 4:
 5:     private OutlookBar        owner              = null;
 6:     private ArrayList         internalArrayList  = null;
 7:
 8:
 9:     public TabCollection( OutlookBar parent ) {
10:         owner = parent;
11:         internalArrayList = new ArrayList( );
12:     }
13:
14:     //ICollection Interface implementation
15:     public int Count {
16:         get { return internalArrayList.Count; }
17:     }
18:
19:     public bool IsSynchronized {
20:         get { return internalArrayList.IsSynchronized; }
21:     }
22:     public object SyncRoot {
23:         get { return internalArrayList.SyncRoot; }
24:     }
25:
26:     public void CopyTo( Array array, int arrayIndex ) {
27:         internalArrayList.CopyTo( array, arrayIndex );
28:     }
29:
30:     //IList interface implementation
31:     public bool IsFixedSize {
32:         get { return false; }
33:     }
34:
35:     public bool IsReadOnly {
36:         get { return false; }
37:     }
38:
39:     //Only used when Interface IList is acquired.
40:     //IList iList = (IList)TabCollection;
41:     object IList.this[ int index ] {
42:         get { return this[ index ]; }
43:         set { this[ index ] = (OutlookBarTab)value; }
44:     }
45:
```

LISTING 8.3   Continued

```
46:    int IList.Add( object o ) {
47:        return this.Add( (OutlookBarTab)o );
48:    }
49:
50:    void IList.Clear( ) {
51:        this.Clear( );
52:    }
53:
54:    public bool Contains( object o ) {
55:        return internalArrayList.Contains( o );
56:    }
57:
58:    public int IndexOf( object o ) {
59:        return internalArrayList.IndexOf( o );
60:    }
61:
62:    void IList.Insert( int index, object o ) {
63:        this.Insert(index, (OutlookBarTab)o );
64:    }
65:
66:    void IList.Remove( object o ) {
67:        this.Remove( (OutlookBarTab)o );
68:    }
69:
70:    void IList.RemoveAt( int index ) {
71:        this.RemoveAt( index );
72:    }
73:
74:    //IEnumerable interface implementation
75:    public IEnumerator GetEnumerator( ) {
76:        return internalArrayList.GetEnumerator( );
77:    }
78:
79:    //TabCollection implementation
80:    public int Add( OutlookBarTab tab ) {
81:        owner.SubscribeToTabEvents( tab );
82:        int idx = internalArrayList.Add( tab );
83:        if( tab.Child != null )
84:            owner.Controls.Add( tab.Child );
85:        owner.ActivateTab( idx );
86:        return idx;
87:    }
88:
89:    public void AddRange( OutlookBarTab[] tabs ) {
90:        foreach( OutlookBarTab T in tabs )
```

LISTING 8.3   Continued

```
 91:                Add( T );
 92:        }
 93:
 94:        public void Remove( OutlookBarTab tab ) {
 95:            RemoveAt( IndexOf( tab ) );
 96:        }
 97:
 98:        public void RemoveAt( int index ) {
 99:            OutlookBarTab T = this[index];
100:            owner.Controls.Remove( T.Child );
101:            internalArrayList.Remove( T );
102:            owner.UnSubscribeToTabEvents( T );
103:
104:            if( internalArrayList.Count > 0 ) {
105:                //Was this the active Tab?
106:                if( index == owner.activeTabIndex ) {
107:                    index++; index %=( Count+1 );
108:                }
109:            }
110:            owner.Invalidate( );
111:        }
112:
113:        public void Insert( int index, OutlookBarTab tab ) {
114:            internalArrayList.Insert( index, tab );
115:            owner.SubscribeToTabEvents( tab );
116:            //is the new tab before or after the current tab?
117: if( index <= owner.activeTabIndex )
118:                owner.activeTabIndex++;
119:            owner.Invalidate( );
120:        }
121:
122:        public void Clear( ) {
123:            foreach( OutlookBarTab tab in internalArrayList )
124:                owner.UnSubscribeToTabEvents( tab );
125:
126:          owner.Controls.Clear( );
127:          internalArrayList.Clear( );
128:          owner.activeTabIndex = -1;
129:          owner.Invalidate( );
130:        }
131:
132:        public OutlookBarTab this[ int index ] {
133:            get {
134:                // The CollectionEditor is famous for passing
```

LISTING 8.3 Continued

```
135:                // the index value of -1. For what reason, I have no idea.
136:                try {
137:                    return (OutlookBarTab)internalArrayList[index];
138:                } catch( Exception e ) {
139:                    System.Diagnostics.Debug.WriteLine( e.Message );
140:        System.Diagnostics.Debug.WriteLine( string.Format(
141:                            "TabCollection[{0}] invalid index", index ) );
142:                }
143:            return null;
144:        }
145:        set {
146:            internalArrayList[index] = value;
147:        }
148:    }
149: }
```

The TabCollection represents a fairly standard collection implementation. All items for the collection are stored in an internal ArrayList. The reason behind developing a custom collection is that there's a need to interact with the OutlookBar control. When a new OutlookBarTab component is added to the collection, it is necessary to add the OutlookBarTabs child control to the Controls collection of the OutlookBar control. Again, the reason for using a nested class to provide the collection is that it allows the collection to access protected methods of the parent class.

Testing the Control

With the collection in place, testing the control is now possible. To test the OutlookBar control, comment out the Designer attribute on the OutlookBar class. Otherwise, VS .NET will not be able to support the control at design-time due to the incapability to locate the designer for it. After all, the designer has not yet been implemented. At this point, create a new Windows Forms application project and add the OutlookBar control to the toolbox. Draw an OutlookBar control on the main form and use the Tabs property to add three OutlookBarTab objects to the control, as shown in Figure 8.2.

With the three tabs in place, compile and run the test application. The activation of tabs is fully working at this point. Of course, the goal of the OutlookBar control is to host other controls and associate those child controls with the various tabs within the control. Although child controls can be added by hand-coding the relationships between the controls and the tab that will host them, a custom designer is required to support this behavior during design-time. The next section discusses the design and implementation of a custom designer for the OutlookBar control.

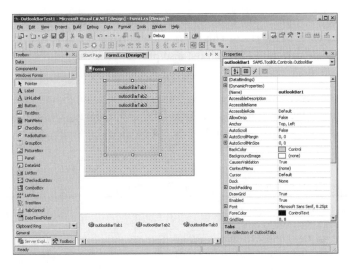

FIGURE 8.2
Testing the OutlookBar *control.*

OutlookBarDesigner

The goal of a control designer is to allow developers to customize the appearance of a control, add child controls, and link event code to the events of a control. The rule of thumb when creating designers is to keep the designer simple and to the point. If you complicate control designs, developers won't want to use your controls. The OutlookBar designer adds support for drag-and-drop during design-time, as well as the capability to activate the hosted tabs within the control similar to the Windows Forms TabControl.

The OutlookBarDesigner requires the use of four services provided by the VS .NET IDE. These services include IDesignerHost, IToolboxService, ISelectionService, and IComponentChangeService. Each of these interfaces was covered in Chapter 5, "Advanced Control Development"; only the relevant methods for these services are covered here.

The IDesignerHost interface is a gateway, so to speak. This interface provides access to the underlying services provided by the root designer. Again, the root designer is the main designer hosted by the VS .NET IDE. For the most part, the IDesignerHost interface is used to obtain services from the root designer. These services include IToolboxService and ISelectionService.

As with other RAD environments, the toolbox is a palette of controls that can be drawn or dragged onto a form. The IToolboxService provides methods for deserializing and creating the controls within the toolbox.

8

OUTLOOKBAR
CONTROL

Changing the active selection—the control currently selected in design mode—requires the use of the ISelectionService interface. This service not only can be used to determine which control or controls are currently selected, but also provides the capability to change the current selection.

The OutlookBar designer will be responsible for responding to drag-and-drop notifications, allowing activation of the contained OutlookBarTabs, and removing unused and unwanted properties from the OutlookBar control. Listing 8.4 provides the source for the OutlookBar designer.

LISTING 8.4   Implementing the OutlookBar Designer

```
 1: using System;
 2: using System.Collections;
 3: using System.ComponentModel;
 4: using System.ComponentModel.Design;
 5: using System.Drawing;
 6: using System.Drawing.Design;
 7: using System.Windows.Forms;
 8: using System.Windows.Forms.Design;
 9: using SAMS.ToolKit.Controls;
10:
11: namespace SAMS.ToolKit.Design
12: {
13:
14:     public class OutlookBarDesigner :
➥System.Windows.Forms.Design.ParentControlDesigner {
15:
16:         private IDesignerHost          designerHost      = null;
17:         private IToolboxService        toolboxService    = null;
18:         private ISelectionService      selectionService  = null;
19:
20:         public override ICollection AssociatedComponents {
21:             get {
22:                 if( base.Control is OutlookBar )
23:                     return ((OutlookBar)base.Control).Tabs;
24:                 else
25:                     return base.AssociatedComponents;
26:             }
27:         }
28:         public IDesignerHost DesignerHost {
29:             get {
30:                 if( designerHost == null )
31:                     designerHost = (IDesignerHost)GetService(
➥typeof( IDesignerHost ) );
32:                 return designerHost;
33:             }
```

LISTING 8.4 Continued

```
34:          }
35:
36:          public IToolboxService ToolboxService      {
37:              get {
38:                  if( toolboxService == null )
39:                      toolboxService = (IToolboxService)GetService(
➥typeof( IToolboxService ) );
40:                  return toolboxService;
41:              }
42:          }
43:
44:          public ISelectionService SelectionService {
45:              get {
46:                  if( selectionService == null )
47:                      selectionService = (ISelectionService)GetService(
➥ typeof( ISelectionService ) );
48:                  return selectionService;
49:              }
50:          }
51:
52:          protected override bool DrawGrid {
53:              get { return false; }
54:          }
55:
56:          public override bool CanParent( System.Windows.Forms.Control
➥ control ) {
57:              return true;
58:          }
59:
60:          protected override void PostFilterProperties( IDictionary
➥ Properties ) {
61:
62:              base.PostFilterProperties( Properties );
63:
64:              string[] props = { "BackColor", "AutoScroll",
65:                                  "AutoScrollMargin", "AutoScrollMinSize",
66:                                  "BackgroundImage" };
67:
68:              foreach( string property in props )
69:                  Properties.Remove( property );
70:
71:          }
72:
73:
74:          protected override void OnDragDrop( DragEventArgs de ) {
```

LISTING 8.4   Continued

```
75:
76:            ToolboxItem toolboxItem =
➥this.ToolboxService.DeserializeToolboxItem( de.Data,
➥this.DesignerHost );
77:
78:            IComponent[] components = toolboxItem.CreateComponents(
➥ this.DesignerHost );
79:
80:            OutlookBar outlookBar = (OutlookBar)this.Control;
81:
82:            Point pt = outlookBar.PointToClient( new Point( de.X,
➥de.Y ) );
83:
84:            int TabIndex;
85:            if( outlookBar.HitTest( HitTestType.CLIENT, pt,
➥out TabIndex ) ) {
86:                //Replace the current control of the active tab
87:                // with the newly dropped control
88:                if( outlookBar.ActiveTab == null ) {
89:                    AddTab( outlookBar, (Control)components[0] );
90:                } else {
91:                    if( outlookBar.ActiveTab.Child != null )
92:                        this.DesignerHost.DestroyComponent(
➥outlookBar.ActiveTab.Child );
93:
94:                    Control old = outlookBar.ActiveTab.Child;
95:                    outlookBar.ActiveTab.Child = (Control)components[0];
96:                    RaiseComponentChanged( TypeDescriptor.GetProperties(
➥ outlookBar.ActiveTab )["Child"], old, outlookBar.ActiveTab.Child );
97:                }
98:            } else {
99:                AddTab( outlookBar, (Control)components[0] );
100:            }
101:
102:            //Set the Selection to the newly dropped control
103:            this.SelectionService.SetSelectedComponents( components );
104:
105:            //Inform the Toolbox that the selected item was used;
➥ this will reset the mouse to the pointer
106:            this.ToolboxService.SelectedToolboxItemUsed( );
107:        }
108:
109:        protected virtual void AddTab( OutlookBar outlookBar,
➥Control control ) {
110:            //The control was dropped on the Tabs, so
111:            // create a new Tab to host the control
```

LISTING 8.4   Continued

```
112:            OutlookBar.TabCollection oldTabs = outlookBar.Tabs;
113:            OutlookBarTab T = (OutlookBarTab)this.DesignerHost.
➥CreateComponent( typeof( OutlookBarTab ) );
114:            T.Text    = string.Format( "outlookBarTab{0}",
➥ oldTabs.Count + 1);
115:            T.Child = control;
116:            outlookBar.Tabs.Add( T );
117:
118:            //Notify the system that the OutlookBar Component is
119:            // changing.  This is necessary for proper serialization of
➥the Tabs collection
120:            this.RaiseComponentChanged( TypeDescriptor.GetProperties(
➥outlookBar )["Tabs"], outlookBar.Tabs, oldTabs );
121:        }
122:
123:
124:        protected override void WndProc( ref Message msg ) {
125:            base.WndProc( ref msg );
126:            if( msg.Msg == 0x00000201 ) {    //left mouse down
127:                OutlookBar outlookBar =
➥this.SelectionService.PrimarySelection as OutlookBar;
128:                if( outlookBar != null ) {
129:                    int tabIndex;
130:                    if( outlookBar.HitTest( HitTestType.TABS, new Point(
➥msg.LParam.ToInt32( ) ), out tabIndex ) )
131: outlookBar.ActiveTabIndex = tabIndex;
132:                }
133:            }
134:        }
135:
136:        private void OnComponentRemoving( object sender,
➥ComponentEventArgs e ) {
137:
138:            //What is being removed?
139:            if( e.Component is OutlookBarTab ) {
140:                OutlookBarTab tab = (OutlookBarTab)e.Component;
141:
142:
143:                //Does the Tab belong to the Current Control?
144:                if( ((OutlookBar)Control).Tabs.Contains( tab ) ) {
145:                    ((OutlookBar)Control).Tabs.Remove( tab );
146:
147:                    if( tab.Child != null )
148:                        DesignerHost.DestroyComponent( tab.Child );
149:                }
150:
```

LISTING 8.4   Continued

```
151:              } else if( e.Component is OutlookBar ) {
152:                  //Destroy all tabs
153:                  OutlookBar bar = (OutlookBar)e.Component;
154:                  int tabCount = bar.Tabs.Count;
155:                  for( int index = 0; index < tabCount; index++ )
156:    DesignerHost.DestroyComponent( bar.Tabs[0] );
157:
158:              } else if( e.Component is Control ) {
159:                  Control control = (Control)e.Component;
160:                  OutlookBar bar = (OutlookBar)Control;
161:                  //Do we own the Control?
162:                  if( bar.Controls.Contains( control ) ) {
163:                      //Find the Tab that owns the control
164:                      foreach( OutlookBarTab tab in bar.Tabs ) {
165:                          if( tab.Child == control ) {
166:                              //Found IT!
167:                              tab.Child = null;
168:                              bar.Controls.Remove( control );
169:                              break;
170:                          }
171:                      }
172:                  }
173:              }
174:          }
175:
176:      public override void Initialize( IComponent component ) {
177:          base.Initialize( component );
178:          IComponentChangeService changeService =
➥(IComponentChangeService)GetService( typeof(IComponentChangeService) );
179:          changeService.ComponentRemoving += new
➥ComponentEventHandler( OnComponentRemoving );
180:      }
181:
182:  public override void Dispose( ) {
183:          IComponentChangeService changeService =
➥(IComponentChangeService)GetService( typeof(IComponentChangeService) );
184:          changeService.ComponentRemoving -= new
➥ComponentEventHandler( OnComponentRemoving );
185:          base.Dispose( );
186:      }
187:
188:      public OutlookBarDesigner() {
189:      }
190:  }
191: }
```

Designers represent a critical element of the control development process. Not only do designers provide for the design-time experience, but they also are part of the serialization process for the code generated for the control.

Dissecting the designer requires looking at the various interfaces and services that the designer uses. Each of the next sections covers a particular aspect of the designers' implementation and services used.

IComponentChangeService

When a control changes during design-time, the code generated, as well as the root designer, needs to be informed of the changes to the control. This allows the designer to make any necessary modifications to the control it is responsible for. In the case of the OutlookBarDesigner, when a child control is added or removed, the designer needs to know if the control belonged to the OutlookBar control, and if so, it updates the OutlookBar control. This is also the case when an OutlookBarTab component is removed. When an OutlookBarTab is removed, the designer needs to remove the child control of the OutlookBarTab from both the root designer and the OutlookBar control itself.

The IComponentChangeService facilitates this notification process. Table 8.8 shows the events provided by the IComponentChangeService interface.

8

OUTLOOKBAR
CONTROL

TABLE 8.8   IComponentChangeService Events

Event	Description
ComponentAdded	Raised when a component is added to the designer during design-time.
ComponentAdding	Raised when a component is in the process of being added.
ComponentChanged	Raised when a component has changed.
ComponentChanging	Raised when a component is in the process of being changed.
ComponentRemoved	Raised when a component has been removed using the IDesignerHost.DestroyComponent method.
ComponentRemoving	Raised when a component is in the process of being removed.

To ensure proper serialization of the OutlookBar control and its associated tabs and child controls, it is necessary to respond when a component is removed from the OutlookBar control. In addition, if the component being removed is the OutlookBar control being designed, all child components need to be destroyed to avoid having orphan components and controls. By subscribing to the events provided by the IComponentChangeService, a designer can properly track the changes within the design-time environment and update the control it is responsible for.

Drag-and-Drop

Support for drag-and-drop functionality is a snap, thanks to the services provided by the .NET base class library. Line 74 of Listing 8.4 provides the overridden method OnDragDrop. The DragEventArgs provides all the necessary information to determine the location of the drop and the currently selected toolbox item. Using this information, the toolbox item can be created using the IToolboxService interface and the control added to the OutlookBar control.

During the processing of the drop notification, the TabCollection of the OutlookBar control is modified, and it is necessary to inform the root-level designer that a property of the currently selected component has been modified. Notification is necessary to ensure that the control will be properly serialized in code during code generation.

The RaiseComponentChanged method is used to notify the root-level designer and code generator about the changes taking place.

Overriding WndProc

To allow for design-time activation of the hosted tabs, the WndProc method is overridden so that processing of the mouse messages can take place. Notice the use of the constant value 0x00000201 for testing the Windows message. This constant value is the raw value for the WM_LBUTTONDOWN message. The class NativeMethods found in the System.Windows.Forms namespace provides a static member name for this message; however, the class is *private*! Not to worry, however; using ILDASM, these constant values can be retrieved. Figure 8.3 shows ILDASM with the NativeMethods class selected and the value for WM_LBUTTONDOWN being displayed.

FIGURE 8.3
Spying with ILDASM.

Summary

With the `OutlookBar`, custom tab collection, and designer in place, the final product is almost complete. This chapter has covered a lot of new ground pertaining to control development and the implementation of a much more sophisticated designer. At this point, extending the current control to add additional features merely requires some imagination and extending the use of the services provided by the .NET base class library covered so far. The goal has been to build on knowledge gained in previous chapters and to apply that knowledge in incremental steps toward the final goal, which is to gain a solid understanding of custom control development.

ImageListView Control

IN THIS CHAPTER

The `OutlookBar` control is nearly complete. All that remains is building the `ImageListView` control that can be hosted inside the `OutlookBar` control or any other `ContainerControl` derived class such as a `Form` or `Panel`.

The `ImageListView` control is built in four stages. The first stage involves creating a soft-control `ScrollButton`. This `ScrollButton` is used for scrolling the contents of the `ImageListView`. The next stage involves the creation of a small component used to track the individual items within the `ImageListView` control. This component, `ImageListViewItem`, is used to store and manage information about an individual item within the `ImageListView` control. Such information includes the text and image index for the item.

After the `ScrollButton` and `ImageListViewItem` components have been created, work will begin on the `ImageListView` control. The `ImageListView` control uses both the `ScrollButton` and `ImageListViewItem` components to create a graphical shortcut-style control. Each image, or `ImageListViewItem`, will act as a button allowing the user to select an item in a similar fashion to clicking a button control.

The final stage of the project involves the creation of a simple designer for the `ImageListView` control. The designer will only provide the necessary support for managing the control and tracking the removal of `ImageListViewItems` from the root designer.

Design

Designing and building the `ImageListView` control appears to be harder than it actually is. The goal of the `ImageListView` control is to mimic the basic look and feel of the list of images hosted within the Outlook shortcut bar. These images include the Inbox, Today, Calendar, and Notes images, to name a few. Figure 9.1 shows our `ImageListView` control at both design-time (on the left) and runtime (on the right).

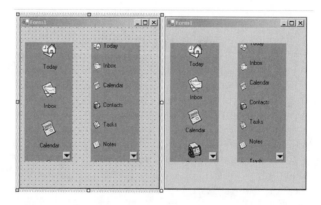

FIGURE 9.1
The `ImageListView` *control.*

The `ImageListView` control supports the following features:

- Large images (32×32)
- Small images (16×16)
- Scrolling
- Hover effect

Scrolling support is provided by "faking" a set of scroll-like buttons in the upper- and lower-right corners of the control. The other features are discussed throughout the remainder of this chapter.

Although the buttons appear to look and act as a standard Windows button, they are in fact just simple classes that provide basic drawing and hit testing. One of the key concepts when building controls is to make them as light as possible. This means that you should not waste unnecessary resources, such as window handles or GDI resources like brushes and pens.

Implementation

Implementation of the `ImageListView` control requires constructing the following components:

- `ScrollButton` component
- `ImageListViewItem` component
- `ImageListView` control
- `ImageListViewDesigner`

Of these four components, only three are tightly coupled: `ImageListViewItem`, `ImageListView`, and `ImageListViewDesigner`. The `ScrollButton` class is designed to be independent so that it can be reused in other projects. This of course raises another key design ideal: reusable components. During the course of developing controls, or any software, there exists a set of shared/common functionality that can be reused. All endeavors in development should look for such reusable components.

Each of the following sections describes the design and implementation of the components required to build the `ImageListView` control.

ScrollButton

Like other soft-controls developed thus far, the `ScrollButton` has two jobs: painting and hit-testing. The first job, painting, involves determining the orientation of the button. The `ScrollButton` can be used to represent either an Up or a Down orientation. The orientation of the button is used to determine the style of arrow to render on the button. Rather than using two bitmaps, or using one bitmap and rotating it, to represent the arrow, the `ScrollButton` uses a `GraphicsPath` primitive to create the polygon for the arrow.

9

IMAGE VIEW LIST
CONTROL

> **NOTE**
>
> The GraphicsPath object allows for a polygon, or path, to be constructed from a set of points or lines. This path can then be filled in the same manner as a rectangle or an arc using standard graphics calls. Developers of custom controls would do well to learn the ins and outs of GDI+.

The decision to create a soft-control rather than a full-blown Control-derived component is based on one simple fact: a full control is not needed. For the ScrollButton to serve its intended purpose, it does not need any of the services or implementation afforded by the Control base class. Sometimes figuring out what's not needed can help to determine the proper starting point for a new component or control.

Note, however, that the ScrollButton could just as easily be developed as a Control-derived or event Button-derived control. The only drawback to this approach is the extra resources consumed by creating an additional window handle and any unseen overhead within the base class implementations. For die-hard ATL/C++ developers, the idea of "don't pay for what you don't use" carries over into C# and .NET. Because the ScrollButton does not use or need any features from the Control base class, why pay the price of using it? Implementation inheritance is like consuming alcoholic beverages. Do it responsibly.

Because the ScrollButton class represents the smallest component, its implementation is shown here first. Listing 9.1 contains the implementation for ScrollButton.

LISTING 9.1   ScrollButton Implementation

```
 1: using System;
 2: using System.Drawing;
 3: using System.Windows.Forms;
 4:
 5: namespace SAMS.ToolKit.Controls
 6: {
 7:     public enum ScrollButtonOrientation {
 8:         Up,
 9:         Down
10:     }
11:
12:     public class ScrollButton {
13:
14:         private static int    SIZE        = 16;
15:         private static int  PADDING       = 5;
16:         private    Rectangle              btnRect;
```

LISTING 9.1   Continued

```
17:         private ScrollButtonOrientation        orientation;
18:
19:         public Point Location {
20:             get { return new Point( btnRect.X, btnRect.Y ); }
21:             set {
22:                 btnRect = new Rectangle( ((Point)value).X,
➡((Point)value).Y, SIZE, SIZE );
23:             }
24:         }
25:
26:   public ScrollButton( ScrollButtonOrientation sbo ) {
27:             orientation = sbo;
28:
29:         }
30:
31:         public bool HitTest( Point pt ) {
32:             return btnRect.Contains( pt );
33:         }
34:
35:         public void Draw( Graphics g, ButtonState state ) {
36:             DrawButton( g, state );
37:             DrawArrow( g, state );
38:         }
39:
40:         private void DrawButton( Graphics g, ButtonState state ) {
41:             if( btnRect.IsEmpty ) return;
42:             ControlPaint.DrawButton( g, btnRect, state );
43:         }
44:
45:         private void DrawArrow( Graphics g, ButtonState state ) {
46:             if( orientation == ScrollButtonOrientation.Up )
47:                 DrawUpArrow( g, state );
48:             else
49:                 DrawDownArrow( g, state );
50:         }
51:
52:
53:         private void DrawUpArrow( Graphics g, ButtonState state ) {
54:             Point[] pts = new Point[3];
55:   pts[0].X = btnRect.Left + (btnRect.Width / 2) +
➡ (state == ButtonState.Pushed ? 1 : 0);
56:             pts[0].Y = btnRect.Top + PADDING +
➡ (state == ButtonState.Pushed ? 1 : 0);
57:
```

9

IMAGEVIEWLIST
CONTROL

LISTING 9.1   Continued

```
58:                pts[1].X = btnRect.Left + 2 +
➡ (state == ButtonState.Pushed ? 1 : 0);
59:                pts[1].Y = btnRect.Bottom - PADDING +
➡ (state == ButtonState.Pushed ? 1 : 0);
60:
61:                pts[2].X = btnRect.Right - 2 +
➡ (state == ButtonState.Pushed ? 1 : 0);
62:                pts[2].Y = btnRect.Bottom - PADDING +
➡ (state == ButtonState.Pushed ? 1 : 0);
63:                RenderArrow( g, pts );
64:            }
65:
66:        private void DrawDownArrow( Graphics g, ButtonState state ) {
67:                Point[] pts = new Point[3];
68:                pts[0].X = btnRect.Left + (btnRect.Width / 2) +
➡ (state == ButtonState.Pushed ? 1 : 0);
69:                pts[0].Y = btnRect.Bottom - PADDING +
➡ (state == ButtonState.Pushed ? 1 : 0);
70:
71:                pts[1].X = btnRect.Left + 2 +
➡ (state == ButtonState.Pushed ? 1 : 0);
72:                pts[1].Y = btnRect.Top + PADDING +
➡ (state == ButtonState.Pushed ? 1 : 0);
73:
74:   pts[2].X = btnRect.Right - 2 +
➡ (state == ButtonState.Pushed ? 1 : 0);
75:                pts[2].Y = btnRect.Top + PADDING +
➡ (state == ButtonState.Pushed ? 1 : 0);
76:
77:                RenderArrow( g, pts );
78:            }
79:
80:        private void RenderArrow( Graphics g, Point[] pts ) {
81:                System.Drawing.Drawing2D.GraphicsPath path =
➡new System.Drawing.Drawing2D.GraphicsPath( );
82:                path.AddLines( pts );
83:                path.CloseFigure( );
84:                Brush blackBrush = new SolidBrush(System.Drawing.Color.Black);
85:                g.FillPath( blackBrush, path );
86:                blackBrush.Dispose( );
87:            }
88: }
89: }
```

By now the basic structure of soft-controls should be ingrained in your mind. The `ScrollButton` introduces a new `Graphics` primitive: the `GraphicsPath`. To draw the arrow or triangle that represents the arrow, a `GraphicsPath` object is constructed based on three points. These three points represent the path of the polygon to be later filled.

The orientation of the arrow is determined by the enum `ScrollButtonOrientation` specified during the construction of the `ScrollButton`. The methods `DrawUpArrow` and `DrawDownArrow`, found in Listing 9.1 on lines 53 and 66, respectively, handle the process of creating the points used to represent the arrow to be drawn. In addition, the arrow is offset when the `ScrollButton` is in a pushed state. This offsetting gives the appearance of the button control being pushed into the screen.

After the points for the arrow have been calculated, the `RenderArrow` method uses these points to construct the `GraphicsPath` object. Notice on line 83 the `path.CloseFigure` method invocation. The `CloseFigure` method call completes the polygon so that when the `GraphicsPath` is filled, a solid triangle will be the output.

Now that the `ScrollButton` is in place, the next step in building the `ImageListView` control is the construction of the `ImageListViewItem` component. The `ImageListViewItem` component is used to manage information reguarding an item within the `ImageListView` control.

ImageListViewItem

Similar to the `OutlookBarTab` component, an `ImageListViewItem` is a component that tracks various information about the item it represents within the `ImageListView` control. This approach is a common theme when building composite controls that contain items such as the `Tab` control, `Menu` control, or `ToolBar` control. Each `ImageListViewItem` is capable of rendering itself in either large or small image mode and provides hit testing and hover state feedback. When the mouse pointer is held over an image, the image is drawn in a popped-up style state to indicate the hover state mode, as shown in Figure 9.2.

As with other controls and components developed so far, a determination of the base class from which to begin needs to be addressed. First, the `ImageListViewItem` needs to be defined. Is it a control? No. What is the `ImageListViewItem`? An `ImageListViewItem` is an object that is to be used to manage the display of text and an associated icon or image. The `ImageListViewItem` depends on its parent, the `ImageListView` control, for location and mouse event processing. In addition, the `ImageListViewItem` needs its parent in order to access the proper `ImageList`, large or small, to obtain the associated image to draw.

The `ImageListViewItem` represents a subcomponent of the `ImageListView` control. This basic definition and the requirements of the `ImageListViewItem` help to establish the base class for it. Listing 9.2 contains the implementation of the `ImageListViewItem` component. A vast majority of the code deals with drawing both the text and the associated image.

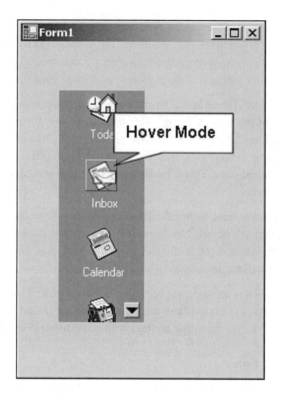

FIGURE 9.2

Hover state feedback.

LISTING 9.2   `ImageListViewItem` Component

```
 1: using System;
 2: using System.ComponentModel;
 3: using System.Drawing;
 4: using System.Windows.Forms;
 5:
 6: namespace SAMS.ToolKit.Controls
 7: {
 8:
 9:
10:     public enum ListViewItemState {
11:         Normal,
12:         Hover,
13:         Pushed
14:     }
15:
```

LISTING 9.2 Continued

```
16:
17:
18:
19:     [ToolboxItem( false )]
20:     public class ImageListViewItem : System.ComponentModel.Component {
21:
22:         private static int EDGE_PADDING = 4;
23:         private static int TEXT_PADDING = 12;
24:         private static int LARGE       = 32;
25:         private static int SMALL       = 16;
26:
27:         private string      text;
28:         private int         imageIndex;
29:         private Rectangle   imageRect;
30:         private Rectangle   textRect;
31:         private bool        drawLarge;
32:         private float       fontHeight;
33:         private Image       image;
34:         private int         fontLines;
35:         private int         height;
36:         private Point       location;
37:
38:         internal ImageListView    parent;
39:
40:         [
41:         Description( "Text displayed for the current item" ),
42:         Category( "Appearance" )
43:         ]
44:         public string Text {
45:             get { return text; }
46:             set {
47:                 text = value;
48:             }
49:         }
50:
51:         [
52:         Description( "Image Index used to display associated image" ),
53:         Category( "Appearance" )
54:         ]
55:         public int ImageIndex {
56:             get { return imageIndex; }
57:             set {
58:                 imageIndex = value;
59:             }
```

LISTING 9.2   Continued

```
60:          }
61:
62:          [ Browsable( false )]
63:          public ImageListView Parent {
64:              get { return parent; }
65:          }
66:
67:          [Browsable( false )]
68:          public int Height {
69:              get { return height; }
70:          }
71:
72:          [Browsable( false )]
73:          public Point Location {
74:              get { return location; }
75:          }
76:
77:          public ImageListViewItem( ) {
78:              parent      = null;
79:              drawLarge   = true;
80:              imageIndex  = -1;
81:              imageRect   = new Rectangle(0,0,0,0);
82:              textRect    = new Rectangle(0,0,0,0);
83:              image       = null;
84:              height      = 0;
85:          }
86:
87:          public bool HitTest( Point pt ) {
88:              return (imageRect.Contains( pt ) || textRect.Contains( pt ));
89:          }
90:
91:
92:          public int CalcHeight( Graphics g, Font font, int width,
➥bool LargeImage ) {
93:
94:              drawLarge = LargeImage;
95:
96: height = ( LargeImage ? LARGE : SMALL );
97:
98:              //calc the height of the Text
99:              SizeF fontSize = g.MeasureString( text, font );
100:             fontHeight = fontSize.Height;
101:             fontLines = 1;
102:             if( LargeImage ) {
```

LISTING 9.2   Continued

```
103:                       height += TEXT_PADDING;
104:                       if( fontSize.Width > width ) {
105:                           //Need to wrap the text
106:                           height += (int)((float)2*fontSize.Height);
107:                           fontLines = 2;
108:                       } else
109:                           height += (int)fontSize.Height;
110:                   }
111:               return height;
112:           }
113:
114:
115:           public void Draw( Graphics g, Font font, Brush foreBrush,
➡Point location, int maxWidth, ListViewItemState state ) {
116:
117:               if( height == 0 || imageIndex == -1) return;
118:               this.location = location;
119:               image = ( drawLarge ? parent.LargeImageList.Images[
➡imageIndex ] : parent.SmallImageList.Images[ imageIndex ] );
120:               if( drawLarge )
121:                   DrawLarge( g,font,foreBrush,location,maxWidth,state );
122:               else
123: DrawSmall( g,font,foreBrush,location,maxWidth,state );
124:           }
125:
126:           public void DrawSmall( Graphics g, Font font, Brush foreBrush,
➡ Point location, int maxWidth, ListViewItemState state   ) {
127:
128:               imageRect = new Rectangle( location.X + EDGE_PADDING,
➡location.Y, SMALL, SMALL );
129:               textRect = new Rectangle( location.X + (2*EDGE_PADDING) +
➡ imageRect.Width, location.Y, maxWidth, (int)fontHeight );
130:
131:               StringFormat fmt    = new StringFormat( );
132:               fmt.Alignment       = StringAlignment.Near;
133:               fmt.LineAlignment   = StringAlignment.Center;
134:               fmt.Trimming        = StringTrimming.EllipsisCharacter;
135:               fmt.FormatFlags     = StringFormatFlags.NoWrap;
136:
137:               g.DrawString( text, font, foreBrush, textRect, fmt );
138:
139:               DrawImage( g, imageRect, state );
140:           }
141:
```

LISTING 9.2   Continued

```
142:          public void DrawLarge( Graphics g, Font font, Brush foreBrush,
➡ Point location, int maxWidth, ListViewItemState state  ) {
143:
144:              imageRect = new Rectangle( (location.X + (maxWidth/2) -
➡ (LARGE/2)), location.Y, LARGE, LARGE );
145:              textRect = new Rectangle( location.X + EDGE_PADDING,
➡ imageRect.Bottom + TEXT_PADDING, maxWidth, fontLines*(int)fontHeight );
146:
147:          StringFormat fmt     = new StringFormat( );
148:          fmt.Alignment        = StringAlignment.Center;
149:          fmt.LineAlignment    = StringAlignment.Center;
150:   fmt.Trimming        = StringTrimming.EllipsisCharacter;
151:
152:          g.DrawString( text, font, foreBrush, textRect, fmt );
153:
154:          DrawImage( g, imageRect, state );
155:
156:      }
157:
158:          private void DrawImage( Graphics g, Rectangle destRect,
➡ ListViewItemState state ) {
159:          Rectangle drawRect = destRect;
160:          switch( state ) {
161:              case ListViewItemState.Normal:
162:                  g.DrawImage( image, drawRect );
163:                  break;
164:
165:              case ListViewItemState.Pushed:
166:                  drawRect.Inflate(-2,-2);
167:                  ControlPaint.DrawBorder3D( g, drawRect,
➡Border3DStyle.Adjust | Border3DStyle.SunkenInner,
➡ Border3DSide.All );
168:
169:                  drawRect.Inflate(2,2);
170:                  drawRect.X +=1;drawRect.Width-=2;
171:                  drawRect.Y +=1;drawRect.Height-=2;
172:                  g.DrawImage( image, drawRect );
173:
174:                  break;
175:
176:              case ListViewItemState.Hover:
177:                  drawRect.Inflate(-2,-2);
178:                  ControlPaint.DrawBorder3D( g, drawRect,
➡Border3DStyle.Adjust | Border3DStyle.RaisedOuter,
➡ Border3DSide.All );
```

LISTING 9.2   Continued

```
179:
180:                        drawRect.X -=1;drawRect.Width+=2;
181:                        drawRect.Y -=1;drawRect.Height+=2;
182:                        g.DrawImage( image, drawRect );
183:                        break;
184:                }
185:        }
186:        }
187: }
```

As noted previously, most of the code from Listing 9.2 deals with drawing both the text and the image for the item. All drawing boils down to determining the size, position, and color of what is going to be drawn. Determining the size of the image, whether large or small, and the size of the text serve to then derive the calculations for size and placement of the text and image.

Implementing various effects, such as a hovering effect when the mouse is over an item or a pushed effect when a mouse click occurs, requires subtle drawing hints. In the case of hovering, a border is added to the image, and the image itself is offset to give the appearance of movement.

Stepping through the drawing code, beginning on line 115 of Listing 9.2, the basic logic is as follows:

1. Is height > 0 ? Yes, go to 2. No, return.
2. Do we have a valid image index ? Yes, go to 3. No, return.
3. Get image. Draw Large? Yes, go to 4. No, go to 5.
4. Calculate image rectangle. Calculate text rectangle to sit below image rectangle. Draw text. Go to 6.
5. Calculate image rectangle. Calculate text rectangle to sit adjacent to image. Draw text. Go to 6.
6. Draw image based on state Hover, Pushed, Normal. See `DrawImage` on line 158.

These six steps outline the drawing logic for the `ImageListViewItem` component. There is no hard-and-fast rule for drawing other than that it should "look right." Defining that look, of course, is left to the developer of the control.

With the `ImageListViewItem` component complete, the next step is to create the `ImageListView` control itself.

9

IMAGEVIEWLIST
CONTROL

ImageListView Control

The next piece of the puzzle for the ImageListView control is implementing the container for all the components listed so far. As with the OutlookBar control, the ImageListView has one primary function: managing the subcomponents it contains. And also like the OutlookBar control, the ImageListView control contains a custom collection in order to maintain and manage the set of ImageListViewItems associated with the control.

The ImageListView control manages one or more ImageListViewItems. Although the ImageListViewItems are capable of drawing themselves, the ImageListView control is responsible for managing their position, scrolling, and handling events such as mouse events.

A custom event is provided to notify any observers, such as the parent form, when a particular ImageListViewItem has been clicked. This custom event provides the index for the item that has been clicked on.

Again, rather than providing extraneous features, the ImageListView control features are kept to a minimum to demonstrate the processing of building a custom control. Table 9.1 lists the properties exposed by the ImageListView control.

TABLE 9.1   ImageListView Control Properties and Description

Property	Description
SmallImageList	ImageList component containing a set of 16×16 images.
LargeImageList	ImageList component containing a set of 32×32 images.
Items	Custom collection of ImageListViewItems.
LargeIcons	Boolean value used to determine whether to show the large or small images.

Before the source listing for the ImageListView control is shown, it should be noted that the listing contains the code for a custom collection. Providing custom collections is a common theme and a task you should become comfortable with. The relevant sections of the custom collection will be discussed following the source listing.

Without further ado, Listing 9.3 contains the source code for the ImageListView control. Following the listing is a discussion of its implementation.

LISTING 9.3   ImageListView Control

```
1: using System;
2: using System.ComponentModel;
3: using System.Collections;
4: using System.Drawing;
```

LISTING 9.3   Continued

```
 5: using System.Windows.Forms;
 6:
 7:
 8: namespace SAMS.ToolKit.Controls {
 9:
10:     public class ImageListViewEventArgs : EventArgs {
11:         private int    itemIndex;
12:
13:         public int ItemIndex { get { return itemIndex; } }
14:
15:         public ImageListViewEventArgs( int index ) {
16:             itemIndex = index;
17:         }
18:     }
19:
20:     public delegate void ItemClickedEventHandler( object sender,
➥ImageListViewEventArgs e );
21:
22:     [
23:     Description( "ImageListView Control" ),
24:     DefaultEvent("ItemClicked" ),
25:     DefaultProperty( "Items" ),
26:     Designer( typeof( SAMS.ToolKit.Design.ItemListViewDesigner ) )
27:     ]
28:     public class ImageListView : Control {
29:
30:         private int             topIndex           = 0;
31:         private int             lastIndex          = 0;
32:         private Point           firstItemLocation  = new Point(0,0);
33:         private Point           lastItemLocation   = new Point(0,0);
34:         private bool            bScrollUp          = false;
35:         private bool            bScrollDown        = false;
36:         private bool            bLargeIcons        = true;
37:         private int             hitIndex           = 0;
38:         private int             hoverIndex         = -1;
39:         private ImageList       largeImageList     = null;
40:         private ImageList       smallImageList     = null;
41:         private ScrollButton    downScroll;
42:         private ScrollButton    upScroll;
43:         private ListViewItemCollection    items;
44:
45:
46:
47:         [
48:         Description( "Event raised when an ImageItem is clicked" ),
```

LISTING 9.3   Continued

```
49:          Category( "Behavior" )
50:          ]
51:          public event ItemClickedEventHandler ItemClicked;
52:
53:          [
54: Description( "Large Image List" ),
55:          Category( "Appearance" )
56:          ]
57:          public ImageList LargeImageList {
58:              get { return largeImageList; }
59:              set { largeImageList = value; Invalidate( );}
60:          }
61:
62:          [
63:          Description( "Small Image List" ),
64:          Category( "Appearance" )
65:          ]
66:          public ImageList SmallImageList {
67:              get { return smallImageList; }
68:              set { smallImageList = value; Invalidate( ); }
69:          }
70:
71:
72:          [
73:          Description( "Image Items Collection" ),
74:          Category( "Appearance" ),
75:          DesignerSerializationVisibility(
➥DesignerSerializationVisibility.Content )
76:          ]
77:          public ListViewItemCollection Items {
78:              get { return items; }
79:              set { items = value; }
80:          }
81:
82:          [
83:      Description( "use large images" ),
84:          Category( "Appearance" )
85:          ]
86:          public bool LargeIcons {
87:              get {
88:                  return bLargeIcons;
89:              }
90:              set {
91:                  bLargeIcons = value;
92:                  Recalc( );
```

LISTING 9.3   Continued

```
 93:                         Invalidate();
 94:                 }
 95:          }
 96:
 97:
 98:
 99:          public ImageListView( ) {
100:                 items = new ListViewItemCollection( this );
101:                 downScroll = new ScrollButton(ScrollButtonOrientation.Down);
102:                 upScroll = new ScrollButton(ScrollButtonOrientation.Up);
103:          }
104:
105:
106:
107:          protected override void OnPaint( PaintEventArgs e ) {
108:                 base.OnPaint( e );
109:
110:                 if( items.Count == 0 ) return;
111:                 if( this.bLargeIcons ) {
112:                     if( this.largeImageList == null ) return;
113:                 } else {
114:                     if( this.smallImageList == null ) return;
115:                 }
116:
117:                 int ClientHeight = this.ClientRectangle.Height;
118:    lastIndex = topIndex;
119:                 int heightAdjust;
120:                 Point pt = new Point(0,0);
121:                 Brush brush = new SolidBrush( this.ForeColor );
122:
123:                 do {
124:                     ImageListViewItem Item = items[ lastIndex++ ];
125:                     heightAdjust = Item.Height;
126:
127:                     DrawItem( e.Graphics, brush, Item, pt,
➥SAMS.ToolKit.Controls.ListViewItemState.Normal );
128:
129:                     pt.Y += heightAdjust + 25;
130:
131:                 } while( pt.Y < ClientHeight && (lastIndex < items.Count));
132:
133:                 lastIndex--;
134:                 //Scrolling?
135:
136:                 this.bScrollUp = topIndex> 0 ? true : false;
```

LISTING 9.3   Continued

```
137:                this.bScrollDown = ((lastIndex+1 < items.Count) ||
➥ (ClientHeight < pt.Y)) ? true : false;
138:
139:                DrawScrollButtons( e.Graphics );
140:
141:            }
142:
143:        protected override void OnSizeChanged( EventArgs e ) {
144:                base.OnSizeChanged( e );
145:                Graphics g = CreateGraphics( );
146:
147:                foreach( ImageListViewItem T in items ) {
148:                    T.CalcHeight( g, Font, this.ClientRectangle.Width,
➥bLargeIcons );
149:                }
150:                this.Invalidate( );
151:            }
152:
153:        protected override void OnMouseMove( MouseEventArgs e ) {
154:
155:                base.OnMouseMove( e );
156:
157:   Point pt = new Point( e.X, e.Y );
158:                Graphics g = CreateGraphics( );
159:                Brush brush = new SolidBrush( this.ForeColor );
160:                bool bHaveHover = false;
161:
162:                if( hoverIndex != -1 ) {
163:                    ImageListViewItem Item = items[ hoverIndex ];
164:                    if( !Item.HitTest( pt ) )
165:                        Item.Draw( g, Font, brush, Item.Location,
➥ this.ClientRectangle.Width, ListViewItemState.Normal );
166:                    else {
167:                        g.Dispose( );
168:                        brush.Dispose( );
169:                        return;
170:                    }
171:                }
172:
173:                for( int index = this.topIndex; index <= this.lastIndex;
➥index++ ) {
174:                    ImageListViewItem Item = items[ index ];
175:                    if( Item.HitTest( pt ) ) {
176:                        Item.Draw( g, Font, brush, Item.Location,
➥ this.ClientRectangle.Width, ListViewItemState.Hover );
```

LISTING 9.3 Continued

```
177:                          hoverIndex = index;
178:                          bHaveHover = true;
179:                          break;
180:                     }
181:               }
182:
183:          if( !bHaveHover )
184:               hoverIndex = -1;
185:
186:          g.Dispose( );
187:          brush.Dispose( );
188:     }
189:
190:     protected override void OnMouseDown( MouseEventArgs e ) {
191:
192:          if( e.Button == MouseButtons.Left ) {
193:               Point pt = new Point( e.X, e.Y );
194:     Graphics g = CreateGraphics( );
195:
196:               //Hit test for scrolling
197:               if( this.bScrollUp )
198:                    if( this.upScroll.HitTest( pt ) ) {
199:                         upScroll.Draw( g, ButtonState.Pushed );
200:                         g.Dispose( );
201:                         return;
202:                    }
203:
204:               if( this.bScrollDown )
205:                    if( this.downScroll.HitTest( pt ) ) {
206:                         downScroll.Draw( g, ButtonState.Pushed );
207:                         g.Dispose( );
208:                         return;
209:                    }
210:
211:               //Hit Test items
212:               for( hitIndex = topIndex; hitIndex <= lastIndex;
➥ hitIndex++ ) {
213:                    ImageListViewItem Item = items[ hitIndex ];
214:                    if( Item.HitTest( pt ) ) {
215:                         Brush brush = new SolidBrush( this.ForeColor );
216:                         Item.Draw( g, Font, brush, Item.Location,
➥this.ClientRectangle.Width, ListViewItemState.Pushed );
217:                         brush.Dispose( );
218:                         g.Dispose( );
```

LISTING 9.3   Continued

```
219:                            return;
220:                        }
221:                    }
222:                }
223:                hitIndex = -1;
224:                base.OnMouseDown( e );
225:            }
226:
227:        protected override void OnMouseUp( MouseEventArgs e ) {
228:
229:            if( e.Button == MouseButtons.Left ) {
230:                Point pt = new Point( e.X, e.Y );
231:                Graphics g = CreateGraphics( );
232:
233:   //Hit test for scrolling
234:                if( this.bScrollUp ) {
235:                    upScroll.Draw( g, ButtonState.Normal );
236:                    if( this.upScroll.HitTest( pt ) ) {
237:                        g.Dispose( );
238:                        this.topIndex--;
239:                        this.Invalidate( );
240:                        return;
241:                    }
242:                }
243:
244:                if( this.bScrollDown ) {
245:                    downScroll.Draw( g, ButtonState.Normal );
246:                    if( this.downScroll.HitTest( pt ) ) {
247:                        g.Dispose( );
248:                        this.topIndex++;
249:                        this.Invalidate( );
250:                        return;
251:                    }
252:                }
253:
254:                //Test Image Items
255:                if( hitIndex != -1 ) {
256:                    ImageListViewItem Item = items[ hitIndex ];
257:                    Brush brush = new SolidBrush( this.ForeColor );
258:                    Item.Draw( g, Font, brush, Item.Location,
➥ this.ClientRectangle.Width, ListViewItemState.Normal );
259:                    brush.Dispose( );
260:                    g.Dispose( );
261:                    if( Item.HitTest( pt ) )
```

LISTING 9.3   Continued

```
262:                              this.OnItemClicked( new
➥ ImageListViewEventArgs( hitIndex ) );
263:                         hitIndex = -1;
264:                     }
265:     }
266:             base.OnMouseUp( e );
267:         }
268:
269:
270:         protected void DrawScrollButtons( Graphics g ) {
271:             if( bScrollUp ) {
272:                 upScroll.Location = new Point(
➥ this.ClientRectangle.Width - 20, 20 );
273:                 upScroll.Draw( g, ButtonState.Normal );
274:             }
275:
276:             if( bScrollDown ) {
277:                 downScroll.Location = new Point(
➥ this.ClientRectangle.Width - 20, this.ClientRectangle.Bottom - 20 );
278:                 downScroll.Draw( g, ButtonState.Normal );
279:             }
280:         }
281:
282:         protected void DrawItem( Graphics g, Brush brush,
➥ ImageListViewItem Item, Point pt, ListViewItemState state ) {
283:             Item.Draw( g, Font, brush, pt, this.ClientRectangle.Width,
➥ state );
284:         }
285:
286:         protected void Recalc( ) {
287:             Graphics g = CreateGraphics( );
288:             foreach( ImageListViewItem T in items )
289:                 T.CalcHeight( g, Font, this.ClientRectangle.Width,
➥ bLargeIcons );
290:
291:             g.Dispose( );
292:         }
293:
294:
295:         protected virtual void OnItemClicked(ImageListViewEventArgs e) {
296:             if( ItemClicked != null )
297:   ItemClicked( this, e );
298:         }
299:
300:         public class ListViewItemCollection : ICollection, IEnumerable,
➥IList {
```

LISTING 9.3   Continued

```
301:
302:            private System.Collections.ArrayList     internalArrayList;
303:            private ImageListView                      owner;
304:
305:
306:            public ListViewItemCollection( ImageListView parent ) {
307:                owner = parent;
308:                internalArrayList = new ArrayList( );
309:            }
310:
311:
312:            //ICollection Interface Implementation
313:            public int Count {
314:                get { return internalArrayList.Count; }
315:            }
316:
317:            public bool IsSynchronized {
318:                get { return internalArrayList.IsSynchronized; }
319:            }
320:
321:            public object SyncRoot {
322:                get { return internalArrayList.SyncRoot; }
323:            }
324:
325:            public void CopyTo( Array array, int arrayIndex ) {
326:                internalArrayList.CopyTo( array, arrayIndex );
327:            }
328:
329:
330:            //IEnumerable Interface Implementation
331:            public IEnumerator GetEnumerator( ) {
332:                return internalArrayList.GetEnumerator( );
333:            }
334:
335:            //IList Interface Implementation
336:            public bool IsFixedSize {
337:    get { return internalArrayList.IsFixedSize; }
338:            }
339:            public bool IsReadOnly {
340:                get { return internalArrayList.IsReadOnly; }
341:            }
342:
343:            object IList.this[ int index ] {
344:                get { return this[ index ]; }
345:                set { this[ index ] = (ImageListViewItem)value; }
```

LISTING 9.3   Continued

```
346:                }
347:
348:            int IList.Add( object o ) {
349:                return this.Add( (ImageListViewItem)o );
350:            }
351:
352:            void IList.Clear( ) {
353:                this.Clear( );
354:            }
355:
356:            public bool Contains( object o ) {
357:                return internalArrayList.Contains( o );
358:            }
359:
360:            public int IndexOf( object o ) {
361:                return internalArrayList.IndexOf( o );
362:            }
363:
364:
365:            void IList.Insert( int index, object o ) {
366:        this.Insert( index, (ImageListViewItem)o );
367:            }
368:
369:            void IList.Remove( object o ) {
370:                this.Remove( (ImageListViewItem)o );
371:            }
372:
373:            void IList.RemoveAt( int index ) {
374:                this.RemoveAt( index );
375:            }
376:
377:            //ListViewItemCollection Implementation
378:            public int Add( ImageListViewItem ilvi ) {
379:                int index = internalArrayList.Count;
380:                Insert( internalArrayList.Count, ilvi );
381:                return index;
382:            }
383:
384:            public void AddRange( ImageListViewItem[] ilvi ) {
385:                foreach( ImageListViewItem T in ilvi )
386:                    Add( T );
387:            }
388:
389:            public void Remove( ImageListViewItem ilvi  ) {
390:                RemoveAt( IndexOf( ilvi ) );
```

9

LISTING 9.3 Continued

```
391:                   }
392:
393:            public void RemoveAt( int index ) {
394:                   internalArrayList.RemoveAt( index );
395:                   owner.Invalidate( );
396:            }
397:
398:            public void Insert( int index, ImageListViewItem ilvi ) {
399:                   internalArrayList.Insert( index, ilvi );
400:                   ilvi.parent = owner;
401:                   ilvi.CalcHeight( owner.CreateGraphics( ), owner.Font,
➥ owner.ClientRectangle.Width, owner.bLargeIcons );
402:                   owner.Invalidate( );
403:    owner.Update( );
404:            }
405:
406:            public void Clear( ) {
407:                   internalArrayList.Clear( );
408:                   owner.Invalidate( );
409:            }
410:
411:            public ImageListViewItem this[ int index ] {
412:                get {
413:                    try {
414:                        return (ImageListViewItem)internalArrayList[
➥index ];
415:                    } catch( Exception ) {
416:                        return null;
417:                    }
418:                }
419:                set {
420:                    try {
421:                        internalArrayList[ index ] = value;
422:                        owner.Invalidate( );
423:                    } catch( Exception ) { }
424:                }
425:            }
426:        }
427:    }
428: }
```

Understanding the code in Listing 9.3 requires breaking it down into the various responsibilities: managing ImageListViewItems, handling mouse events, and providing scrolling.

Managing `ImageListViewItems`

The management of items within the control is twofold. First is the custom collection that interacts with the `ImageListView` control whenever an item is added or removed. Second is managing the location of the items within the drawing area of the control itself.

The custom collection is fairly similar to the custom collection created from the `OutlookBar` control. The differences pertain to the interaction with its parent. In the case of the `ImageListView` control, when an item is added to the collection, the new item must calculate its size and the parent needs to be invalidated so that the new item will appear. The `Insert` method, on line 398 of Listing 9.3, contains this insertion logic.

The next major task of managing `ImageListViewItems` is to determine their position within the client area of the `ImageListView` control. During the drawing of each item, its calculated height is used to determine the location of the next `ImageListViewItem`. In the event that there are more items to be drawn than space is available, scrolling buttons need to be displayed. Scrolling support is discussed later.

Drawing logic is contained within the `OnPaint` method, on line 107 of Listing 9.3. The drawing logic is as follows:

1. Get index for top item to draw.
2. Draw item.
3. Use height of item to determine location of next item to draw.
4. Will next item be visible based on its location? If yes, go to step 2.
5. If more than two items, need scrolling support.

This set of steps is repeated until there are no more items to draw or step 5 is reached.

Handling Mouse Events

Mouse events are the main means of interaction with the `ImageListView` control. In fact, the handling of mouse events represents a significant portion of the code for the `ImageListView` control. The mouse events used are `OnMouseMove`, `OnMouseDown`, and `OnMouseUp`.

Starting with the `OnMouseMove` event, on line 153 of Listing 9.3, the logic is as follows:

1. Is there an item currently being drawn in hover mode? If no, go to step 3.
2. Is the mouse over the item in hover mode? If yes, nothing to do and return from `OnMouseMove`; otherwise, draw the item in normal mode.
3. Loop through visible items and hit-test. If the mouse is over an item, draw the item in hover mode, save the item's index, and exit `OnMouseMove`.

The MouseMove event is used to provide visual feedback to the user. This visual feedback is accomplished by drawing the item under the mouse in hover mode. That is, the item appears to be raised up from the control.

The next mouse event, OnMouseDown, on line 190, is used to determine whether an item or ScrollButton has been hit. The MouseDown method logic is as follows:

1. Is there a scroll-up button? If no, go to step 3 else step 2.
2. Has the scroll-up button been hit? If yes, draw the ScrollButton in a pressed state and exit OnMouseDown, else step 3.
3. Is there a scroll-down button? If no, go to step 5 else step 4.
4. Has the scroll-down button been hit? If yes, draw the ScrollButton in a pressed state and exit OnMouseDown, else step 5.
5. For each visible item, hit-test the item. If an item has been hit, draw the item in a pressed state and exit OnMouseDown.

The final mouse event, OnMouseUp, on line 227 of Listing 9.3, is used to determine whether an item or ScrollButton has been clicked. If an item has been clicked, the OnItemClicked method is invoked for the current item. The OnItemClicked method in turn raises the ItemClicked event. If a ScrollButton has been hit, the topIndex member is adjusted up or down depending on the ScrollButton that was clicked.

Scrolling

The scrolling functionality for the control is provided through the adjustment of the member topIndex. The topIndex member determines which ImageListViewItem will be drawn at the top of the control. Adjusting which item is drawn at the top enables the illusion of scrolling to be obtained. As seen by the implementation, there is no scrolling of the actual window contents. Rather, the item to be drawn first is adjusted.

At this point, the control is functional but not well behaved within the designer, because it will not clean up any items it contains when the control itself is deleted. To realize all the work done so far, there is only one final step: creating a simple designer. This final step is discussed in the following section.

ImageListViewDesigner

For the ImageListView control to be considered a well-behaved control, it must clean up after itself during design-time. Without a designer, the ImageListView control will orphan ImageListViewItems when deleted from a form. Orphaning of the ImageListViewItems happens when the ImageListView control is deleted and there is no designer logic to destroy subcomponents associated with the ImageListView control.

The ImageListViewDesigner will take on the responsibility of destroying all
ImageListViewItems when the ImageListView control is deleted. Subscribing to the
OnComponentRemoving event of the IComponentChangeService allows for this cleanup to take
place. When the component being removed is the ImageListView control, all the
ImageListViewItems are destroyed. Listing 9.4 provides the implementation of the designer.

LISTING 9.4   ImageListViewDesigner

```
 1: using System;
 2: using System.Collections;
 3: using System.ComponentModel;
 4: using System.ComponentModel.Design;
 5: using System.Drawing;
 6: using System.Drawing.Design;
 7: using System.Windows.Forms;
 8: using System.Windows.Forms.Design;
 9: using SAMS.ToolKit.Controls;
10:
11:
12: namespace SAMS.ToolKit.Design
13: {
14:
15:     public class ItemListViewDesigner : ControlDesigner {
16:
17:
18:         private void OnComponentRemoving( object sender,
➥ComponentEventArgs e ) {
19:             IDesignerHost designerHost = (IDesignerHost)GetService(
➥typeof(IDesignerHost) );
20:             //What is being removed?
21:             if( e.Component is ImageListView ) {
22:                 //Destory all Items
23:                 ImageListView ilv = (ImageListView)e.Component;
24:
25:                 while( ((ImageListView)e.Component).Items.Count > 0 ) {
26:                     designerHost.DestroyComponent(
➥ ((ImageListView)e.Component).Items[0] );
27:  ((ImageListView)e.Component).Items.RemoveAt( 0 );
28:                 }
29:             }
30:         }
31:
32:         public override void Initialize( IComponent component ) {
33:             base.Initialize( component );
34:
```

LISTING 9.4 Continued

```
35:               IComponentChangeService changeService =
➥ (IComponentChangeService)GetService(typeof(IComponentChangeService));
36:               changeService.ComponentRemoving += new ComponentEventHandler(
➥OnComponentRemoving );
37:          }
38:
39:       public override void Dispose( ) {
40:
41:               IComponentChangeService changeService =
➥ (IComponentChangeService)GetService(typeof(IComponentChangeService));
42:               changeService.ComponentRemoving -=
➥new ComponentEventHandler( OnComponentRemoving );
43:
44:               base.Dispose( );
45:          }
46:
47:       public ItemListViewDesigner() {
48:          }
49:    }
50: }
```

Again, the only function of the designer is to remove orphaned ImageListViewItems during the removal of the ImageListView control. The OnComponentRemoving event handler, located on line 18 of Listing 9.4, accomplishes this task. To properly clean up during the removal of the ImageListView control, the designer iterates through the Items collection of the ImageListView control and has the IDesignerHost service destroy each component. It is necessary to use the IDesignerHost service to destroy these components in order for the components to be removed from the Icon Tray area as well as remove all generated code from the InitializeComponent method that relates to the now deleted components.

With the completion of the designer, the process of building a basic OutlookBar control is finally finished.

Testing the OutlookBar Control

Testing the final control is a victory that should be savored. The various controls, components, and designers for the OutlookBar control and its related controls demonstrate the basic requirements for creating custom controls for Windows Forms. Figure 9.3 shows the test application displaying a MessageBox indicating which item was clicked on.

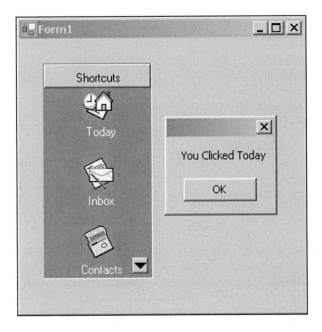

FIGURE 9.3
The OutlookBar *client.*

To test the OutlookBar control, compile the solution containing all the code developed thus far. This will result in the dll SAMS.ToolKit.dll being created. This dll houses all the components, controls, and designers developed to this point.

Creating the client application requires starting a new Windows Forms project and adding the OutlookBar and ImageListView controls to the Toolbox. Adding the controls to the Toolbox requires customizing the Toolbox and browsing to the location of the newly compiled dll.

To create the test application, drag the OutlookBar control onto the main form. Next, drag an ImageListView control onto the OutlookBar control. A new tab is automatically created.

Associate an ImageList component with the ImageListView control containing a set of large images. The images can be of anything. The images shown in Figure 9.3 were borrowed from Microsoft Outlook.

After the ImageList has been associated with the ImageListView control, use the Items property editor to add ImageListViewItems and set the text and image index for them. Listing 9.5 shows the result of the test client code.

LISTING 9.5 OutlookBar Client

```
 1: using System;
 2: using System.Drawing;
 3: using System.Collections;
 4: using System.ComponentModel;
 5: using System.Windows.Forms;
 6: using System.Data;
 7:
 8: namespace OutlookBar_Test
 9: {
10:     /// <summary>
11:     /// Summary description for Form1.
12:     /// </summary>
13:     public class Form1 : System.Windows.Forms.Form
14:     {
15:         private SAMS.ToolKit.Controls.OutlookBar outlookBar1;
16:         private System.Windows.Forms.ImageList LargeImages;
17:         private SAMS.ToolKit.Controls.ImageListView imageListView1;
18:         private SAMS.ToolKit.Controls.OutlookBarTab outlookBarTab1;
19:         private SAMS.ToolKit.Controls.ImageListViewItem
➥ imageListViewItem1;
20:         private SAMS.ToolKit.Controls.ImageListViewItem
➥ imageListViewItem2;
21:         private SAMS.ToolKit.Controls.ImageListViewItem
➥ imageListViewItem3;
22:         private SAMS.ToolKit.Controls.ImageListViewItem
➥ imageListViewItem4;
23:         private SAMS.ToolKit.Controls.ImageListViewItem
➥ imageListViewItem5;
24:         private SAMS.ToolKit.Controls.ImageListViewItem
➥ imageListViewItem6;
25:         private SAMS.ToolKit.Controls.ImageListViewItem
➥ imageListViewItem7;
26:         private System.ComponentModel.IContainer components;
27:
28:         public Form1()
29:         {
30:             //
31:             // Required for Windows Form Designer support
32:             //
33:             InitializeComponent();
34:
35:             //
36:             // TODO: Add any constructor code after
➥InitializeComponent call
```

LISTING 9.5   Continued

```
37:            //
38:        }
39:
40:        /// <summary>
41:        /// Clean up any resources being used.
42:        /// </summary>
43:        protected override void Dispose( bool disposing )
44:        {
45:            if( disposing )
46:            {
47:                if (components != null)
48:                {
49:                    components.Dispose();
50:                }
51:            }
52:            base.Dispose( disposing );
53:        }
54:
55:        #region Windows Form Designer generated code
56:        /// <summary>
57:        /// Required method for Designer support - do not modify
58:        /// the contents of this method with the code editor.
59:        /// </summary>
60:        private void InitializeComponent()
61:        {
62:            this.components = new System.ComponentModel.Container();
63:            System.Resources.ResourceManager resources =
➥new System.Resources.ResourceManager(typeof(Form1));
64:            this.outlookBar1 = new SAMS.ToolKit.Controls.OutlookBar();
65:            this.LargeImages = new System.Windows.Forms.ImageList(
➥this.components);
66:            this.imageListView1 =
➥new SAMS.ToolKit.Controls.ImageListView();
67:            this.outlookBarTab1 =
➥new SAMS.ToolKit.Controls.OutlookBarTab();
68:            this.imageListViewItem1 =
➥ new SAMS.ToolKit.Controls.ImageListViewItem();
69:            this.imageListViewItem2 =
➥new SAMS.ToolKit.Controls.ImageListViewItem();
70:            this.imageListViewItem3 =
➥new SAMS.ToolKit.Controls.ImageListViewItem();
71:            this.imageListViewItem4 =
➥ new SAMS.ToolKit.Controls.ImageListViewItem();
72:            this.imageListViewItem5 =
➥new SAMS.ToolKit.Controls.ImageListViewItem();
```

LISTING 9.5   Continued

```
73:            this.imageListViewItem6 =
➥new SAMS.ToolKit.Controls.ImageListViewItem();
74:            this.imageListViewItem7 =
➥new SAMS.ToolKit.Controls.ImageListViewItem();
75:  this.outlookBar1.SuspendLayout();
76:            this.SuspendLayout();
77:            //
78:            // outlookBar1
79:            //
80:            this.outlookBar1.Location = new System.Drawing.Point(24, 24);
81:            this.outlookBar1.Name = "outlookBar1";
82:            this.outlookBar1.Size = new System.Drawing.Size(112, 216);
83:            this.outlookBar1.TabIndex = 0;
84:            this.outlookBar1.Tabs.AddRange(new
➥SAMS.ToolKit.Controls.OutlookBarTab[] {
85:                          this.outlookBarTab1});
86:            this.outlookBar1.Text = "outlookBar1";
87:            //
88:            // LargeImages
89:            //
90:            this.LargeImages.ColorDepth =
➥System.Windows.Forms.ColorDepth.Depth8Bit;
91:            this.LargeImages.ImageSize = new System.Drawing.Size(32, 32);
92:            this.LargeImages.ImageStream =
➥ ((System.Windows.Forms.ImageListStreamer)(resources.GetObject(
➥"LargeImages.ImageStream")));
93:            this.LargeImages.TransparentColor =
➥System.Drawing.Color.Transparent;
94:            //
95:            // imageListView1
96:            //
97:            this.imageListView1.BackColor =
➥System.Drawing.SystemColors.ControlDark;
98: this.imageListView1.ForeColor =
➥System.Drawing.SystemColors.ControlLightLight;
99:            this.imageListView1.Items.AddRange(new
➥SAMS.ToolKit.Controls.ImageListViewItem[] {
100:                                      this.imageListViewItem1,
101:                                      this.imageListViewItem2,
102:                                      this.imageListViewItem3,
103:                                      this.imageListViewItem4,
104:                                      this.imageListViewItem5,
105:                                      this.imageListViewItem6,
106:                                      this.imageListViewItem7});
107:          this.imageListView1.LargeIcons = true;
```

LISTING 9.5   Continued

```
108:              this.imageListView1.LargeImageList = this.LargeImages;
109:              this.imageListView1.Location = new
➥System.Drawing.Point(1, 25);
110:              this.imageListView1.Name = "imageListView1";
111:              this.imageListView1.Size = new
➥System.Drawing.Size(110, 190);
112:              this.imageListView1.SmallImageList = null;
113:              this.imageListView1.TabIndex = 0;
114:              this.imageListView1.ItemClicked +=
➥new SAMS.ToolKit.Controls.ItemClickedEventHandler(
➥this.imageListView1_ItemClicked);
115:
116:              this.outlookBarTab1.Alignment =
➥System.Drawing.StringAlignment.Center;
117:              this.outlookBarTab1.Child = this.imageListView1;
118:              this.outlookBarTab1.ForeColor =
➥System.Drawing.SystemColors.ControlText;
119:              this.outlookBarTab1.Text = "Shortcuts";
120:
121:              this.imageListViewItem1.ImageIndex = 0;
122:              this.imageListViewItem1.Text = "Today";
123:
124:              this.imageListViewItem2.ImageIndex = 1;
125:              this.imageListViewItem2.Text = "Inbox";
126:
127:              this.imageListViewItem3.ImageIndex = 2;
128:              this.imageListViewItem3.Text = "Contacts";
129:
130: this.imageListViewItem4.ImageIndex = 3;
131:              this.imageListViewItem4.Text = "Calendar";
132:
133:              this.imageListViewItem5.ImageIndex = 4;
134:              this.imageListViewItem5.Text = "Tasks";
135:
136:              this.imageListViewItem6.ImageIndex = 5;
137:              this.imageListViewItem6.Text = "Notes";
138:
139:              this.imageListViewItem7.ImageIndex = 6;
140:              this.imageListViewItem7.Text = "Trash";
141:
142:              this.AutoScaleBaseSize = new System.Drawing.Size(5, 13);
143:              this.ClientSize = new System.Drawing.Size(292, 273);
144:              this.Controls.AddRange(new System.Windows.Forms.Control[] {
145:                                          this.outlookBar1});
146:              this.Name = "Form1";
```

9

IMAGEVIEWLIST CONTROL

LISTING 9.5   Continued

```
147:                this.Text = "Form1";
148:                this.outlookBar1.ResumeLayout(false);
149:                this.ResumeLayout(false);
150:
151:        }
152:        #endregion
153:
154:        /// <summary>
155:        /// The main entry point for the application.
156:        /// </summary>
157:        [STAThread]
158:        static void Main()
159:        {
160:            Application.Run(new Form1());
161:        }
162:
163:        private void imageListView1_ItemClicked(object sender,
➥SAMS.ToolKit.Controls.ImageListViewEventArgs e) {
164:            string msg = string.Format("You Clicked {0}",
➥this.imageListView1.Items[ e.ItemIndex ].Text );
165:    MessageBox.Show( this, msg );
166:            }
167:        }
168: }
```

Listing 9.5 is 99% generated during the design process of the test application. The only hand-coded method is the imageListView1_ItemClicked event handler on line 163, and even the stub for this was genereated by double-clicking on the ImageListView control.

The imageListView1_ItemClicked event handler uses the ImageListViewEventArgs parameter to get the text of the ImageListView item and displays a message box stating which item was clicked on. Of 168 lines of code, only 2 lines have to be typed. Isn't code generation wonderful?

Summary

These last four chapters have covered a lot of ground. The only magic to creating custom controls is imagination, creativity, and desire. At this point, the nuts and bolts of control development have been explored, and all that remains is to add features to both the controls and the designers developed so far. Using Chapter 5, "Advanced Control Development," as a reference, you should be able to extend the OutlookBar to add new features or create a new custom control from scratch. The best way to learn to develop controls is to write them. Look at the various UI elements found in VS .NET and start creating controls.

Control Deployment

IN THIS CHAPTER

The last major area of control development has to do with distributing controls to customers. Control deployment consists of three basic topics:

- Licensing
- Hosting controls in Internet Explorer
- GAC (Global Assembly Cache) versus local assemblies

Each of these topics requires assessing how, when, and where controls will be used.

Licensing

Almost every type of software application includes some type of licensing agreement that governs the rights and uses of the software. In addition to the licensing agreement, a product key may also be required during the installation and setup for the software package. Licensing is used to govern the rights of the user with respect to the use of a product and how that product is deployed, used, and even distributed.

.NET provides a licensing system for components such as the custom controls developed in this book. The licensing system is based on the COM version of licensing providing support for both design-time and runtime licensing for a component. By licensing components, a vendor can govern the use of the component and help ensure that the user of the component has the proper licensing for development and distribution of the component.

> **NOTE**
>
> For those of you not familiar with COM, don't worry—it's not important anymore. COM is mentioned only because the current licensing system is based on COM licensing. There are plenty of texts covering every grueling aspect of COM if you feel inclined to investigate. Personally, after many years of COM-based development, I'm glad to see it go.

Types of Licensing

The type of license depends on the expected use of a component. Demo versions of a component, such as the IconButton, may be distributed free and require no license for use. Generally, the demo version has only a subset of the functionality available for use, along with the restriction that the component cannot be used in a commercial application without purchase of the component.

Another option for licensing is a one-time fee for the product such as when buying a software package. The software generally includes an EULA, or End User License Agreement. The terms and conditions of the EULA will define the rights of the user with regard to the software.

Specialized server-based products often require the purchase of a Per-CPU license, in which the license fee is based on the number of CPUs within the server hosting the software or component. This style of licensing is generally found in server applications such as databases, email systems, and Web servers.

When considering a licensing system, try to keep in mind that the licensing should be unobtrusive and effective for both parties. Creating a complicated and intrusive licensing system often turns away potential customers who view the licensing schema as an unnecessary burden.

Licensing Controls

The .NET framework provides for both simple file-based licensing and custom licensing that can be implemented as needed to fulfill the licensing requirements of the component author. In the simplest form of licensing, a small text file is used to contain a single line of text regarding the license of the component. This scheme provides no real security or means of enforcement for the license. With custom licensing, the enforcement and use of the component and licensing are governed by the implementation of the custom `LicenseProvider` derived class. Custom licensing is covered in the "Providing Custom Licensing section" of this chapter.

To support licensing, the .NET Framework provides the classes listed in Table 10.1

TABLE 10.1   Licensing Classes

Class	Description
License	Abstract base class of all licenses.
LicenseContext	Specifies when a licensed component can be used.
DesigntimeLicenseContext	Specifies a design-time licensing context.
LicenseProvider	Abstract base class for all license provider classes.
LicenseProviderAttribute	Attribute used to specify the `LicenseProvider` for the licensed component.
LicenseManager	Used to add a license to a component and manage the `LicenseProvider`.
LicFileLicenseProvider	Implementation of a `LicenseProvider` that is consistent with the .NET Framework licensing system.
LicenseException	Exception thrown when an error is encountered when trying to validate or grant a component's license.

The .NET licensing classes provide for simple licensing or serve as a starting point for developing custom licensing schemas. The next two sections cover simple licensing using the `LicFileLicenseProvider` class and creating a custom-licensing schema by inheriting from `LicenseProvider` to implement the licensing validation.

Simple Licensing: `LicFileLicenseProvider`

Creating a simple licensed component requires very little effort and entails only the four following steps:

1. Create a LIC (license) file.
2. Use the `LicenseProviderAttribute` to specify the `LicenseProvider` for the component.
3. Create an instance of the license.
4. Dispose the license when the component is disposed of.

The LIC, or license file, is a simple text file containing a single text string in the following format:

`"Component is a licensed component."`

Here, `Component` is the fully qualified name of the licensed component. In addition, the LIC file should have the same name as the component. Using the `IconButton` control, the LIC file would be as follows:

Filename: `SAMS.ToolKit.Controls.IconButton.LIC`

Contents: `SAMS.ToolKit.Controls.IconButton is a licensed component.`

The LIC file must be located in the directory containing the assembly of the licensed control. Figure 10.1 shows the LIC file for the `IconButton` loaded in VS .NET.

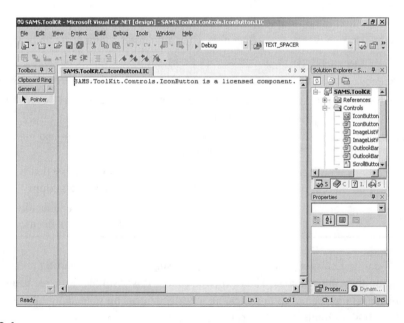

FIGURE 10.1
The `IconButton` *LIC file.*

To implement the simple licensing for the IconButton, the source for the control needs to be updated to add the LicenseProviderAttribute and the creation and disposal of the license. Listing 10.1 shows the modifications to the IconButton source necessary to support basic LIC file–based licensing.

LISTING 10.1   Licensed IconButton

```
 1: using System;
 2: using System.Windows.Forms;
 3: using System.Drawing;
 4: using System.ComponentModel;
 5:
 6:
 7: namespace SAMS.ToolKit.Controls {
 8:     /// <summary>
 9:     /// IconButton Class
10:     /// </summary>
11:     [
12:     System.ComponentModel.Description( "SAMS IconButton Control" ),
13:     System.ComponentModel.Designer(
➥typeof( SAMS.ToolKit.Design.IconButtonDesigner ) ),
14:     System.ComponentModel.LicenseProvider(
➥typeof( System.ComponentModel.LicFileLicenseProvider ) )
15:     ]
16:     public class IconButton : System.Windows.Forms.Control {
17:
18:         private License    license = null;
19:
20:         public IconButton( ) {
21:
22:             //validate the license
23:             license = LicenseManager.Validate( typeof(
➥SAMS.ToolKit.Controls.IconButton ), this );
24:
25:             InitializeComponent(  );
26:         }
27:
28:         protected override void Dispose( bool disposing ) {
29:             if( license != null ) {
30:                 license.Dispose( );
31:                 license = null;
32:             }
33:             base.Dispose( disposing );
34:         }
35:  //rest of IconButton implementation
36: }
```

Rather than relisting the entire `IconButton` source, Listing 10.1 shows only the modifications to the `IconButton` needed in order to implement licensing. The first modification is the addition of the `LicenseProviderAttribute` on line 14. This attribute is used to specify the type of license provider to create when validating the license for the component. The .NET Framework supports simple file-based licensing by providing an implementation of the `LicenseProvider` abstract base class in the form of `LicFileLicenseProvider`.

With the attribute in place, the next step is to declare a private member of type `License`. The declaration of this member is found on line 18 of Listing 10.1. Remember that the `License` class is an abstract base class for all license types. To obtain a valid license, the `LicenseManager` is used to validate the license for the control. This validation can be found within the constructor for the `IconButton` starting on line 20. If the validation fails, the `LicenseManager` throws a `LicenseException`. When this exception is not caught, an instance of the control will not be created.

In fact, using VS .NET to create a Windows application and hosting the `IconButton` on a form can demonstrate this point. To make the license validation fail, remove the LIC file from the directory containing the `SAMS.ToolKit.dll` assembly. Next, drag the `IconButton` from the Toolbox onto the form. VS .NET generates a message box stating that a valid license for the control could not be created, as shown in Figure 10.2.

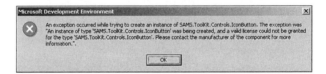

FIGURE 10.2
License validation failure.

Licenses created by a component should be disposed of when the component itself is disposed of. Line 28 of Listing 10.1 shows the `Dispose` method of the `IconButton` disposing of the contained `License`.

To see the results of the licensing implementation, create a new Windows application and add the `IconButton` to the Toolbox and then to the form. If the LIC file is in place, the `IconButton` will be created without any noticeable difference with respect to other test applications created to this point. However, there is a difference, and that difference is in how the licensing is enforced and used.

Every Windows application contains a `license.licx` file, located in the project directory. This license file contains the necessary licensing information for all licensed controls used by the application. This licx file is compiled as a binary resource and embedded within the output assembly. This allows the application to validate all licenses and does not require the various LIC files for licensed components to be distributed along with the application. Figure 10.3 shows the `license.licx` file for the test Windows application.

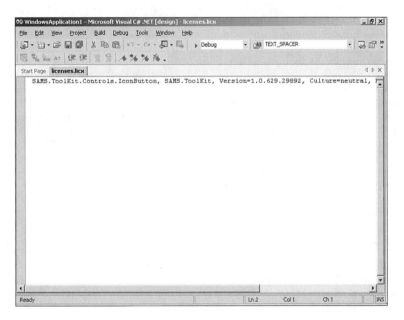

FIGURE 10.3

The License.licx *file.*

The simple file-based licensing schema does not provide much in the way of security or the enforcement of proper use of the control based on an agreed license. To provide a more robust licensing schema, it's necessary to create a custom licensing solution.

Providing Custom Licensing

To provide a custom licensing implementation, at least two classes need to be created. These two classes will represent the license and the license provider implementation. The licensing scheme is implemented by deriving from the `LicenseProvider` base class and implementing the `GetLicense` method. In addition, a custom license class needs to be created by deriving from the abstract `License` class and implementing the `LicenseKey` property and the `Dispose` method.

Custom Licensing implementations vary based on need. For the purpose of demonstration, a file-based custom provider will be developed. Other implementations might make use of a Web Service or some other verification means, such as registry entries or a product key entered by the developer. In development of a custom provider, there is no steadfast rule for "how"—only that the licensing system makes sense for the product.

To demonstrate a custom license provider, the `IconButton` will be licensed by using an xml file that contains an entry for the `IconButton` control along with a key value to be used as the license key. This xml file will be named `sams.licensing.xml` and located within the same directory as the `SAMS.ToolKit.dll` assembly. Listing 10.2 shows the xml file to be used as the license file.

LISTING 10.2   Custom License XML File

```
1: <?xml version="1.0"?>
2: <sams>
3:    <control name="SAMS.ToolKit.Controls.IconButton" key="custom_key_value"/>
4: </sams>
```

The next step in providing a custom licensing schema is to provide the implementation for a license and license provider. Listing 10.3 shows the implementation for the `CustomLicenseProvider` and `CustomLicense` classes.

LISTING 10.3   Custom License Provider Source

```
 1: using System;
 2: using System.ComponentModel;
 3: using System.ComponentModel.Design;
 4: using System.Xml;
 5: using System.Xml.XPath;
 6: using System.IO;
 7: using System.Reflection;
 8: using System.Diagnostics;
 9:
10: namespace SAMS.ToolKit.Licensing
11: {
12:     public class CustomLicense : System.ComponentModel.License {
13:         private string                          licenseKey = null;
14:         private CustomLicenseProvider    owner     = null;
15:
16:     public CustomLicense( CustomLicenseProvider owner, string key ) {
17:             this.owner       = owner;
18:             this.licenseKey  = key;
19:         }
20:
21:         public override string LicenseKey {
22:             get { return licenseKey; }
23:         }
24:
25:         public override void Dispose( ) {
26:         }
```

LISTING **10.3**   Continued

```
27:      }
28:
29:     public class CustomLicenseProvider : LicenseProvider  {
30:
31:
32:        protected bool IsKeyValid( string key, Type type ) {
33:            return (key == null ? false : true);
34:        }
35:
36:
37:        public override License GetLicense( LicenseContext context,
38:                                             Type type,
39:                                             object instance,
40:                                             bool allowExceptions ) {
41:
42:           CustomLicense    license    = null;
43:           if( context == null ) return null;
44:
45:
46:           if( context.UsageMode == LicenseUsageMode.Runtime ) {
47:               //See if the key is stored
48:               string key = context.GetSavedLicenseKey( type, null );
49:               if( key != null && IsKeyValid( key, type ) )
50:          license = new CustomLicense( this, key );
51:           }
52:
53:           if( license == null ) {
54:               //locate sams.license.xml file
55:               ITypeResolutionService resolver =
➥(ITypeResolutionService)context.GetService( typeof(
➥ ITypeResolutionService ) );
56:
57:               string location = resolver.GetPathOfAssembly(
➥type.Assembly.GetName( ) );
58:
59:               string licenseFile = Path.GetDirectoryName( location )
➥ + "\\sams.license.xml";
60:
61:               Debug.WriteLine( string.Format("License file location :
➥ {0}", licenseFile ) );
62:
63:
64:               try {
65:                   XmlDocument    doc = new XmlDocument( );
```

LISTING 10.3   Continued

```
66:                    doc.Load( licenseFile );
67:                    string xpathExpression = string.Format(
➥"descendant::control[@name='{0}']", type.FullName);
68:                    XmlNode controlNode = doc.SelectSingleNode(
➥xpathExpression );
69:                    if( controlNode != null ) {
70:                        //get the key value
71:                        string key = controlNode.Attributes.GetNamedItem(
➥ "key" ).Value;
72:             if( key != null ) {
73:                            license = new CustomLicense( this, key );
74:                            //Save the license in the current context
75:                            context.SetSavedLicenseKey( type,
➥license.LicenseKey );
76:                        }
77:                    }
78:                } catch( Exception e ) {
79:                    if( allowExceptions )
80:                        throw new LicenseException( type, instance,
➥ "License not valid" );
81:                    else
82:                        return null;
83:                }
84:            }
85:            return license;
86:        }
87:    }
88: }
```

The verification of the license takes place in the GetLicense method of the CustomLicenseProvider class; this method begins on line 37. The location of the license key depends on the current LicenseContext.UsageMode. The UsageMode can be either Runtime or Designtime. During runtime, the license key should be located within the current LicenseContext object because the application's .licx file is part of the assemblies manifest. Remember that the .licx file will contain the necessary license information for validation during execution so that the component license file does not need to be distributed along with the application.

During design-time, the CustomLicenseProvider attempts to locate the custom xml-based license file located in the same directory as the control assembly. If the license key is valid, the license information is stored within the current LicenseContext object, and an instance of the CustomLicense is returned. Otherwise, the CustomLicenseProvider throws an exception of type LicenseException, if allowed; otherwise, it returns null.

> **NOTE**
>
> For the purpose of the example, a non-empty string will suffice for the licensing requirements. In addition, the license key is extracted using an XPath expression into the xml file. The subject of XML and XPath are beyond the scope of this text. However, information about XPath expressions and their usage is available from www.w3c.org.

To use the new custom licensing, the `LicenseProvider` attribute of the `IconButton` should be updated as shown in Listing 10.4.

LISTING 10.4 Adding Licensing Support to the `IconButton`

```
1:      System.ComponentModel.LicenseProvider( typeof(
➥SAMS.ToolKit.Licensing.CustomLicenseProvider ) )
2:      ]
3:      public class IconButton : System.Windows.Forms.Control {
```

No other changes to the `IconButton` class are necessary to make use of the new custom licensing implementation.

The licensing support provided by the .NET Framework allows for custom licensing schemas to be implemented with little effort, thus allowing vendors to enforce proper use of their intellectual property.

Hosting Controls in Internet Explorer

Internet Explorer (IE) supports the `OBJECT` tag for hosting classic ActiveX controls. In .NET, the `OBJECT` tag can be used to also host Windows Forms controls and provide accesses to the properties of the hosted control. For those of you familiar with hosting ActiveX controls, the syntax for the `OBJECT` tag will seem very familiar. The only difference is the `CLASSID` attribute used to identify the control to be created. The general form of the `OBJECT` tag is as follows:

```
<OBJECT ID="<var-name>" CLASSID="http:<assembly>#<qualified-name>"
➥height="<height>" width="<width>">
  <PARAM NAME="<property-name>" VALUE="<property-value>">
</OBJECT>
```

IE places the following constraints when hosting .NET controls within the browser:

- It requires Full-Trust for COM Interop (Event Handling).
- The assembly must be in the current virtual directory or in the Global Assembly Cache.
- Permissions for the virtual directory must be set to "Scripts only." Setting permissions to "Scripts & Executables" will not allow the control to be hosted.

As long as these conditions are met, hosting a control is a fairly simple process. Listing 10.5 shows a basic aspx page for hosting the IconButton developed earlier.

LISTING 10.5   Hosting the IconButton

```
1: <%@ Page language="c#" Codebehind="WebForm1.aspx.cs"
➥AutoEventWireup="false" Inherits="IEIconButton.WebForm1" %>
2: <!DOCTYPE HTML PUBLIC "-//W3C//DTD HTML 4.0 Transitional//EN" >
3: <html>
4:     <head>
5:         <title>WebForm1</title>
6:         <meta name="GENERATOR" Content="Microsoft Visual Studio 7.0">
7:         <meta name="CODE_LANGUAGE" Content="C#">
8:         <meta name="vs_defaultClientScript" content="JavaScript">
9:         <meta name="vs_targetSchema" content=
➥"http://schemas.microsoft.com/intellisense/ie5">
10:     </head>
11:     <body MS_POSITIONING="GridLayout">
12:         <form id="WebForm1" method="post" runat="server">
13:             <object id="MyButton" classid=
➥"http:SAMS.ToolKit.dll#SAMS.ToolKit.Controls.IconButton"
➥height="25" width="100"
14:             VIEWASTEXT>
15:                 <param name="Text" value="Hello World">
16:             </object>
17:         </form>
18:     </body>
19: </html>
```

The output produced from Listing 10.5 is shown in Figure 10.4.

FIGURE 10.4
Hosting the IconButton *in Internet Explorer.*

GAC (Global Assembly Cache) Versus Local Assemblies

Deploying any .NET application, or any .NET assembly for that matter, requires determining where the physical assemblies will be installed. One of the major advantages of the .NET platform is the capability for xcopy-style deployment of applications and components.

> **NOTE**
>
> For those of you who don't remember the days of DOS, xcopy-style deployment means to simply copy the application and its dependencies to a target destination. No registration of components is required, except changes to the operating system itself. In Microsoft's words, it just works.

With classic COM, all COM servers require registration before the COM object can be used by client applications. This registration process involves creating entries within the registry that identify the location of the COM server along with the various co-classes, Prog-Id's, and version information. The various entries are used by the COM runtime to locate and create an instance of a particular COM server co-class.

With .NET, there is no need to register assemblies for use because the runtime searches specific locations to locate the required assemblies for any given .NET application. The runtime first searches the directory containing the client application and then, if it's not found, continues the search using the system PATH environment variable and the Global Assembly Cache.

The question still remains, should the assemblies be located within the application directory or within the Global Assembly Cache? The answer to this question depends on the intended use of a given assembly. Application-specific assemblies should be stored within the application's home directory, whereas system-wide assemblies, or assemblies that will be used by multiple applications, might be better located within the GAC. In addition, to provide side-by-side versioning of assemblies, GAC deployment is necessary. The next section explores component versioning and describes side-by-side versioning.

Assembly Versioning

Versioning ofcomponents, or DLL hell as it is often referred to, has always proven to be somewhat troublesome in nature. One of the design goals of .NET was to enable assemblies to run side-by-side based on version. This versioning system allows assemblies to be updated without breaking existing clients who depend on an earlier version of the assembly.

The only caveat about supporting versioning is that the versioned assembly must be signed. That is, a public-private key pair that identifies the assembly must be provided. The process of signing an assembly is covered in the .NET SDK documentation, as well as other books, including *C# and the .NET Framework*, by Sams Publishing.

Summary

This chapter brings to a conclusion the process of designing, creating, and deploying custom controls. There's a saying that imitation is the sincerest form of flattery. With the number of vendors providing custom UI elements to mimic those found in the latest Microsoft products, there must be something to that old saying. To expand your own knowledge of building custom controls, it's often helpful to pick a particular control and try implementing your own control that looks and feels like the original. Examples for controls can be found on codeguru.com, on codeproject.com, and in any application that offers some UI element you find interesting. As with all endeavors in life, practice makes perfect.

This is the last chapter, but the following appendix, "Extender Providers," offers an interesting look at dynamically extending controls. Extenders can be used with your newly created custom controls or to extend common controls.

Extender Providers

IN THIS CHAPTER

Although not a control, Extender Providers allow for properties to be added to .NET components. The ToolTip component is an example of an Extender Provider. The ToolTip component allows a ToolTip window to be associated within one or more controls on a form. The ToolTip component adds the ToolTip property to each control on the form. This ToolTip property is then displayed in the Property Browser when a control is selected.

To see how to implement and use Extender Providers, two separate components will be created. The first component will be used to highlight a control when the mouse passes over it. This Extender Provider will enable the highlight to be specified during design-time. In addition to this first extender, a second extender will be implemented to provide feedback for menu options. This second extender will demonstrate how to apply extenders to classes such as the MenuItem component that are not derived from the Control base class.

Creating Extender Providers

Extender Providers are created by implementing the IExtenderProvider interface. This interface has only a single method: bool CanExtend(object target). This method is used to determine whether the provider can extend the target object. Generally, Extender Providers are designed to work only with specific types of components as in the case of the ToolTip Extender Provider. The ToolTip will only add the ToolTip property to Control-derived objects and will not extend MenuItems.

Adding properties to objects being extended is twofold. First the Extender Provider must use the ProvideProperty attribute. This attribute is applied to the Extender Provider class. Listing A.1 shows an example based on the ToolTip extender provider.

LISTING A.1   Defining an Extender Provider

```
 1: [ ProvideProperty( "ToolTip", typeof ( Control ) ) ]
 2: public class ToolTip : Component, IExtenderProvider {
 3:
 4:     //IExtenderProvider Interface Implementation
 5:     bool IExtenderProvider.CanExtend( object target ) {
 6:             if( target is Control )
 7:                 return true;
 8:             else
 9:                 return false;
10:     }
11: }
```

The ProvideProperty attribute takes two arguments for its constructor. The first argument is the name of the property to provide. In the case of the ToolTip component, the property name happens to be ToolTip. Note that the name of the property being provided does not have to be the same as the name of the Extender Provider. Listing A.2 shows the start of the `BorderPainterExtender` component that will be developed as our first foray into Extender Providers.

LISTING A.2   The `BorderPainterExtender` Class Description

```
 1: [ ProvideProperty( "BorderColor", typeof( Control ) ) ]
 2: public class BorderPainterExtender : Component, IExtenderProvider {
 3:
 4:     //Implement the IExtenderProvider interface
 5:     bool IExtenderProvider.CanExtend( object target ) {
 6:         if( (target is Control) && !(target is Form) )
 7:             return true;
 8:         else
 9:             return false;
10:  }
11: }
```

The `BorderPainterExtender` will only extend controls hosted on a `Form` and will not provide a border to a `Form`-derived control. This brings up the second argument to the `ProvideProperty` attribute. In addition to the need to specify the name of the property to be provided, the base class or type of target being extended needs to be specified. In the case of the ToolTip and `BorderPainterExtender`, the target object must be of type `Control`.

With the basics of the `BorderPainterExtender` in place, you now need to understand how the property is added to the targets. The properties are provided via a set of method calls. These method calls allow for obtaining and setting the property value. The syntax for these methods is as follows:

```
public type GetPropertyName( object target )
public void SetPropertyName( object target, type value )
```

PropertyName is replaced with the name specified within the `ProvidePropertyAttribute`. Notice that the properties are provided via method calls and not the property syntax. This is because the Extender Provider requires an additional parameter: the object associated with the property. When a ToolTip extender is placed on a `Form`, that single ToolTip extender provides the ToolTip property to every control on the `Form`. Hence only a single instance of the ToolTip is used to extend all the controls on the `Form`.

For a single extender to service all controls on the `Form`, the extender needs to track the provided property or properties for each control. This association can be accomplished by using a hashtable to map the control to its associated property. Listing A.3 extends the `BorderPainterExtender` to demonstrate this.

LISTING A.3   Next Step in the `BorderPainterExtender`

```
1: [ ProvideProperty( "BorderColor", typeof( Control ) ) ]
2: public class BorderPainterExtender : Component, IExtenderProvider {
3:
4:      protected Hashtable                  borderColors;
5:
6:      public BorderPainterExtender( ) {
7:          borderColors = new Hashtable( );
8:      }
9:
10:     //Provide Get/Set methods
11:     public Color GetBorderColor( object target ) {
12:         return (Color)borderColors[ target ];
13:     }
14:
15:     public void SetBorderColor( object target, Color color ) {
16:
17:         if( color.IsEmpty ) {
18:             borderColors.Remove( target );
19:         } else {
20:             borderColors[ target ] = color;
21:         }
22:     }
23:
24:      //Implement the IExtenderProvider interface
25:      bool IExtenderProvider.CanExtend( object target ) {
26:              if( (target is Control) && !(target is Form) )
27:                 return true;
28:              else
29:                 return false;
30:      }
31: }
```

The `BorderPainterExtender` has now been updated to associate the target object with a specified color. The methods `GetBorderColor` and `SetBorderColor` on lines 11 and 15, respectively, demonstrate how to expose the provided property. Again, the reason for this approach is that there exists only one instance of the extender and that extender will service all controls within the current `Form`.

During design-time, the property will be added to the list of properties available to the selected control. Figure A.1 shows the Property Browser with the `BorderColor` property added to the selected `Label`.

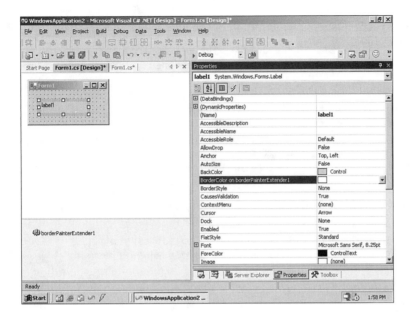

FIGURE A.1

The extended property BorderColor *shown in the Property Browser.*

Notice the BorderPainterExtender1 icon shown in the Icon Tray in Figure A.1. Extender
Providers can be added to the Toolbox and used during design-time. In addition, notice the
name of the property: BorderColor on BorderPainterExtender1. This property name comes
from the fact that there may be another BorderPainterExtender added to the form. A way to
distinguish which extender is hosting the property is necessary.

> **NOTE**
>
> To add an extender to the Toolbox, create a .NET dll assembly containing the exten-
> der. Next, customize the Toolbox and load the .NET dll assembly just as you would
> any other assembly. The extender will then be available in the Toolbox. This is how
> the ToolTip extender is provided.

To complete the BorderPainterExtender component, the BorderPainterExtender will moni-
tor two mouse events: MouseEnter and MouseLeave. These events will be used to determine
which control to paint a border around. The complete listing is shown in Listing A.4.

LISTING A.4   Complete Implementation of the `BorderPainterExtender`

```
 1: [ ProvideProperty( "BorderColor", typeof( Control ) ) ]
 2: public class BorderPainterExtender : Component, IExtenderProvider {
 3:
 4:     protected Hashtable      borderColors;
 5:     protected Control        activeControl;
 6:     protected Rectangle      borderRect;
 7:
 8:     public BorderPainterExtender( ) {
 9:         borderColors    = new Hashtable( );
10:         borderRect      = new Rectangle( );
11:         activeControl   = null;
12:     }
13:
14:     bool IExtenderProvider.CanExtend( object target ) {
15:         return ((target is Control) && !(target is Form));
16:     }
17:
18:     public Color GetBorderColor( object target ) {
19:         try {
20:             return (Color)borderColors[ target ];
21:         } catch( Exception ) {
22:             return new Color( );
23:         }
24:     }
25:
26:     public void SetBorderColor( object target, Color color ) {
27:
28:         if( color.IsEmpty ) {
29:   borderColors.Remove( target );
30:             ((Control)target).MouseEnter -=
➥new EventHandler( OnMouseEnter );
31:             ((Control)target).MouseLeave -=
➥new EventHandler( OnMouseLeave );
32:             if( target == activeControl )
33:                 EraseBorder( );
34:
35:         } else {
36:
37:             if( !borderColors.Contains( target ) ) {
38:                 ((Control)target).MouseEnter +=
➥new EventHandler( OnMouseEnter );
39:                 ((Control)target).MouseLeave +=
➥new EventHandler( OnMouseLeave );
40:             }
41:             borderColors[ target ] = color;
```

LISTING A.4   Continued

```
42:                    if( activeControl == target )
43:                        DrawBorder( );
44:            }
45:        }
46:
47:        protected void EraseBorder( ) {
48:            DrawRectangle( activeControl.Parent.BackColor );
49:        }
50:
51:        protected void DrawBorder( ) {
52:            borderRect = new Rectangle( activeControl.Left, activeControl.Top,
53:                                activeControl.Width, activeControl.Height );
54:            borderRect.Inflate( 2, 2 );
55:
56:            DrawRectangle ( (Color)borderColors[ activeControl ] );
57:        }
58:
59:        protected void DrawRectangle( Color color ) {
60:            Pen        borderPen = new Pen( color, 2 );
61:            Graphics g          = activeControl.Parent.CreateGraphics( );
62:
63:            g.DrawRectangle( borderPen, borderRect );
64:            g.Dispose( );
65:            borderPen.Dispose( );
66:        }
67:
68:        protected void OnMouseEnter( object sender, EventArgs e ) {
69:            activeControl = (Control)sender;
70:            DrawBorder( );
71:        }
72:
73:        protected void OnMouseLeave( object sender, EventArgs e ) {
74:            EraseBorder( );
75:            activeControl = null;
76:    }
77: }
```

To understand how the BorderPainterExtender works, locate the SetBorderColor method located on line 26. This method serves two purposes. First, if the color passed in is uninitialized, the target object is removed from the collection and the mouse event handlers are also removed. Otherwise, the color is associated with the target and the mouse events are monitored. Now, whenever the mouse enters a control being extended by the BorderPainterExtender, a border of the specified color is drawn around the control.

In addition to drawing a border around the control, when the mouse moves out of the control the border will be removed. Figure A.2 shows the `BorderPainterExtender` in action.

The association between the extender and a target happens when the provided property, in this case `BorderColor`, is set within the Property Browser for a given control. Remember that when an extender is added to a form, all target controls will have the specified property added to them. However, the association occurs only if the property value is set. If the property value is deleted or nulled out, the association will also be removed.

FIGURE A.2
`Label` *with a red border provided by the* `BorderPainterExtender`.

Extender Providers are flexible mechanisms for adding properties to .NET components. Any object in .NET can be an Extender Provider, even a control.

Control-Based Extender Providers

As stated previously, any component can serve as an Extender Provider. All that is necessary is to implement the `IExtenderProvider` interface, add the necessary `ProvideProperty` attributes, and implement the `Get/Set` methods for the property. Creating a control that implements the `IExtenderProvider` interface is the same as it was for the `BorderPainterExtender` sample described previously. To demonstrate this, the next Extender Provider will be derived from a `Label` control. In addition, this new Extender Provider will only extend `MenuItems` to provide a `MenuItemHelpText` property. Figure A.3 shows the completed `MenuItemExtender` displaying some help text for the selected `MenuItem`.

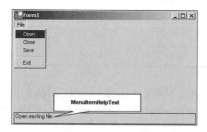

FIGURE A.3
A `Label` *control implementing* `IExtenderProvider`.

The `MenuItemExtender` only provides the `MenuItemHelpText` property to `MenuItems`. This is accomplished in two ways: First, the target base class is specified in the `ProvideProperty` attribute by specifying `typeof( MenuItem )`. Second, the `CanExtend` method returns `true` only if the target is a `MenuItem`. The code for implementing the `MenuItemExtender` is simple, to say the least. Listing A.5 contains the implementation.

LISTING A.5   MenuItemExtender Source

```
 1: [ ProvideProperty( "MenuItemHelpText", typeof( MenuItem ) ) ]
 2: public class MenuItemExtender : Label, IExtenderProvider {
 3:
 4:     protected Hashtable        menuItemHelpText;
 5:
 6:     //Hide the base class's Text Property
 7:     [Browsable(false)]
 8:     public new string Text {
 9:         get { return base.Text; }
10:         set { base.Text = value; }
11:     }
12:
13:     //Implement IExtenderProvider
14:     bool IExtenderProvider.CanExtend( object target ) {
15:         return (target is MenuItem);
16:     }
17:
18:     public MenuItemExtender( ) {
19:         menuItemHelpText = new Hashtable( );
20:     }
21:
22:     //Provide Get/Set Methods for the MenuItemHelpText property
23:     public string GetMenuItemHelpText( object target ) {
24:         string text = string.Empty;
25:     if( menuItemHelpText.ContainsKey( target ) )
26:             text = (string)menuItemHelpText[ target ];
27:         return text;
28:     }
29:
30:     public void SetMenuItemHelpText( object target, string text ) {
31:         MenuItem mi = (MenuItem)target;
32:         if( text == null || (text.Length == 0) ) {
33:             menuItemHelpText.Remove( mi );
34:             mi.Select -= new EventHandler( OnMenuItemSelect );
35:         } else {
36:             menuItemHelpText[ mi ] = text;
37:             mi.Select += new EventHandler( OnMenuItemSelect );
```

LISTING A.5   Continued

```
38:          }
39:      }
40:
41:      protected void OnMenuItemSelect( object sender, EventArgs e ) {
42:          base.Text = (string)menuItemHelpText[ sender ];
43:      }
44:  }
```

Not unlike the BorderPainterExtender, the MenuItemExtender implements the IExtenderProvider interface to dynamically add a property to all MenuItem-derived objects on the current form. Any Component-derived class can implement the IExtenderProvider interface to provide dynamic properties to controls during design-time.

The MenuItemExtender associates simple help text with a MenuItem first by providing the dynamic property MenuItemHelpText and second by subscribing to the Select event for the given MenuItem. When the Select event occurs, the method OnMenuItemSelect is invoked. This method then assigns the associated help text with the Text property. Because the MenuItemExtender is derived from a Label, the Text will then be displayed.

Summary

Extender Providers are a useful idea and an easy way to add additional properties to existing controls. Other uses for extenders include adding layout management such as Flow, Grid, or GridBag layout to a Form at design-time. Of course, you'll also have to implement the layout logic, but using extenders allows for assigning various layouts to different elements of a form. The uses for extenders are limited only by your imagination and necessity.

INDEX